D1110314

Health Care Budgeting
and Financial Management
for Non-Financial
Managers

Health Care Budgeting and Financial Management for Non-Financial Managers

WILLIAM J. WARD, JR.

A New England Healthcare Assembly Book

AUBURN HOUSE
Westport, Connecticut • London

Library of Congress Cataloging-in-Publication Data

Ward, William J., Jr.
Health care budgeting and financial management for non-financial
managers / William J. Ward, Jr.
p.   cm.
"A New England Healthcare Assembly book."
Includes bibliographical references and index.
ISBN 0-86569-211-4 (alk. paper). – ISBN 0-86569-231-9 (pbk. :
alk. paper)
1. Health facilities – Finance.   2. Health facilities – Accounting.
I. Title.
RA971.3.W36   1994
362.1'1'0682 – dc20   93-24757

British Library Cataloguing in Publication Data is available.

Library of Congress Catalog Card Number: 93-24757
ISBN: 0-86569-211-4
0-86569-231-9 (pbk.)

First published in 1994

Auburn House, 88 Post Road West, Westport, CT 06881
An imprint of Greenwood Publishing Group, Inc.

Printed in the United States of America

The paper used in this book complies with the
Permanent Paper Standard issued by the National
Information Standards Organization (Z39.48-1984).

10 9

Contents

Contents

Illustrations

FIGURES

TABLES

Preface

This text was developed as the result of a perceived need for non-financial managers to understand enough about financial management in health care to be successful in their day-to-day activities while not smothering them with an "everything you ever wanted to know about financial management, but were afraid to ask" approach.

It is an introductory text, containing enough information to be useful and completely sufficient for non-financial managers and providing a firm foundation for additional study.

Acknowledgments

Thanks are owed to three people who helped me bring this text to life. Liz Kramer made the necessary contacts with the publisher. Dee Kelley and my daughter Lisa were invaluable helpers with the manuscript.

My wife, Judy, and our three children, Lisa, Colin, and Maggie, offered encouragement all along the way. They were always supportive, even when I spent hours away from them while I was writing. The book is dedicated to them.

Health Care Budgeting and Financial Management for Non-Financial Managers

Chapter 1

Introduction

Historically, health care managers have evolved from apprenticeships within technical areas. Radiology managers, for example, have risen through the technician ranks, head nurses through the nursing ranks, and so on. Often, the best technical persons have been elevated to management only to find that the skills that served them so well as technicians are insufficient in their new roles.

PURPOSE AND STRUCTURE OF THIS TEXT

Some management skills can be acquired while on the job. Organizational skills can be learned over time if the work environment allows. Leadership qualities can be present from experience outside the workplace (e.g., scouting, fraternal and social clubs, and community or neighborhood improvement associations). Other management skills, however, are highly technical in nature and do not lend themselves to an on-the-job-training approach. Among these are financial management skills.

The purpose of this text is to present the cadre of "up through the ranks" managers with a basic level of financial management principles, including understanding financial statements and ratios, preparing an operating budget, and using financial analysis to help with decision making. Those chapters that present analytical techniques also contain review problems. The solutions can be found in Appendix 1.

LEARNING TO SPEAK THE LANGUAGE

Financial management, like most scientific disciplines, has a language—a jargon—all its own. In order to function effectively, one must understand that language. This is no different from the tourist who studies French before touring

France or the baseball fan who learns the difference between a "Baltimore chop" and a "Texas leaguer."

In health care, words and phrases such as *STAT*, *q4h*, *PRN*, and *NPO* are liberally sprinkled throughout the language. To the uninformed, casual observer, these four simple statements take on a significance far in excess of their true meanings. Not understanding the language places one at a distinct disadvantage. It can throw a person off stride and place him or her on the defensive in any conversation. Consider, for example, this hypothetical scenario.

A senior administrator enters the office of a unit manager and asks for an explanation of salary performance during the most recent three-month period. "How much of this salary variance is caused by a labor rate variance? How much is the efficiency variance?" And, he asks, "What effect did volume have on the quarterly performance?" How will the unit manager respond? If he does not understand what was requested, he will not be able to provide a proper answer. If he guesses, he may respond with wrong or misleading information. If he answers that he does not understand what the senior administrator is asking, he runs the risk of appearing to be ignorant.

Beware of individuals whose reliance on the language of finance is such that they casually toss catchy phrases and buzzwords into a conversation in a way that only confuses the listener. Remember that a good communicator is one who is easily understood by all listeners. The responsibility to be a good communicator lies with the speaker, not the listener. The speaker must comprehend the listener's level of understanding and match his or her remarks to that level. The listener, too, has a responsibility: to stop the speaker and politely explain that there is a lack of understanding and that a further explanation is needed.

For the brief scenario involving the senior administrator and the unit manager, the "English language" version is as follows.

For the most recent three-month period, the actual salary level was different from the level budgeted (a variance). The senior administrator wanted to know how much of that difference was the result of hourly pay rates that were different from the rates budgeted, how much was the result of the staff's working harder than was planned for in the budget or not working as hard as was planned, and how much of the difference was a result of seeing more or fewer patients than were envisioned in the budget.

The Glossary contains financial terms that will be used throughout this text.

OVERCOMING THE MYSTIQUE

For some reason a mystique surrounds financial management. It is a misconception that mere mortals are not expected to do well when it comes to financial management techniques. The reality, however, is that financial management and the techniques associated with it are not as complicated as they seem. Beyond basic comprehension skills, one need only be able to multiply, divide, add, and subtract to achieve success. The notion that "if you can balance your checkbook, you can be a good financial manager" is true in most cases. As an assist, Appendix 2 contains over two dozen formulas commonly used in financial management.

TODAY'S HEALTH CARE DILEMMA

Health care, specifically the high cost of health care and the resulting need for reform, was one of the hottest topics of discussion during the 1992 presidential campaign year. Why health care reform? The answer lies in the fact that some 34 million Americans have no insurance coverage. At the same time, premium costs for those who are insured are growing at 15 percent per year. There is no coordinated cost containment program. Politicians are quick to grasp the fact that 34 million Americans represent a sizable block of votes. Health care progressed rapidly from an annoyance to a national campaign issue.

The recession, too, contributed to the situation. A large and vocal segment of the population lost their coverage when they lost their jobs. In turn, the states felt the effects in the form of lowered tax revenues and a swelling of medical assistance roles. The decreased state tax revenues, coupled with "balanced budget" spending caps, resulted in significant Medicaid program cuts.

But what exactly is this health care delivery system that many say is in such dire need of reform? Some facts and figures can help define it. There are just under 5,500 community hospitals operating 933,000 beds. Another 1.6 million beds are operated by the nation's 16,000 nursing homes. There are more than 601,000 active physicians.

Of the billions spent on health care, nearly 60 percent is paid to hospitals and physicians (Figure 1-1). Nursing homes at 8 percent represent a real "sleeper" in that the aging of the population will increase their share over the next several years.

The bill for these services falls largely to government—Medicare and Medicaid—along with other federal and state entitlement programs (Figure 1-2). Private insurance covers a third of the cost.

In 1990, despite spending $650 billion on health care, America was the only developed nation with 15 percent of the population uninsured. Americans spent more per capita than anyone else but were not rewarded with increased life expectancy (Figure 1-3).

Health care represents more than 12 percent of the gross national product, and by the year 2000 it is expected to top 17 percent. If the trend continues, health care spending will top $1.5 trillion in the year 2000 (Figure 1-4). Curiously, however, if the domestic auto industry was performing like this, there likely would be no calls for reform. People would be patting Lee Iacocca and the others on the back and telling them what a super job they had done.

Figure 1-1
Where Does All the Money Go?

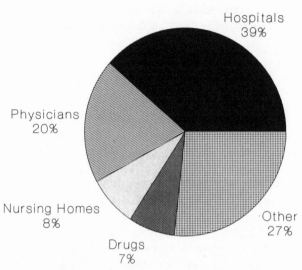

Hospitals and physicians are responsible for nearly 60 percent of health care spending. Although consuming only 8 percent, the aging of the population will increase the nursing home share sharply over the next several years.

Figure 1-2
Who Pays the Bills?

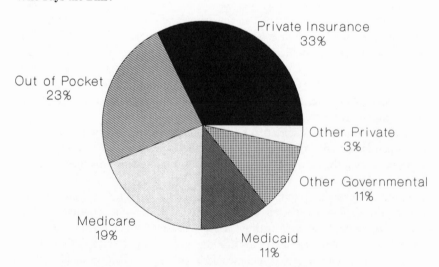

The bill for health care services falls largely to federal and state government agencies. Private insurance covers a third of the cost. With nearly one dollar in four coming out-of-pocket, the public's concern is easy to understand.

Figure 1-3
Spending More But Living Less

	Per Capita Spending	Life Expectancy
United States	$2,354	76
Canada	$1,683	77
Germany	$1,232	75
Japan	$1,035	78
United Kingdom	$ 836	76

Although Americans spent more per capita than anyone else, they were not rewarded with increased life expectancy.

Figure 1-4
U.S. Health Care Expenditures
(in Billions of Dollars)

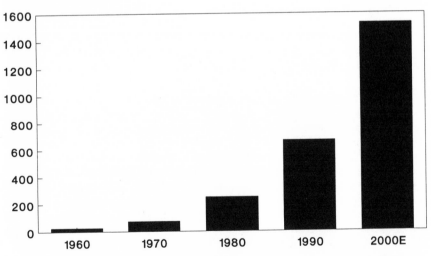

If the trend continues, health care spending will top $1.5 trillion by the year 2000. This same performance by the domestic auto industry would be cause for celebration.

5

The Effect on Providers of Care

Health care has usually been considered a "recession-proof" industry. In a recession, people may put off buying a new home or a refrigerator. They may make do with the old car for another year. But people still get sick, regardless of the economy. The difference is that now the sick have no money, no coverage, and little or no state assistance to pay for their care. The burden then falls to the providers, who have felt the pinch of federal and state budget cuts and experienced a rise in collection problems.

Hospitals have been particularly hard hit. Profit margins are falling; hospitals are closing. As the largest segment of the health care industry, hospitals have become heavily regulated, both voluntary—the Joint Commission on the Accreditation of Healthcare Organizations (JCAHO)—and mandatory. The health care field has experienced increasing scrutiny—particularly by the media. The ABC "Primetime Live" series offered reports on the abusive health care delivery system. It began with a hidden camera exposé of the Department of Veterans Affairs Medical Center in Cleveland and followed that with a revealing story about Humana's excessive profits. Unfortunately, the story failed to state exactly how much profit Humana actually did make.

To comprehend fully how the health care delivery system in the United States got into this mess, it is necessary to understand two critical elements—the public's expectations of the system and the way health care is financed.

The Public's Expectations

The following open letter to the American public may help explain how the public and the health care delivery system worked together to create the dilemma now facing the country.

[Dear American Public:]
I can't stand it any longer—it's me—I am guilty—I did it. I listened to your demands for more of everything, and I supplied them. You wanted more and better educated people to take care of you, and I supplied them. You wanted new and higher levels of care, and I brought them to you. The pressure to create bright, beautiful facilities became a goal for you, and I have responded. You wanted more time in life and I gave it to you. You wanted me close by—and you wanted me to be ready for anything at any time—and I am. You wanted me to pull you into this life and you want me to gently caress your hand as you leave it, and I do. And yes, it costs. It costs a lot more than you like and much more than I would like—and I will continue to create the best possible system for you to use. And I will always be aware of the resources I consume and the financial burden I contribute to— but I will be here—it's me—I did it—I'm guilty.

[Sincerely]
"Your American Health Care System" [1]

The health care delivery system gave the public everything it wanted, but now the public does not like the price. The public wanted excess capacity, standby capacity, but now the public does not like the price. The public wants to abuse its bodies, have transplants and other high-technology treatments available — *without rationing* — but now the public does not like the price. Health care providers are doing things today that were unimagined just a decade ago, but now the public does not like the price.

Thus, health care providers find themselves in a difficult position: the public wants more but wants to pay less for it, and smart politicians are encouraging this.

How Health Care Is Financed

To achieve an understanding of how health care is financed, it is necessary to begin with a lesson in basic economic theory — supply and demand.

The normal economic system exists in a monetary environment. The parties involved include suppliers (those who provide goods and services) and consumers (also referred to as orderers or payers who demand goods and services). As Figure 1-5 illustrates, this is essentially a two-sided exchange. The exchange between supplier and consumer is accomplished via the exchange of money (or the promise of money) for supplies or services. The system has operated in this

Figure 1-5
Normal Economic Environment

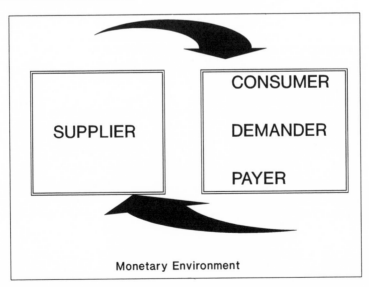

In a normal economic environment, there are essentially two parties — suppliers and consumers (also referred to as orderers or payers). The former supply goods and services, and the latter demand goods and services. Money, or the promise of it, is exchanged between the two parties, thus establishing a market price for the goods and services.

Figure 1-6
Economic Equilibrium

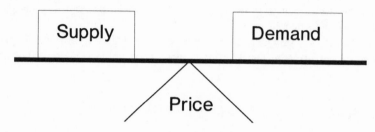

When free of artificial constraints like price controls or production limits, price can establish an equilibrium so that the amount supplied equals the amount demanded and the amount demanded equals the available supply.

Figure 1-7
Price Sensitivity

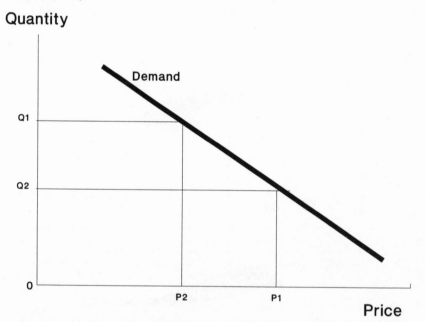

The principle of price sensitivity holds that the change in demand for desirable goods or services is a function of the change in the price of those goods or services. As can be seen here, a decrease in the price from P2 to P1 results in an increase in the quantity demanded from Q1 to Q2. Conversely, an increase in the price from P1 to P2 results in a decrease in the quantity demanded from Q2 to Q1.

simplified manner in this country for many years. In the early days, wampum belts and animal skins were quite successful as the unit of exchange.

In the world of supply and demand, price acts as the great equalizer. It establishes an equilibrium (Figure 1-6) so that supply equals demand and demand equals supply. Given an economy free of outside pressures (price controls and so on) the absence of equilibrium will cause prices to rise or fall so that equilibrium can once again be established. One need only look to the gasoline crisis of the 1970s to see how price and equilibrium go hand in hand. At 30¢ to 40¢ per gallon, demand exceeded supply. With prices controlled and unable to rise, equilibrium was not easily achieved. Because of the lifting of controls, price has been able to float freely up and down to maintain constantly the balance of supply and demand. The long lines at the gas stations during the 1970s were caused by the disequilibrium between supply and demand.

This ability of price to act as the great equalizer is rooted in an economic principle called price elasticity or, as it is sometimes called, price sensitivity. Simply stated, this principle holds that the amount of change in demand for goods and services is a function of the amount of change in the price of those goods and services. As can be seen in Figure 1-7, as price decreases, demand for desirable goods and services increases, and vice versa. It follows, therefore, that as price decreases to zero, demand for desirable goods and services will increase to the point of becoming insatiable. This is important to remember as it relates to health care because during the late 1960s and into the 1970s, the price to the average American who was "demanding" health care became, by virtue of insurance coverage, zero. The result was an insatiable demand for health care. As supply increased to meet this insatiable demand, the cost to the nation for health care grew at an alarming rate.

This can be understood more clearly by examining the differences evident in the health care economic environment as compared with the normal economic environment. As depicted in Figure 1-8, the monetary environment has remained, but notice that it has shrunk and no longer includes all of the parties. Notice, too, that the relationship between the parties has undergone a significant change. Supply continues to be provided by a single party. Demand, which previously included three parties (orderer, consumer, and payer) within the monetary environment, is now divided into three separate parties — orderer and consumer, who function outside the monetary environment, and payer, who continues to function inside the monetary environment. The problem in the health care economic system began with these significant changes. The cause of the problem stems from the fact that price exists inside the monetary environment, where it can exert its balancing force. However, the demand for health care services, originating with the orderer and consumer, lies outside the monetary environment; therefore, price is not able to influence demand. Since neither the orderer nor the consumer (physician and patient) is concerned with price, demand becomes insatiable. Efforts to alter this via increased shifting of insurance premium costs to

Figure 1-8
Health Care Economic Environment

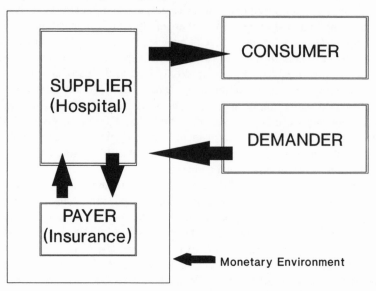

The economic environment as applied to health care is significantly different. Note that there are now four parties instead of two. Note, also, that the supply of, and the demand for, health care services no longer include the payer for those services. Because the monetary environment does not include the orderer or consumer, price is unable to establish a balance between supply and demand.

employees, deductibles, and copayments have met with little success. They have, however, been successful in convincing the public that health care has become too expensive.

The lack of price sensitivity on the part of the public finds its genesis in the growth of health insurance coverage since the end of the World War II (Figure 1-9). As more and more people became insured, the price (the amount paid out-of-pocket) plummeted, and demand increased. Adding fuel to the fire, insurance coverage often encouraged the use of high-cost services to the exclusion of less expensive ones. Certain treatments, for example, were covered only if performed in an inpatient setting, even though the same services could be provided in the less expensive outpatient area. The reversal of this half-century of growth in coverage in the early 1990s has led to an increasing public outcry over the high cost of health care.

Coupled with this was the introduction of Medicare and Medicaid in the mid-1960s. These two programs instituted a reimbursement methodology called cost reimbursement. The underlying principle was that since the government covered so many patients, the programs should get a good "deal" from hospitals by buying services at cost. In theory, at least, this was fine, but in practice it introduced the

Figure 1-9
Health Insurance Coverage

Percentage of the Population Covered

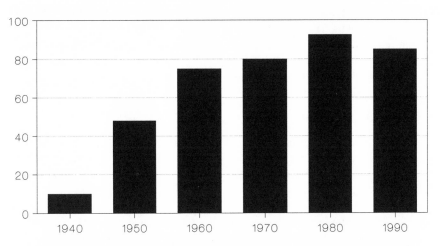

As more people became insured, the price to consumer (the amount paid out-of-pocket) plummeted. With price unable to establish equilibrium, demand increased. The reversal of this half-century of growth in coverage in the 1990s has led to an increasing public outcry over the high cost of health care.

notion to providers of care that "the more you spent, the more you got." In effect, cost reimbursement taught hospitals to spend money – to supply health care services to meet expanding demand at any cost. The flaw in the cost reimbursement logic can be illustrated by the following example.

An automobile dealer is approached by a wealthy gentleman, who explains that he is in the market for automobiles for all of his 15 grandchildren. "I want to buy an automobile for each; however, since I am buying so many, I do not want to pay the sticker price; I want to pay only cost." With that, the gentleman explains where to deliver each automobile and where to send the bill. If you were the automobile dealer, would you send the 15 grandchildren the least expensive or most expensive automobiles?

Substituting Medicare and Medicaid for the wealthy gentleman, hospital for automobile dealer, program beneficiary for grandchildren, and hospital service for automobile produces the following version of the story.

A hospital is approached by Medicare and Medicaid, which explain that they are in the market for hospital service for their program beneficiaries. "We want to buy hospital service for each; however, since we are buying so much, we do not want to pay the going price. We want to pay only cost." With that, Medicare and Medicaid explain where to deliver the hospital service and where to sent the bill. If you were the hospital, would you supply the program beneficiaries with the least expensive or most expensive hospital service?

In the nearly three decades following the birth of Medicare and Medicaid, government spending has risen sharply. Because one of the rules of cost reimbursement required that the prices charged (cost) to non-Medicare/Medicaid patients had to be higher than the cost to Medicare/Medicaid, the prices charged to those patients and their insurers climbed as well.

Is There a Solution?

Will the United States be able to get out of this financing mess? The answer is probably yes, but only if care is taken to avoid "trendy" approaches, if a number of popular myths can be debunked, if the multiple agendas of the various characters in this melodrama can be avoided, and if all of the parties can begin to focus on the real problem and not just the symptoms.

There are a number of trendy ideas making the rounds these days. First among these is the notion that the United States can solve its problems by importing the Canadian system. The problem with this is that the Canadian approach to life in general is completely different from ours. Canadians believe in peace, order, and good government. Americans believe in life, liberty, and the pursuit of happiness. There is a high price to be paid for the reckless pursuit of happiness. The fundamental differences in the two populations can be illustrated with a couple of examples. Imagine that road construction forces the closure of a lane of traffic on a busy highway. Traffic is required to merge from several lanes to just two. Canadian drivers automatically, almost instinctively, merge. Not Americans. The second example involves the New York and Toronto subway systems. In New York City, a train pulls to a stop, the doors open, and the crowd on the platform starts to push into the cars before the passengers in the cars can exit. It is chaotic almost to the point of anarchy. In Toronto, quite the opposite is the case. The kind of health system that provides care for an orderly population can never be expected to succeed in dealing with an American population that wants instant gratification.

National health insurance is making a return appearance as a possible solution, but it is far from a new idea. It was first proposed by Teddy Roosevelt as part of the Bull Moose Party platform at the start of the century. Hopefully, it will fare no better at the end of this century. The government has clearly demonstrated its inability to deal effectively with health care during the last quarter-century and will likely repeat its failings again and again. One need only look to Amtrak and the postal service to get an idea of the kind of health care that could be in store with a federally operated system of national health insurance.

Another of the trendy ideas is the "play or pay" approach. But rather than deal head-on with the real underlying problem, "play or pay" perpetuates the problem by continuing to isolate price from demand.

A number of popular myths must be debunked because they contribute to a misconception on the part of the public. The first of these is that increasing the employee share of insurance premiums will reduce overall cost because employees will think twice before using the health care delivery system and, thus, consume less. In fact, this technique encourages employees to use what can be construed as something for which they have already paid the price.

Another popular myth involving insurance is that insurance companies should insure everyone, even those with expensive, preexisting conditions. Usually the most poignant cases are used to illustrate the "unfairness" of the situation. If the social objective is to insure all, regardless of risk, then everyone should understand that doing so amounts to cost shifting. The very idea behind insurance is to provide a hedge against uncertainty. Insuring those with expensive-to-treat preexisting conditions means taking on an obligation that is certain to occur—there is no risk; there is certainty. At best, this represents cost shifting. At worst, it is a prescription for bankrupting the insurance industry when the premiums increase higher and faster than is now the case.

The final popular myth in need of debunking is that profits in health care are wrong. The nonprofit providers should make no profits. If they do, it is proof that they are abusing the public. The for-profit providers had better not make too much profit—however much "too much" might be. Again, the "Primetime Live" exposé of Humana's "excessive profits" reinforces the myth instead of educating the public about profits and the need for them if health care providers, be they for-profit or nonprofit, are to survive. Profits provide the funds necessary to replace aging physical plants, acquire modern equipment, develop new and improved programs, and so on. Lacking profits to fund this, where will the money come from? Depreciation on yesterday's equipment will in no way pay for tomorrow's.

Critical Players in the Health Care Dilemma

In order to achieve a solution, all of the parties must take an active role, or there will be no lasting solution, only a quick fix that will cure one or more of the symptoms at the expense of the other parties. All of the parties will have to give up something if there is to be a lasting solution. Everyone will have to compromise. Just who are all these parties, and what stake does each have?

Most of the money spent on health care goes to the providers of care: hospitals, nursing homes, physicians, and so on. They will be interested in a reimbursement stream that satisfies their need to cover the realistic costs of doing business, including a stream of profits necessary to assure survival and growth. Indirect providers like drug companies and manufacturers of durable medical goods will need enough of a profit stream to cover research and development and provide sufficient return on investment to keep stockholders happy. In exchange for this, they may find themselves more regulated.

The people paying the bills must be involved. Insurers, employers, and government programs want to reduce the amounts they pay out for health care. For insurers, the driver is premium competition. For employers, the picture is more complex. A reduction of fringe benefit costs translates into an increased ability to offer competitive benefits programs to attract and retain good employees. An overall decrease in cost translates into improved business competitiveness. The government, too, wants to keep down the cost of entitlement programs. To achieve this objective, the payers must be willing to stop the gamesmanship that exists. One insurance company, for example, requires a preadmission second opinion for trauma cases! Others refuse to divulge the criteria used in determining if they will pay for a particular admission. In effect, they are gaming the system and taking whatever steps they can in order to avoid paying claims.

Those who shape public perception and understanding, the politicians, most certainly must be involved. These are the folks telling the general public that there is a free lunch. This must stop. Instead of telling the public what it wants to hear, they must begin telling the public what it needs to hear. The risk for politicians is that telling the public anything it does not want to hear is usually a prescription for losing an election. These are, however, our leaders, and they should lead!

Last, the people the health care industry is supposed to serve, the public, must take an active part in the dialogue. Expectations will have to be changed. Access, immediacy, and cost will all be affected by the compromises that all parties must make. The public will need to take more responsibility for its own well-being.

The Real Problem

Understanding the following formula is essential to resolving the dilemma: Cost = Price × Volume. Simply stated, the cost of health care is a function of two variables, the prices charged for the various services provided and the volume of services provided. Up until now, attempts to solve the dilemma have focused mainly on price. State-sponsored rate control, Medicare's Prospective Payment System, and so on have attacked price. Volume has not been effectively influenced. It must be understood that volume is a function of supply and demand. Those initiatives that have dealt with volume have concentrated on the supply side. The demand side, however, has been almost completely ignored. The demand for health care services is not being controlled. As an inescapable result, the cost of health care is not being controlled, despite all the efforts.

In reality, the problem is not the high cost of health care. The excessive and uncontrolled demand for health care is the real underlying problem. In effect, we have been treating the symptoms and not the underlying disease. Is it any wonder the patient is getting sicker?

A number of factors influence the demand for health care services and thus drive up cost. The first of these is the broad category of life-style choices: the ways in which Americans consciously choose to live that cause the system to be used more than necessary.

When a motorcyclist expresses his constitutional right not to wear a helmet and slams his cycle and body into a roadside utility pole, the cost of putting him back together again is accounted for as part of "the high cost of health care."

Abortion is far more costly than contraception as a form of birth control. The cost of abortion services is accounted for as part of "the high cost of health care."

Diet and exercise are involved, too. Americans overeat and underexercise and wonder why heart disease is one of the leading causes of death. The American public seems bent on mistreating the body for 40 or so years and then relying on transplants and other costly high-tech interventions to make it all well again. Again, the cost is accounted for as part of "the high cost of health care." Life in the fast lane is an expensive proposition. The public needs to recognize this fact.

When a 14-year-old can walk into a public school with a loaded handgun and kill two classmates, this social problem is accounted for as part of "the high cost of health care."

As a society, we have "medicalized" behavior problems. Spouse abuse, child abuse, alcohol and drug abuse, and a host of other antisocial behaviors are thought of as diseases. The sense of personal responsibility for one's behavior has given way to a belief that the health care system should "find a cure" for these diseases. Needless to say, the cost of these abhorrent behaviors is accounted for as part of "the high cost of health care."

Abuse of the medical malpractice insurance system has done wonders to drive up cost. A man and a woman look in the mirror. Both are ugly beyond description. They have a baby who looks just like them. They sue the obstetrician for malpractice! A bit exaggerated, perhaps, but the example serves to illustrate the fact that the public has come to expect a financial reward as the outcome of almost any untoward event that we do not like.

Last, technology has made significant advances. So much more can now be done to heal the human body, and these advances justifiably cost more—and they are worth it. As with most other things in life, there is abuse, which adds needless cost to the national health care bill. But the benefits of technological advances far outweigh the cost.

What Is Really Needed

Two elements must be blended together to produce an effective, lasting solution: a national health policy and the leadership, at the local and national level, to develop, implement, and maintain it.

A national health policy must be developed to reduce needless demand, promote healthy life-styles, mandate preventive care, eliminate excess capacity, promote or provide basic insurance coverage, and protect against catastrophic loss.

How often does the general public present at a hospital emergency room with a cold or the flu? Cases like these belong at the drugstore or perhaps at a general practitioner's office, but certainly not an expensive emergency room. How much cosmetic surgery is really necessary? This kind of needless demand fails to improve the health status of Americans but succeeds in adding to the high cost of health care.

Healthy life-styles will allow Americans to reduce the demand for health care. Less demand translates into less cost. Preventive care has been shown to save cost.

The excess capacity in the delivery system must be reduced or eliminated. Too many hospitals are operated at occupancy rates that cannot be justified. There need to be fewer hospitals, but the difficulty lies in selecting the ones to close. Most hospital executives would agree, so long as the hospitals chosen for closure are someone else's hospitals. With so many empty beds in the civilian sector, can a separate, parallel Veterans Administration (VA) medical system be justified? If the idea is to provide for the brave men and women who put their lives on the line for the country, why not give them a "gold card" and let them use whatever hospitals and doctors they want—just like the rest of us?

As a nation, we need either to promote or provide *basic* health insurance coverage and protection against *catastrophic* loss. A base level of coverage should be available to all citizens, with expanded coverage available for those who are willing to pay for it. There should be some form of "stop-loss" protection against catastrophic illness, but it should be structured in a way that avoids the "everything for everyone" dilemma. The role of government should be limited to encouraging, perhaps mandating, others to provide the insurance coverage as opposed to being the insurer itself.

The second, and perhaps the most critical, element is leadership, at both the national and the local level. Leadership is needed at the local level because the creative solutions necessary to achieve success are best developed locally to meet the needs of a diverse population as opposed to a uniform solution in which everything is either black or white with no shades of gray. The role of national leadership will be to develop the national framework upon which diverse, but nonetheless effective, local solutions will be assembled.

The leadership agenda must place cost containment as a high priority. While the high cost of health care is largely a result of demand for service, providers must make sure that each unit of service is delivered at the lowest possible cost. To date, this has not been a priority. Systems available in other industries could be borrowed and adapted to health care, but there has been a reluctance to do so.

Leadership is needed to involve all the parties: those demanding care, those receiving it, and those paying the bills. All will need to compromise so a solution can be achieved, but none will be willing to be the first to compromise. Leadership must force the necessary compromises, while assuring that none of the parties is disadvantaged.

If an effective, lasting solution is to be achieved, a fundamental change in the public's perception of the health care system is essential. A program of public education is key. America's leaders must be willing to tell the public what it must hear, not just what it wants to hear. Leadership will be needed to convince the public that health is the responsibility of the individual, not "the system." If an effective, lasting solution is to be achieved, leadership is needed to help make the difficult choices that must be made if success is to be achieved. Because, as a society, Americans have grown accustomed to instant gratification, the leadership must force the focus to be on the long term. The problems with our health care system did not spring up overnight, and the solutions will, likewise, not spring up overnight. Further, because the solutions will be somewhat painful, America's leaders must "stay the course," or else one set of problems will merely be exchanged for another.

FROM COST REIMBURSEMENT TO COMPETITION TO . . .

Since the mid-1970s, the single word that most accurately describes the health care financing system is *change*. Retrospective cost-based reimbursement has given way in many states to prospective rate control. Emphasis has shifted from per diem to per case. Competition has entered the system in the form of alternatives to expensive institutionalized care. Health maintenance organizations, preferred provider organizations, surgicenters, and the like are siphoning patients and forcing hospitals to be more competitive. Words like *advertising, marketing*, and *competition* have entered the lexicon of health institutions, which until only a few years ago were able to sit back and wait for the patients to arrive.

As a result health care managers at all levels are dealing, and will continue to deal, with an environment that is increasingly more difficult, an environment that is characterized by an alphabet soup of agencies and programs designed to accomplish one thing—lower the cost of health care. What follows is a descriptive listing of such agencies and programs.

HCFA—The Health Care Financing Administration (pronounced Hic'fa) is the federal agency within the Department of Health and Human Services that administers Medicare and Medicaid.

PPO—Preferred provider organization refers to a group of physician or institutional providers to which patients are directed by their insurance plan. Generally, these organizations provide lower-cost health care and are, thus, the "best buy" for the buck.

HMO—A health maintenance organization is a provider of an agreed-upon set of basic and supplemental health care services. HMOs seek to provide a less costly alternative to conventional coverage by stressing health maintenance and preventive care and by utilizing lower-cost hospitals when possible.

PRO—A professional review organization represents a utilization control mechanism used by the Medicare program to reduce both the number and length of hospital stays incurred by program beneficiaries. Each admission is reviewed, and hospitals are denied reimbursement for days of stay, procedures, or entire admissions that a local PRO determines to be inappropriate.

DRGs—Diagnosis related groups represent a method of grouping disease entities into a relatively small number (492) of "products" for analysis and reimbursement purposes.

First developed at Yale University and extensively tested in New Jersey, DRGs have been criticized for not accounting for differences from case to case and for not giving proper recognition to patient acuity. Of the 492, 5 are no longer valid, leaving 487 workable, defined DRGs.

PPS – The prospective payment system is the methodology used by Medicare to reimburse hospitals. The system establishes a price for each diagnosis related group. Hospitals whose costs exceed the established price lose the difference. Those whose costs are less than the established price are allowed to keep the difference.

MANAGEMENT RESPONSE

Having examined the health care financing system and the pressures being brought to bear, we can now look at the response that managers at all levels of the health care system must make in order to insure survival of their institutions. Whether in nursing, finance, or operations, managers have one overriding objective: to win at this real-life game. This means that managers in health care must begin to employ, if they have not already done so, many of the techniques used in the manufacturing and service industries but as yet not widely subscribed to in health care. Industrial engineering techniques and quantitative methods must be used to examine the flows of patients, providers, materials, and technologies. Emphasis must be placed on the maximization of all resources.

Information systems must no longer be limited to patient billing, laboratory test results reporting, or simplified clinical information. New systems must be developed to bring clinical data together with artificial intelligence to improve diagnosis and treatment. Computer-driven treatment protocols already exist in some institutions. Hospitals can store medical records information, radiology images, and the like optically and network this information with physicians and clinics to develop and control provider networks, thereby locking in market share. Other systems will need to accumulate data by DRG, ICD-9 code, physician, insurer, and so on to facilitate decision analysis. It is possible to establish and monitor practitioner performance against criteria such as length of stay, ancillary usage, surgical outcome, and so on as part of an institution's quality assurance program.

Cost accounting systems can aid in establishing standard costs for treatments. When linked with industrial engineering expertise, standards can be established for nursing hours, supply usage, and so on. Variance analysis can be used to determine the underlying causes of differences between actual performance and budgeted or standard performance.

Market analysis can be focused on two objectives: analyzing where the patients are and determining on which lines of business, which diagnoses, an institution should concentrate.

Finally, managers must rely more on analytical methods to support the decision-making process. Techniques such as benefit/cost analysis, break-even analysis, and the like will be integrated with long-range planning, operations budgeting, and forecasting to achieve a better financial outcome.

THE BALANCING ACT

As health care managers begin to focus more and more on financial results (the "bottom line"), it is vitally important to remember what health care is about: the provision of health services to the public. Survival requires a balance between the dictates of the bottom line and the mandates of modern health care.

The delivery of health services without regard for the financial aspect invites disaster; likewise, the fixation on dollars and cents to the exclusion of concern for the delivery of health services is equally disaster-prone. Balance requires understanding — understanding by those involved with caregiving of the financial impact of their actions and understanding by those involved with financial management of the effect their actions have on the delivery of care.

It is possible, even desirable, to combine the two disciplines in such a way as to provide high-quality, cost-effective health care. That is the challenge to managers for the 1990s and beyond. Meeting that challenge will mean success, both personally and for the individual manager's institution. This text is designed to help managers meet that challenge.

NOTE

1. Reprinted by permission from "We'd Like To Be More Optimistic About 1987 – But," *Rate Controls* 2, no. 2A (February 16, 1987).

Chapter 2

Financial Statements

Perhaps the best way to begin the discussion of financial management is at the end, with the financial statements. These provide a summary of what transpired during a given period of time (e.g., the month of January, last fiscal year) or the financial status on a particular date (e.g., June 30, December 31). Two principal financial statements that are produced for every company are the balance sheet and the income statement.

THE BALANCE SHEET

The balance sheet (Figure 2-1) can be thought of as a family portrait. It depicts the status of the business on a particular date, just as a family portrait freezes action at a particular time. Like the family portrait, it is a snapshot as opposed to a movie. It does not cover what happened over the course of time, but rather is a picture of an instant in time.

The balance sheet tells what is owned by the company (assets), what is owed (liabilities), and the difference between what is owned and what is owed (equity). Assets are generally described as current assets (cash, short-term securities, accounts receivable, and inventories) and long-term or fixed assets (typically, property, plant, and equipment). Liabilities are generally classed as either current liabilities (amounts that are due and payable during the next 12-month period) or long-term liabilities (representing those debts that will not be paid during the next 12 months). Equity, a surrogate for the value of the company, is the difference between what is owned (assets) and what is owed (liabilities). Depending on the type of company, this may be referred to as owners' equity, stockholders' equity, fund balance, the capital account, or, simply, capital.

There are essentially three ways that a balance sheet can be displayed. Often, it

Figure 2-1
Balance Sheet

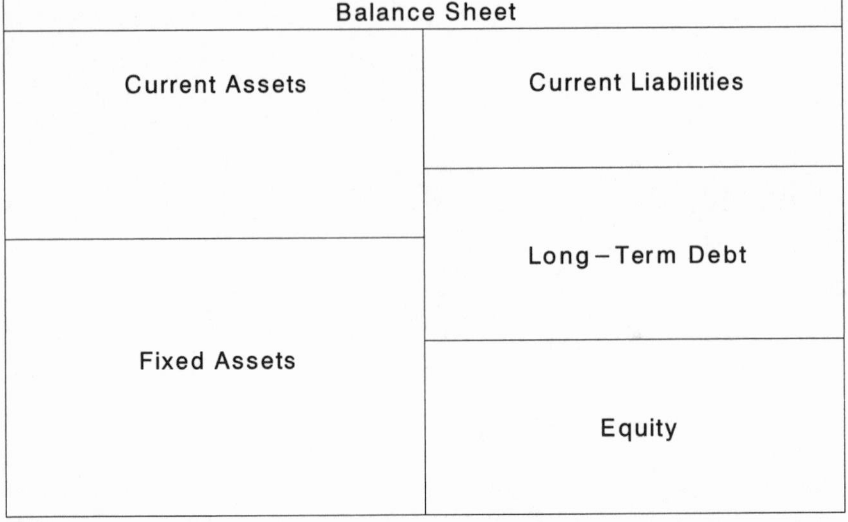

Balance Sheet	
Current Assets	Current Liabilities
	Long–Term Debt
Fixed Assets	Equity

The balance sheet is much like a family portrait. It shows the status of the business on a particular date.

is prepared on a single page with assets on the left and liabilities and equity on the right. If the balance sheet contains a significant amount of information, it may be displayed on two facing pages with assets on the left-hand page and liabilities and equity on the right-hand one. Occasionally, a balance sheet will be stacked vertically on a single page with assets at the top and liabilities and equity at the bottom. Regardless of the format, the amounts shown represent the balances of the various items as of the date of the financial statement, hence the title balance sheet. Another way to think of this is that the left side is *balanced* by the right side.

It is possible to learn more by examining an actual balance sheet to see what information is presented. Table 2-1 displays the balance sheet of the Real General Hospital. Notice that a substantial amount of information is presented. The initial reaction might be that it is impossible to understand all of these numbers. It is possible, however, if the information presented is examined methodically. Two columns of numbers are displayed for each of two dates—June 30, 19X2, and June 30, 19X1. For the Real General Hospital, these are the final days of fiscal years 19X2 and 19X1. To the left of the balances are the descriptions for the dollars displayed.

Current assets are grouped together. These include cash and other assets that will be converted to cash or consumed within one year from the date (June 30 in this example) of the balance sheet. The $2,921,054 (June 30, 19X2) and

Table 2-1
The Real General Hospital Balance Sheet

	June 30, 19x2		June 30, 19x1	
ASSETS				
CURRENT ASSETS				
Cash		$2,921,054		$2,097,775
Short Term Investments		15,000,000		9,000,000
Accounts Receivable – Patients				
Self Pay & Others	$900,714		$837,681	
Commercial Insurance	3,602,856		3,071,492	
Blue Cross	2,251,785		1,675,360	
Medicare	3,377,678		2,699,190	
Medicaid	1,125,893		1,023,830	
HMOs	1,986,750		1,642,515	
Total	$13,245,676		$10,950,068	
Less: Allowance for Uncollectible Accounts	1,806,638	11,439,038	1,353,700	9,596,368
Other Accounts Receivable		771,366		899,424
Inventories		2,145,673		2,023,155
Prepaid Expenses		471,625		497,599
TOTAL CURRENT ASSETS		$32,748,756		$24,114,321
PROPERTY PLANT AND EQUIPMENT				
Land		$4,852,826		$4,852,826
Land Improvements	$531,767		$531,767	
Buildings	20,269,167		19,005,393	
Fixed Equipment	15,066,837		14,367,460	
Major Movable Equipment	26,352,185		24,893,466	
Total	$62,219,956		$58,798,086	
Less: Accumulated Depreciation	25,122,042	37,097,914	21,768,688	37,029,398
Construction in Progress				500,561
TOTAL PROPERTY, PLANT AND EQUIPMENT		$41,950,740		$42,382,785
TOTAL ASSETS		$74,699,496		$66,497,106
LIABILITIES AND FUND BALANCE				
CURRENT LIABILITIES				
Accounts Payable		$6,789,161		$6,634,302
Accrued Liabilities		1,318,253		1,210,215
Salaries, Wages and Payroll Taxes Payable		1,841,380		1,437,894
Advances from Third Party Payors		2,817,256		1,319,451
Accrued Vacation		1,260,095		1,189,986
TOTAL CURRENT LIABILITIES		$14,026,145		$11,791,848
LONG TERM LIABILITIES				
Bonds Payable		$25,870,440		$26,122,680
Deferred pension liability		462,042		565,332
TOTAL LONG TERM LIABILITIES		$26,332,482		$26,688,012
FUND BALANCE				
Fund Balance – Beginning of Period		$28,017,246		$24,550,147
Excess of Revenue over Expenses for the Periods				
Ending June 30, 19X2 and 19X1		6,323,623		3,467,099
TOTAL FUND BALANCE		$34,340,869		$28,017,246
TOTAL LIABILITIES AND FUND BALANCE		$74,699,496		$66,497,106

$2,097,775 (June 30, 19X1) of "cash" can be made up from several sources—the general operating cash account, the payroll account, one or more change funds in the cashier's office, and so on. Short-term investments ($15 million and $9 million) usually represent excess cash invested in marketable securities, certificates of deposit, notes issued by commercial companies, and so on. The purpose of such investments is to put to work any cash that will not be needed in the short term.

The listing of current assets continues with "accounts receivable—patients," which represents the amounts owed to Real General for health care services rendered to patients. In this construct, the amounts are accounted for on the basis of who will pay the hospital for the services—patients who pay directly (self-pay and other), commercial insurance (Travelers, Prudential, and so on), Blue Cross, Medicare, Medicaid, and health maintenance organizations (HMOs). After the total accounts receivable is summed ($13,245,676 and $10,950,068), a deduction called the "allowance for uncollectible accounts" is made. This allowance accounts for the fact that, for one of three reasons, the entire amount owed will not be collected. In this example, $1,806,638 and $1,353,700 will likely be written off as bad debts (amounts owed by people who can afford to pay but who refuse to pay), charity care (for those persons who are willing to pay but are unable), or contractual adjustments (in effect, discounts to major third-party payers for prompt payment, volume of business, or reductions related to a "lower of cost or charges" approach).

"Other accounts receivable" represents the amount the hospital expects to collect for nonpatient care services. In some cases one hospital may provide the laundry service for one or more other hospitals, and the amount listed may represent the value of services so rendered but for which payment has not yet been received. The value of goods and supplies held in the storeroom or warehouse is listed as "inventories." This can include medical/surgical supplies, office supplies, fuel oil, food, and so on, which have been purchased but not yet issued to using departments. The last current asset listed, "prepaid expenses," represents the value to be received in the future as a result of payments made on or before the balance sheet date. Examples include such things as service contracts and unexpired insurance.

"Property, plant, and equipment," occasionally referred to as "fixed assets," are grouped together and segregated from current assets. While it is expected that current assets will be consumed within 12 months, fixed assets have an anticipated useful life that is considerably longer, as much as 30 to 50 years in the case of buildings. Land is treated separately and is not depreciated because, unlike buildings and equipment, land does not wear out, thus its book value remains constant.

The balance sheet of the Real General Hospital lists land improvements (such things as ground-level parking lots, sidewalks, and so on), buildings, fixed equipment (which includes major systems and built-ins like pneumatic tubes, air-conditioning chillers, paging systems, and so on), and major movable equipment (monitors, infusion pumps, and all the other pieces of equipment used in the hospital). Some balance sheets include construction in progress (the accumulated value of projects not yet completed) and minor equipment with their listing of fixed assets.

Usually, predetermined criteria determine if a piece of equipment should be "capitalized," that is, recorded in the books and records of the company as an asset, or expensed immediately upon purchase. If the item has a useful life of more than one year, has an acquisition cost greater than an institution-specified amount (usually in the range of $300 to $500), and is large enough to be identified with a tag of some kind, it is customary to capitalize it and not charge it directly to expense. An office chair costing $165 would not be capitalized because, while it does have a useful life of several years and is large enough to be identified and tagged, it is not expensive enough. Operating room instruments, though long-lasting and costly, are usually too small to be individually identified, and no one would think of trying to affix an asset tag to a surgical instrument. A personal computer would likely be capitalized because it meets all three criteria: life, cost, and size.

Accumulated depreciation represents that portion of an asset's life, expressed in dollar terms, that has been consumed over time in generating revenue. There are a number of depreciation methods. The straight line method is the one used by nonprofit institutions. It is calculated by dividing the historical cost of the asset by its useful life. The resulting annual depreciation expense amount is added to accumulated depreciation each year. Fixed assets have different life expectancies and thus are depreciated at different rates. Buildings, for instance, might be depreciated over a 30-year lifetime, with 1/30th of the historical value (purchase price) written off each year. Major movable equipment, like beds, lab machinery, and so on, might be depreciated over only an 8-year or 10-year life, with 1/8th or 1/10th of historical value written off each year.

An important accounting concept applies in determining the value of assets on the balance sheet: the concept of the going concern. This concept holds that unless there is substantial evidence otherwise, it is assumed that a business entity like a hospital, a nursing home, or a clinic will continue to operate ad infinitum. Assets that have not yet been consumed in the course of business activity are, therefore, shown not at their value to someone who might buy them (market value) but at their acquisition cost. The current market value of these assets is irrelevant because a "going concern" would not sell them but would retain them for use in the business.

The total assets of Real General Hospital ($74,699,496 at June 30, 19X2, and $66,497,106 at June 30, 19X1) must be "balanced" by liabilities and equity.

Current liabilities include "accounts payable," which represent amounts owed to vendors who have sold goods and services to the hospital but who have not yet been paid. "Accrued liabilities" represent actual liabilities that are owed but not yet billed by the vendor or not yet fully processed through the accounts payable system. An example would be supplies received and entered into the inventory but not yet invoiced by the vendor. "Salaries, wages, and payroll taxes payable" is the liability for earnings that have not yet been disbursed to employees and the related taxes that have not yet been paid to the appropriate taxing authorities. This liability is often segregated from other accounts payable.

Included with the current liabilities is the value of any "advances from third-party payers" that the institution has received. These funds are generally provided by some third parties as a substitute for more rapid payment of specific individual claims. The amount is negotiated periodically and represents, in essence, a cash advance. Finally, "accrued vacation" displays the institution's liability for vacation days earned but not yet used by employees. Recognizing this liability as it accumulates is important for two reasons. First, it is a legitimate indebtedness. Second, it prevents sudden expense spikes if and when long-tenured employees with a significant number of accumulated vacation days leave the organization.

The "long-term liabilities" represent that class of indebtedness that will not be paid during the next 12-month business cycle. At the Real General Hospital, this category includes "bonds payable," which will be repaid over many years, and "deferred pension liability," representing amounts owed to a retirement plan.

"Fund balance," Real General's way of referring to equity, represents the difference between total assets and the combination of current liabilities and long-term debt. It is reported as two elements. The balance at the end of the prior year is carried forward as the "beginning of period" value. Added to this is the profit for the current year (as shown on the statement of revenues and expenses).

Notice that the balance sheet of the Real General Hospital displays values for both current and prior fiscal years as of June 30. This allows for a comparison by providing a benchmark of sorts to help determine whether the financial picture on June 30 of the current year represents an improvement over June 30 of the previous year. In other words, has the "family" in the "family portrait" improved with age or not? While the amount of short-term investments does represent an improvement over June 30, 19X1, can the same be said for total accounts receivable? Is there more of a gap between current assets and current liabilities than last year? Is the level of current liabilities better or worse than last year?

All that can be seen at this juncture are absolute values. The hospital has more current assets than a year ago, but it also has more current liabilities. The total of accounts receivable from patients after allowances is up by nearly $2 million, but it cannot be determined whether this is an improvement or not. Comparing current and prior year balances will tell only if asset and liability values are higher or lower in the absolute. To determine "better" or "worse" requires the use of a technique called financial ratio analysis, which will be covered later in this chapter.

THE INCOME STATEMENT

Variously referred to as the income statement, statement of revenue(s) and expense(s), or simply "the P&L" (Profit and Loss), the income statement represents a summary financial report of activity during an accounting period (month, quarter, or fiscal year). The statement heading tells the period of time covered. The Real General Hospital's P&L is presented in Table 2-2. It is called a *comparative* statement of revenues and expenses because a comparison to the prior fiscal year is presented. As indicated by the column headings, the report is "for the 12 months ended," meaning the amounts shown represent activity for a full fiscal year. Like on the balance sheet, the descriptions are printed on the left, and the values are displayed on the right.

The amounts reported as "gross patient service revenue" ($92,805,908 and $77,185,080) represent the total amount of revenue derived from health care services during the period of time that the report covers. Revenues from all services (inpatient room and board, outpatient visit charges, ancillary charges for diagnostic and therapeutic work) are included. Some institutions report this revenue in greater detail, specifying revenue for inpatient routine (room and board), inpatient ancillary, outpatient routine (facility or visit charges), and outpatient ancillary. Occasionally, different nomenclature is used to describe the revenues (e.g., gross revenues are sometimes called gross charges), but regardless of the name, the first amounts reported in the P&L represent the patient revenues.

Following the revenues is a series of deductions. "Contractual allowances"

Table 2-2
The Real General Hospital Comparative Statement of Revenues and Expenses

| | For the 12 Months Ended June 30, | |
	19X2	19X1
Gross Patient Service Revenue	$92,805,908	$77,185,080
Less Deductions		
Contractual Allowances	$5,907,416	$4,755,060
Provision for Bad Debts	2,342,708	1,505,041
Provision for Charity Care	676,844	690,246
Total Deductions	$8,926,968	$6,950,347
Net Patient Service Revenue	$83,878,940	$70,234,733
Other Operating Revenue	3,342,121	3,615,015
Total Operating Revenue	$87,221,061	$73,849,748
Operating Expenses		
Salaries and Wages	$38,204,953	$34,436,411
Fringe Benefits	7,517,926	6,460,602
Supplies and Purchased Services	29,916,553	25,573,883
Interest Expense	1,867,590	1,491,970
Depreciation	3,390,416	2,419,783
Cost of Operations	$80,897,438	$70,382,649
Excess of Revenue over Expenses	$6,323,623	$3,467,099

(sometimes also referred to as contractual adjustments or third-party discounts) represent the amount of gross charges written off and not billed to the major third parties because of preexisting discounting or "lower of cost or charges" agreements. The provisions for bad debts and charity care represent the amount of revenue the institution believes will not be collected, even though billed, because patients will not or cannot pay. This reduction of revenue is recognized on the P&L just as the reduction of the accounts receivable is recognized on the balance sheet. The "total deductions" line is simply the sum of the three types of deductions. Some institutions report in less detail, using a single "deductions" or "deductions from revenue" line while others go into greater detail. Regardless, the essential principle is the recognition that certain properly charged amounts will not be collected. The amount remaining after deductions is the net patient revenue.

The report continues with "other operating revenue," which represents income to the hospital from such auxiliary operations and enterprises as gift shops, parking lots, baby picture concessions, television and telephone rentals, and so on. Total operating revenue is the total of all of the institution's revenue streams.

Shifting gears, the report moves to the cost of generating the revenues and summarizes them in four to six categories. People costs are always listed first, whether referred to as "salaries and wages," as Real General does, or simply as salaries. This refers to the cash compensation paid to staff of the institution. The cost of providing health care insurance, pension, tuition assistance, and other nonwage compensation for employees is reported as "fringe benefits." Some P&Ls report a single line called "salaries and benefits" that merges the two costs.

"Supplies and purchased services" represent the expense associated with the consumption of medical and other supplies and the use of services such as medical transcription, legal, accounting, and so on.

"Interest expense" refers to the cost of borrowing money to meet the cash needs of the institution. Interest income, which may have been earned by the investment of excess cash, would be reported as "other operating revenue." The two would never be combined or netted and reported on a single line in an income statement.

Usually, the last expense item to be reported is "depreciation." It is a noncash expense, not purchased like the other expense items. It represents in dollars the portion of the useful life of the fixed assets consumed during the accounting period for which the P&L was prepared. The logic behind the depreciation of fixed assets (except land, which is never depreciated) is that a portion of any asset's life is consumed in the generation of revenue. Just as the cost of supplies consumed in generating revenue is deducted from revenue, so, too, the cost of that portion of the fixed asset that was consumed is similarly deducted.

"Cost of operations" is the sum of the expenses previously listed and is deducted from total operating revenue to arrive at the "excess of revenue over expenses." This may also be referred to as operating gain or loss. It is, to use a popular expression, the bottom line.

It is worthwhile to note that the accounting for revenue in the health care industry differs from that in most other industries. Elsewhere, sales, the equivalent of patient revenue outside the health care industry, are not reported as a gross amount and then reduced by discounts and other deductions but rather are reported as a single net amount. (Recently, some hospitals have begun to use P&Ls that begin with net revenue rather than gross.) The reason this is significant is that in some respects health care institutions overreport revenue. Consider, for example, the scenario in which a hospital begins to experience increasing bad debt and charity care write-offs owing, perhaps, to an economic downturn or a reduction in insurance coverages. If one assumes that the costs of rendering care do not change over time and that the service profile remains constant for comparison purposes, a graph of patient revenues might resemble Figure 2-2. The impression is one of strong growth in gross revenue. However, net revenue has remained flat over time. Clearly the reporting treatment of patient revenue has given a misleading message.

A recent decision by the Financial Accounting Standards Board (FASB) has resulted in another change in the way a hospital P&L displays the provision for bad debts. Rather than showing the provision for bad debts as a deduction from revenue, it is now to be shown with operating expenses. Table 2-3 displays the state-

Figure 2-2
Trend in Gross and Net Revenue

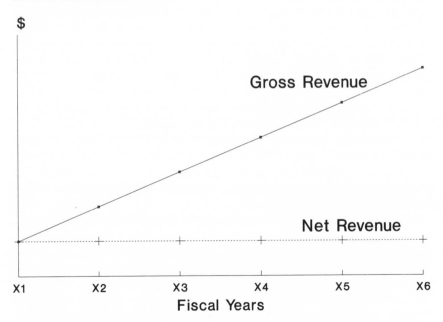

This graph clearly shows that the reporting treatment of patient revenue has given a misleading message.

Table 2-3
The Real General Hospital
Comparative Statement of Revenues and Expenses
(Depicting FASB Reporting Changes)

	For the 12 Months Ended June 30,	
	19X2	19X1
Net Patient Service Revenue	$86,221,648	$71,739,774
Other Operating Revenue	3,342,121	3,615,015
Total Operating Revenue	$89,563,769	$75,354,789
Operating Expenses		
Salaries and Wages	$38,204,953	$34,436,411
Fringe Benefits	7,517,926	6,460,602
Supplies and Purchased Services	29,916,553	25,573,883
Provision for Bad Debts	2,342,708	1,505,041
Interest Expense	1,867,590	1,491,970
Depreciation	3,390,416	2,419,783
Cost of Operations	$83,240,146	$71,887,690
Excess of Revenue over Expenses	$6,323,623	$3,467,099

ment of revenues and expenses for the Real General Hospital, restated to show these two recent changes in reporting treatment.

Because data from the previous fiscal year, 19X1, are printed side by side with the current year, it is possible to gain a reasonable understanding of what happened during the year and how the financial events of the current year differed from those of the previous year. Reviewing the P&L in Table 2-2, one can note that gross revenue grew significantly, by greater than 20 percent; the amount of total deductions grew by almost one-third; other operating revenue decreased; and total operating expense increased by more than $10 million. On the excess of revenue over expense line, the profit has nearly doubled.

Comparative data are of great value in reviewing financial statements. Whether the comparison is to a relevant prior period, to a budget for the reporting period, or to a series of data elements comprising a trend, the presence of comparative amounts gives the reviewer a perspective. It provides a yardstick against which to measure the reported financial results.

Despite the fact that Real General Hospital's balance sheet and statement of revenues and expenses provide the data necessary to make the comparison with the prior year's results, a major weakness remains. The numbers displayed represent absolute values—the absolute value of cash, the absolute value of total deductions, the absolute value of the operating gain or loss, and so on. In order to have a complete understanding, *relative* values (ratios) must also be examined. Consider, for example, the selected absolute values for two hypothetical nursing homes (Table 2-4).

Home B has more cash on hand and more current assets than Home A. It also

Table 2-4
Financial Information

	Nursing Home A	Nursing Home B
Cash	$ 10,000	$ 20,000
Total Current Assets	300,000	384,000
Total Current Liabilities	150,000	320,000

has a higher level of current liabilities. The question that cannot be answered accurately using only these absolute values, however, is, Which nursing home is better able to pay its bills? Is it Home B because it has more cash on hand or because it has more total current assets than Home A? Or is it Home A, which has fewer total current liabilities? To find the answer, a financial ratio, which expresses a *relative* value rather than an *absolute* value, must be used.

FINANCIAL RATIOS

One of the tools used in assessing the financial condition of a company is financial ratio analysis — the examination of one absolute value expressed in relative terms as a ratio to another absolute value. It is possible to draw a parallel between financial ratios and diagnostic test results that the medical profession uses in determining the health status of a patient. In the business arena, financial analysts function like "dollar doctors" trying to determine the health status of a company along with symptoms, diagnosis, treatment recommendations, if any, and so on.

There are over a hundred different ratios measuring everything from the ability to satisfy creditors, to efficiency, to turning profits. For the purposes of this text, three groups of financial ratios will be considered: liquidity, asset activity, and profitability.

Measures of Liquidity

The first group of these ratios deals with liquidity — the ability to pay current obligations.

Current Ratio. The current ratio represents the number of dollars of current assets available to cover each dollar of current liabilities.

$$\text{Current Ratio} = \frac{\text{Total Current Assets}}{\text{Total Current Liabilities}}$$

A health care institution with $100,000 of total current assets and $50,000 of total current liabilities would have a current ratio of 2.0.

$$\text{Current Ratio} = \frac{\$100,000}{\$50,000}$$
$$= 2.0$$

This means that for each dollar of current liability, there are two dollars of current assets available to cover the debt. It is now possible to answer the question concerning Nursing Homes A and B (Table 2-5). Which nursing home is better able to pay its bills? The correct answer (based not on absolute values but rather on the financial ratio that measures liquidity—the current ratio) is Home A, which has a current ratio that is nearly double that of Home B.

Working Capital. The same values used in determining the current ratio are used to determine working capital, but instead of division, subtraction is used. Using the same example as before, a health care institution with $100,000 of total current assets and $50,000 of total current liabilities would have $50,000 of working capital.

Total Current Assets	$100,000
− Total Current Liabilities	50,000
Working Capital	$ 50,000

Quick Ratio. The quick ratio, sometimes referred to as the acid test ratio or simply the acid test, is a more demanding measure of liquidity. The inventory value is eliminated from the calculation because it may not be converted to cash as quickly as the other current assets. The quick ratio, therefore, is a more conservative financial ratio than the current ratio.

$$\text{Quick Ratio} = \frac{\text{Total Current Assets} - \text{Inventory}}{\text{Total Current Liabilities}}$$

Given a health care institution with total current assets of $17,400,000 (including $1,200,000 of inventory) and total current liabilities of $7,200,000, the quick ratio would be:

$$\begin{aligned} \text{Quick Ratio} &= \frac{\$17,400,000 - \$1,200,000}{\$7,200,000} \\ &= \frac{\$16,200,000}{\$7,200,000} \\ &= 2.25 \end{aligned}$$

Table 2-5
Expanded Financial Information

	Nursing Home A	Nursing Home B
Cash	$ 10,000	$ 20,000
Total Current Assets	300,000	384,000
Total Current Liabilities	150,000	320,000
Current Ratio	2.0	1.2

These two ratios are among the most commonly used indicators of liquidity. As a rule the higher the value, the better. As a trend, increasing ratio values are favorable. Avoid the mistake, however, of assuming that a high value is always a good sign and a low value is a bad sign. An institution with an excessively high current or quick ratio may, for example, not be investing enough funds in its property, plant, and equipment; this may cause a serious obsolescence problem at a later date.

Asset Activity Measures

The second group of ratios also deals with liquidity, but expressed in terms of asset activity—the time needed to convert balance sheet items into cash. Of interest are accounts receivable, inventory, and accounts payable.

Accounts Receivable. The average age of accounts receivable measures the approximate number of days that the receivables remain outstanding (unpaid). It tells how fast bills are turned into cash. It is, in essence, a ratio of the receivable and the average daily patient revenue (the patient revenue for a given period of time divided by the number of calendar days in that period of time).

$$\text{Average Age} = \frac{\text{Receivable}}{(\text{Revenue} \div \text{Calendar days})}$$

There are three different ways to state the average age of accounts receivable: (1) "gross"—the calculation is based on the receivable balance, before any adjustment for allowances, and *gross* patient service revenue; (2) "net"—the calculation is based on the receivable value after an adjustment is made for allowances and *net* patient service revenue; and (3) "net-net"—the receivable part of the equation is further reduced by the value of any advances from third-party payers. In comparing accounts payable performance, it is important to compare like days, avoiding the erroneous comparison of gross days in one instance with net-net in another.

Using the June 30, 19X2, data from the Real General Hospital's balance sheet, the calculations would be:

$$
\begin{aligned}
\text{Average Age (Gross)} \quad &= \frac{\$13,245,676}{\$92,805,908 \div 365 \text{ days}} \\
&= \frac{\$13,245,676}{\$254,263} \\
&= 52.1 \text{ days}
\end{aligned}
$$

$$
\begin{aligned}
\text{Average Age (Net)} \quad &= \frac{\$13,245,676 - 1,806,638}{\$83,878,940 \div 365 \text{ days}} \\
&= \frac{\$11,439,038}{\$229,805} \\
&= 49.8 \text{ days}
\end{aligned}
$$

$$\text{Average Age (Net-Net)} = \frac{(\$13,245,676 - 1,806,638 - 2,817,256)}{(\$83,878,940 \div 365 \text{ days})}$$
$$= \frac{\$8,621,782}{\$229,805}$$
$$= 37.5 \text{ days}$$

This means that, on average, it takes between one and two months to turn a bill into cash, and the hospital must plan its use of resources with this in mind.

Accounts Receivable Turnover. This is a measure of the number of times each year that the accounts receivable are completely replaced or turned over.

$$\text{Turnover} = \frac{365 \text{ Days}}{\text{Average Age}}$$

Using the previous data, the accounts receivable turnover is 9.7 or 10 times on a net-net basis (365 days ÷ 37.5 days).

Average Inventory Age. This measures the number of days of supplies on hand in inventory, based on the institution's average daily use of supplies. The calculation requires several steps and a piece of data not found on the balance sheet. Step One is to determine the average inventory value by combining the inventory value at the end of the current period with the value at the end of the prior period and dividing by two. For an institution with inventory values as of June 30, 19X5, and June 30, 19X6, of $181,600 and $211,500, respectively, the average inventory value would be $196,550 ($181,600 + $211,500 = $393,100; $393,100 ÷ 2 = $196,550).

Step Two uses the piece of data not found on the balance sheet—the annual amount of inventory purchases. This can be obtained from the finance department or from the records in materials management. For this exercise assume that $1,592,400 of items were purchased for the inventory during the year. This value is used to calculate inventory turnover, the number of times that the inventory is completely replaced each year.

$$\text{Inventory Turnover} = \frac{\text{Annual Inventory Purchases}}{\text{Average Inventory Value}}$$
$$= \frac{\$1,592,400}{\$196,550}$$
$$= 8.1$$

Step Three in the calculation process is to divide 365 by the number of times the inventory turns over each year. This tells how many days there are between turns, which equate to the average number of days of inventory on hand.

$$\text{Inventory Age} = \frac{365}{\text{Inventory Turnover}}$$
$$= \frac{365}{8.1}$$
$$= 45.06 \text{ days}$$

If all purchases were to stop, about a month and a half (45 days) would pass before the inventory value dropped to zero. The lower the number of days of average inventory age, the better; however, a proper balance must be struck so that critical supplies are not out of stock. Noncritical items are of less concern and may occasionally be out of stock without causing operational disruption. As a trend, declining values are good. Inventory age that is higher than necessary means that money is being tied up unnecessarily in inventory when it could be used more productively.

Consider, for example, what would happen if the manager responsible for inventory were to reduce the average age to 30 days. At that level, over $65,000 would be available for other onetime uses such as equipment purchases, facility renovations, and so on. The value of the 15-day decrease in inventory age is calculated by dividing the average inventory value by the average inventory age. The result is the value of each "day" of inventory. In this case, $196,550 divided by 45.06 days yields a value of $4,362 for each "day" of inventory. The decrease from 45 days to 30 days is, thus, worth $65,430 (15 × $4,362 = $65,430).

Accounts Payable Age. This is a measure of the average age of bills owed to creditors. Once again, a piece of data not present on the balance sheet is needed to make the calculation; the information necessary is the annual credit purchases. The finance or accounting department can supply these data. For this example, assume values of $199,920 for the accounts payable balance and $1,737,400 for annual credit purchases.

$$\text{Average Age} = \frac{\text{Accounts Payable}}{(\text{Annual Credit Purchases} \div 365)}$$
$$= \frac{\$199,920}{(\$1,737,400 \div 365)}$$
$$= \frac{\$199,920}{\$4,760}$$
$$= 42 \text{ days}$$

The lower the age, the faster bills are being paid. In times of tight money, the age generally will increase as efforts are made to conserve cash. Monies not used to pay current bills can be used for other purposes, up to a point. The payment terms generally extended by creditors cannot be consistently abused by late payment of bills without risking the loss of a vendor. Paying too quickly is also poor practice because it does not allow available cash to work for the institution.

Profitability Measures

The third group of ratios deals with profitability—how well the company uses its financial resources to generate profits.

Return on Investment. Sometimes referred to as return on assets, this ratio is a measure of the ability to use company assets to generate profits. Of all the financial ratios, it is the most important. The reason that the terms *assets* and *investments* are used interchangeably stems from the fact that a company's primary investment is in itself—its assets. The interpretation of this ratio is quite simple: the higher, the better. Consequently, increasing values over time represent a favorable trend. For an institution with a bottom line of $960,000 and total assets of $12,260,000, the calculation is as follows.

$$\text{Return on Investment} = \frac{\text{Net Operating Gain}}{\text{Total Assets}}$$
$$= \frac{\$960,000}{\$12,260,000}$$
$$= 0.078 \text{ or } 7.8\%$$

This means that the hospital's investment in its own assets has earned 7.8 percent, a good return. It is the single most important ratio because it measures overall management effectiveness.

The Collection Rate. This is an indicator of the amount of the revenue charged that is actually collected. The higher the value, the better, and, as a trend, increasing values are, of course, favorable. If a health care provider suffers from a declining collection rate trend, the eventual outcome can be bankruptcy. Consequently, the collection rate must be monitored carefully and frequently so that corrective actions can be taken quickly if necessary. For a provider with net patient revenue of $53,100,000 and gross charges of $60,300,000, the collection rate would be calculated as follows:

$$\text{Collection Rate} = \frac{\text{Net Patient Revenue}}{\text{Gross Patient Revenue}}$$
$$= \frac{\$53,100,000}{\$60,300,000}$$
$$= 0.881 \text{ or } 88.1\%$$

Operating Margin Ratio. This ratio measures the proportion of total operating revenue that is retained as operating gain. It is a measure of profitability; nevertheless, comparison to industry averages should be made carefully. Above average values can be misleading if there is a greater than average need for working capital, debt repayment, or investment in plant and equipment (all of which are funded from operating margin). Conversely, a hospital with substantial endowment distributions or income from other outside sources such as philanthropy may have lower operating margin requirements, and, thus, a lower ratio may be quite acceptable. Given a total operating revenue of $70 million and an operating gain of $2.5 million, the calculation would be.

$$\text{Operating Margin Ratio} = \frac{\text{Operating Gain}}{\text{Total Operating Revenue}}$$
$$= \frac{\$2,500,000}{\$70,000,000}$$
$$= 0.357 \text{ or } 3.6\%$$

REVIEW PROBLEMS

1. Examine the balance sheet and income statement of the Real General Hospital. Calculate the following for Fiscal Year 19X1.

- Current ratio
- Working capital
- Quick ratio
- Average age of accounts receivable (on a gross, net, and net-net basis)
- Accounts receivable turnover
- Return on investment
- Collection rate
- Operating margin ratio

2. If the Real General Hospital's inventory purchases during 19X2 were $15,528,884, how many times did the inventory turn over during the year; and what is the average inventory age?

3. How much cash would be provided for alternative use if the average value of the inventory was reduced to 30 days?

Chapter 3

Cost and Cost Behavior

In health care, the focus of management responsibility is, for the most part, the control of operating expense – cost. To exercise this responsibility more effectively, managers must understand cost types, cost behavior over the course of time, which costs are fixed, which are variable, which are a bit of both, how cost is translated into price, and so on. This understanding begins with cost accounting.

COST ACCOUNTING

The subject of cost accounting, quite naturally, is cost (expense) and cost behavior. In the health care industry, cost accounting has assumed a retrospective posture, providing information regarding what costs were and how they behaved in the past. In other industries, cost accounting has been concerned not only with historical cost levels and behavior but also with what the level of costs should be and how they should behave. This orientation to the future was beneficial in supporting management in the exercise of control in order to deliver products and services that could be sold in a competitive marketplace. In a highly competitive environment, management could ill afford to sit back and take a retrospective view of cost performance. Rather, upper management needed to establish cost standards for the future and hold line management responsible for compliance.

Historically, management in the health care industry has not adopted this prospective, standards-based, cost-controlling orientation. Some of the cost-control techniques employed in other industries are discussed in Chapter 8.

COST CONCEPTS AND TYPES

Basically, there are three types of costs—fixed, variable, and semivariable.

Fixed costs tend to remain constant over the course of many accounting or reporting periods. Such costs are not influenced by changes in volume or intensity of service. The salary of a nursing unit head nurse or supply clerk would be an example of fixed costs. These salary levels are not influenced by changes in the volume of patients treated in the nursing unit. In graphic form, fixed costs appear as the flat, horizontal line in Figure 3-1.

Variable costs, on the other hand, rise and fall in relation to changes in the level of activity. This relationship is illustrated in Figure 3-2. Anesthesia supplies, for instance, are consumed as a function of the number and duration of surgical cases.

Caution must be exercised in establishing which measure of volume is appropriate for determining the relationship. The use of anesthetic agents is driven more by the number of minutes than by the number of cases. Thus, even if surgical procedures were declining, anesthetic agent costs might increase as a result of an increase in the length of cases (Table 3-1).

As the table indicates, the total monthly cost of anesthesia supplies is increas-

Figure 3-1
Performance of Fixed Costs

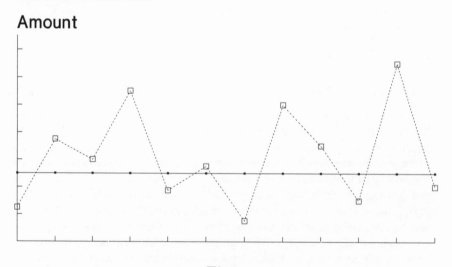

This graphic example of the performance of fixed costs indicates that they are not influenced by fluctuations in volume.

Figure 3-2
Performance of Variable Costs

Amount

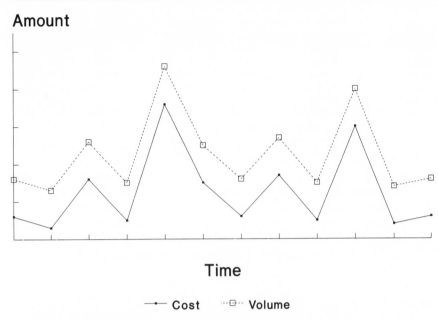

Time

—•— Cost   ···□··· Volume

Variable costs, as shown here, rise and fall accordingly with volume.

ing at approximately 12 percent per month. At the same time, surgical cases are decreasing. As a result, the cost per case is escalating rapidly. But are the data complete? Are all the facts available? Do anesthesia supplies represent a variable cost? Additional data present a different picture and highlight the importance of selecting the proper measure of volume when working with variable costs (Table 3-2).

A more thorough compilation of the data, to include total minutes and cost per minute, reveals quite a different picture. Use of the proper volume measure (in this case, minutes) reveals that anesthesia supplies are, indeed, variable with vol-

Table 3-1
Anesthesia Supply Cost per Case Analysis

Month	Total Cost	Surgical Cases	Cost per Case
April	$9,663	250	$38.65
May	11,558	240	48.16
June	13,387	230	58.20
July	14,852	220	67.51
August	16,296	210	77.60
September	17,379	200	86.90

Table 3-2
Anesthesia Supply Cost per Minute Analysis

Month	Total Cost	Surgical Cases	Cost per Case	Total Minutes	Cost per Minute
April	$9,663	250	$38.65	10,000	$0.9663
May	11,558	240	48.16	12,000	0.9632
June	13,387	230	58.20	13,800	0.9701
July	14,852	220	67.51	15,400	0.9644
August	16,296	210	77.60	16,800	0.9700
September	17,379	200	86.90	18,000	0.9655

ume; the average cost per minute of time is $0.9666, with a standard deviation of $0.0158 and a range of $0.0069.

Semivariable costs, as the name implies, are partially fixed and partially variable. Typical of this type of costs would be those for workers who are able to deal with a range of workload. Radiology and lab technicians who are able to produce a range of relative value units (RVUs) and CAP (College of American Pathologists) workload units, respectively, represent examples of semivariable costs. Another approach to semivariable costs is to think of them as fixed over a certain

Figure 3-3
Performance of Semivariable Costs

Amount

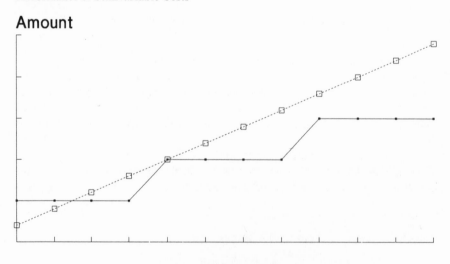

Time

—•— Cost   ··□·· Volume

As graphically indicated here, semivariable costs are fixed over a range of volume, then become variable given the addition of a single unit of volume before becoming fixed again.

range of volume and then variable up to the next range of volume. A visual representation would resemble the steplike line in Figure 3-3.

Note that as volume rises, cost remains fixed through certain ranges of volume. In a long-term care facility with a patient-to-staff ratio of 8 to 1, for example, staffing costs are essentially fixed in the range of 1 to 8 patients; one full-time equivalent employee (FTE) is required. A 9th patient will trigger a change in staffing (and in this semivariable cost, as well) to add an additional FTE. However, that second FTE remains fixed as volume grows through the 16th patient. At that point the addition of a 17th patient would set the process in motion again. Thus, in this example, for a volume of 1 to 8 patients, the staffing cost is fixed. It becomes variable with the 9th patient, remains fixed for patients 10 through 16, becomes variable again with the 17th patient, holds fixed for patients 18 through 24, and so on.

Understanding the performance of semivariable costs is important to the decision-making process. In the previous example, the addition of a 9th patient, if not followed by a 10th, 11th, and so on, would be a poor choice because the level of productivity decreases sharply, and cost increases just as sharply with the addition of a single patient. With 8 patients the productivity ratio is 8 to 1. The addition of a single patient drops the productivity ratio to 4.5 to 1, a productivity drop of approximately 56 percent. Concurrently, there is a labor cost increase of 100 percent. If revenue increased by only 12.5 percent (1 added patient = 1/8th = 12.5 percent), this would prove to be a poor business decision. A "before and after" view of the financial performance may illustrate the point (Table 3-3).

As can be seen from the abbreviated P&L, the decision to add a single patient was unwise. The impact of semivariable costs was not properly understood. It

Table 3-3
Old Age Medical Center
Profit and Loss Statement

Operating Facts	Before	After
Daily Patient Rate	$82	$82
Number of Patients	8	9
Number of Staff FTEs	1	2
Staff Cost at $12 per Hour	$96	$192
Daily Non-Staff Cost per Patient	$62	$62

Profit and Loss Statement	Before	After
Gross Revenue (at $82 per Patient)	$656	$738
Operating Expenses		
Staff Cost	$96	$192
Non-Staff Costs ($62 x 8)	496	
Non-Staff Costs ($62 x 9)		558
Total	$592	$750
Profit or Loss	$64	($12)

was assumed that the staff cost was totally variable when, in fact, it was really semivariable.

The kind of economies and diseconomies of scale or size represented by semivariable costs is covered further in this chapter as part of the discussion of marginal cost and decision making on the margin.

COST BEHAVIOR OVER TIME

The passage of time has an effect on cost behavior. Fixed costs, for example, take on greater, if not total, variability over the course of time. The fixed cost associated with a department manager's salary can become 100 percent variable if the department is closed.

In addition, the proportion of costs will change as volumes change. In a department in which costs are considered half fixed and half variable, a change in volume will affect this 50/50 proportion. Consider the example of a department with $500,000 of fixed costs, $500,000 of variable costs, and 10,000 units of service. The expense profile at this level of volume is 50 percent fixed and 50 percent variable. If volume were to double, would the department still be 50 percent variable? No, variable costs would then comprise two-thirds of total costs. This is illustrated in Figure 3-4.

Note that the proportion of variable costs has doubled, and the department's cost profile is now one-third to two-thirds. If this was not recognized, the ques-

Figure 3-4
Proportion of Fixed and Variable Costs
Before and After an Increase in Volume

Variable Costs = $500,000 50% Variable	Variable Cost Addition $500,000	New Variable Costs = $1,000,000 Now 66.67% Variable
Fixed Costs = $500,000 50% Fixed		Fixed Costs = $500,000 33.33% Fixed
Total Cost $1,000,000	Added Cost $500,000	Total Cost $1,500,000
10,000 Units	10,000 Units	20,000 Units

Before an increase in volume, variable costs were equally proportionate to fixed costs; after the increase, the proportion shifts in favor of variable costs.

tion of whether to expand the department might result in a faulty decision based on an improper understanding of the underlying costs. If management allowed volume to grow to 30,000 units of service based on the erroneous assumption of a 50/50 cost profile, insufficient resources would be allotted and a poor P&L outcome would result. The risk of making a decision with limited knowledge is that unwise decisions can result. Given today's environment, it is far wiser for a manager, at any level within the organization, to gain the proper understanding of cost behavior to support wise, prudent decision making rather than court disaster.

MARGINAL ANALYSIS

The term *marginal analysis* refers to the technique of considering only incremental data as part of a financial analysis or decision process. Only the changes in financial condition are considered, as opposed to the "before and after" style of analysis used in the Old Age Medical Center example of semivariable costs. Using the same data as that example, a marginal analysis would resemble Table 3-4.

The marginal P&L displays only increments, only the difference between before and after. In effect, the marginal P&L provides a financial statement of the decision itself—the profitability of adding a single patient. In using this kind of analysis, a manager would make a decision "on the margin" and in this case would avoid adding this single patient.

Marginal analysis is helpful in making decisions because it reduces the scope of supportive analytical work and because it focuses attention on the financial re-

Table 3-4
Old Age Medical Center
Marginal Profit and Loss Statement

Operating Facts	Before	After
Daily Patient Rate	$82	$82
Number of Patients	8	9
Number of Staff FTEs	1	2
Staff Cost at $12 per Hour	$96	$192
Daily Non–Staff Cost per Patient	$62	$62

Marginal Profit and Loss Statement

P & L Item	Amount
Gross Revenue ($82 x 1 Patient)	$82
Operating Expenses	
Staff Cost (1 added FTE)	$96
Non–Staff Costs ($62 x 1 Patient)	62
Total	$158
Profit or Loss (from a $64 profit to a $12 loss)	($76)

ality of the decision itself, not the overall financial condition after a decision has been made. In other words, will the change improve the financial condition of the institution? If it will, the change should be made to pursue the improvement, assuming no non-financial barriers lie in the path. If it does not improve the financial condition, the change should be avoided. It is also possible to compare marginal P&Ls for several available options to help select the most beneficial one. In this situation the use of marginal analysis greatly reduces the amount of analytical work that must be performed to support properly the decision-making process.

Using marginal analysis to examine a proposal concentrates the decision-making energy on the proposal, not the final result of its implementation. Consider the example in Table 3-5. In this case, a proposal is put forth that will generate $50,000 of revenues, cost $10,000, and have a $40,000 profit.

The proposal should be judged on its own set of facts, not the financial situation that would exist after adoption of the proposal. If only the "after" column was examined, the decision likely would be rejected because the P&L shows a $60,000 loss. Marginal analysis, however, examines only the changes, an improvement of $40,000 to the bottom line, and accepts the proposal.

Because marginal analysis focuses on the financial reality of a decision, it is the approach of choice in benefit/cost ratio analysis, which is discussed in Chapter 8.

REAL-WORLD IMPLICATIONS

What would happen if a hospital's costs were really 50 percent fixed and 50 percent variable, but a regulator took the view that costs were 100 percent variable? If volume were to increase, one dollar of improvement would accrue to the hospital for each 50¢ of real cost increase (only the variable costs would increase). Conversely, if volume were to decline, one dollar would be lost for each 50 cent of cost decrease (again, only the variable costs would change – in this case decreasing).

In an era in which volumes are declining, this can be disastrous. The 1990s represent such an era, and the prospective payment system (PPS) considers hospital costs to be 100 percent variable. An understanding of cost behavior can be used proactively and creatively to take advantage of economies of scale. The pro-

Table 3-5
Marginal Analysis

	Before Adoption	Proposal	After Adoption
Revenue	$100,000	$50,000	$150,000
Expense	200,000	10,000	210,000
Profit or (Loss)	($100,000)	$40,000	($60,000)

file of fixed and variable costs must be known to determine real behavior of costs as volume changes. Also, the regulator's view must be known to determine revenue potential.

Consider, for example, a hospital with costs that are 50 percent variable. As depicted in Table 3-6, the hospital's current level of operation results in a volume of 400 cases, with its costs evenly split between fixed and variable. The hospital wishes to make an average profit of $100 on each case. For purposes of illustration, it is assumed that revenues are fully collectible. Given these facts, the hospital charges $2,600 for each case.

In a competitive environment, if the hospital leadership fully understood the behavior of its fixed and variable costs, it might be possible to pursue market share aggressively by lowering the price per case to $1,975 to attract HMO business. In this case, Scenario A, as volume doubles because of the aggressive pursuit of market share in a price-competitive marketplace, the fixed costs remain constant, the targeted average profit per case is achieved, and total profits double.

Scenario B displays the same hospital's data. In this scenario, however, no consideration is given to price sensitivity. Rather, market share is increased using more conventional methods. The result of doubling the number of cases while maintaining the average price per case is a significant increase in total profits to $580,000.

COST ALLOCATION

Cost allocation involves the transfer or allocation of costs from one department to another. The purpose of such allocations is to develop a price for a service, determine the relationship of total revenue and total costs for a department or service, and to determine profitability on a product line or departmental basis. In health care, most cost allocations involve cost transfers from overhead centers (non–revenue-producing departments like housekeeping and security which are unable to bill patients for services) to revenue centers (revenue-producing departments like labs and radiology, which do bill for services). When used as part of a product line management approach, allocations involve the transfer of revenues, write-offs, costs, and profits from ancillary centers (labs, radiology, nuclear

Table 3-6
Real-World Scenarios

	Current Situation	Scenario A	Scenario B
Number of Cases	400	800	800
Variable Costs	$500,000	$1,000,000	$1,000,000
Fixed Costs	500,000	500,000	500,000
Target Profit per Case	100	100	100
Average Price per Case	2,600	1,975	2,600
Total Profit	40,000	80,000	580,000

medicine, pharmacy, operating rooms, and so on) to direct patient care centers (inpatient units and clinics).

Several methods are used to allocate costs; these range from the simplest single step-down methodology (so named because the allocation worksheet resembles a set of steps leading down) to highly sophisticated multiple simultaneous equation methodologies. Examples of overhead centers and the statistical bases used to allocate their costs are shown in Table 3-7.

Using the simplest step-down allocation methodology, the cost of dietary services would be allocated only to those revenue centers where patient meals were served. Laundry and linen costs would be shared among the users on the basis of the number of pounds they utilized. If a nursing unit used 15,000 pounds of laundry (of a total consumption of 300,000 pounds), it would receive a cost allocation of 5 percent (15,000 ÷ 300,000) of the laundry department's cost.

The cost allocations can be determined by using two large worksheets—one for the statistics used in the allocation calculations, the other for recording the actual dollar allocation amounts.

The first step in the cost allocation process is the completion of the worksheet that compiles the statistics used as the bases of the various allocations—direct cost and revenue by department, patient meals, and so on. Table 3-8 traces a single step-down cost allocation process at Miscellaneous General Hospital. For purposes of illustration, the number of departments has been limited.

The statistics worksheet lists department names in the far left column. The statistics relative to each department are listed in the remaining columns. Headings indicate which kind of statistic is to be listed in each column. The first column captures the amount of direct costs for each department. This statistic will be used to allocate the cost of hospital administration. One reason for using direct cost in this instance is that the larger the department, using direct cost as a surrogate, the more service or attention it receives from hospital administration. No value is entered on the hospital administration line in this column because its costs will be allocated only to other departments, not to itself. If one did enter an

Table 3-7
Bases Used in the Allocation of Overhead Costs

Overhead Cost Center	Basis of Cost Allocation
Administration	Total direct costs of those departments receiving the cost allocation
General Accounting	Total direct costs of those departments receiving the cost allocation
Patient Billing	Departmental revenue
Dietary Services	Patient meals
Housekeeping	Square feet
Social Work	Discharges
Laundry and Linen	Pounds of laundry processed
Admitting Office	Admissions

Table 3-8
Miscellaneous General Hospital Cost Allocation Step-down,
Worksheet 1 – Allocation Statistics

Departments	Direct Cost ($000s)	Revenue ($000s)	Patient Meals	Square Feet	Discharges & Deaths	Laundry Pounds	Admissions
Hospital Administration							
General Accounting	665.0						
Billing	395.0						
Dietary	655.8						
Housekeeping	370.0						
Social Work	67.6			600			
Laundry	248.3			5,000			
Admitting	101.3			1,300			
2 North	704.4	1,338.4	12,167	9,000	764	14,190	739
2 South	690.3	1,311.6	11,923	9,000	760	13,905	735
3 East	721.7	1,372.8	12,480	8,500	685	14,560	660
3 West	700.6	1,331.5	12,104	8,500	682	14,135	657
I C U	361.5	759.2	1,519	4,000	93	5,310	190
Radiology	966.7	1,836.7		8,000		1,400	
O R	930.0	1,789.6		6,100		5,700	
Labs	718.0	1,634.2		3,000			
Total	$8,296.2	$11,374.0	50,193	63,000	2,984	69,200	2,981

Table 3-9
Miscellaneous General Hospital Cost Allocation Step-down,
Worksheet 2 – Allocation Amounts ($000s)

Departments	Direct Cost	Allocation Amounts From Departments on the Left To Departments Below the Double Line								Total Cost
Hospital Admin.	$950.0	950.0								
General Acctg.	665.0	76.1								
Billing	395.0	45.2								
Dietary	655.8	75.1								
H'keeping	370.0	42.4								
Social Work	67.6	7.7								
Laundry	248.3	28.4								
Admitting	101.3	11.6								
2 North	704.4	80.7								
2 South	690.3	79.0								
3 East	721.7	82.6								
3 West	700.6	80.2								
I C U	361.5	41.4								
Radiology	966.7	110.7								
O R	930.0	106.7								
Labs	718.0	82.2								
Total	$9,246.2	$950.0								

50

Table 3-10
Miscellaneous General Hospital Cost Allocation Step-down,
Worksheet 2 – Allocation Amounts ($000s)

Departments	Direct Cost	Allocation Amounts From Departments on the Left / To Departments Below the Double Line								Total Cost
Hospital Admin.	$950.0	950.0								
General Acctg.	665.0	76.1	741.1							
Billing	395.0	45.2	38.4	478.6						
Dietary	655.8	75.1	63.7		794.6					
H'keeping	370.0	42.4	35.9			448.3				
Social Work	67.6	7.7	6.6			4.3	86.2			
Laundry	248.3	28.4	24.1			35.6		336.4		
Admitting	101.3	11.6	9.8			9.3			132.0	
2 North	704.4	80.7	68.4	56.3	192.6	64.0	22.8	69.0	32.7	$1,291.0
2 South	690.3	79.0	67.0	55.2	188.8	64.0	22.7	67.6	32.5	1,267.1
3 East	721.7	82.6	70.1	57.8	197.6	60.5	20.4	70.8	29.2	1,310.6
3 West	700.6	80.2	68.0	56.0	191.6	60.5	20.3	68.7	29.1	1,275.1
I C U	361.5	41.4	35.1	31.9	24.0	28.5		25.8	8.4	556.7
Radiology	966.7	110.7	93.9	77.3		56.9		6.8		1,312.3
O R	930.0	106.7	90.3	75.3		43.4		27.7		1,273.4
Labs	718.0	82.2	69.7	68.8		21.3				960.0
Total	$9,246.2	$950.0	$741.1	$478.6	$794.6	$448.3	$86.2	$336.4	$132.0	$9,246.2

51

amount, the allocation calculations would be such that there would always remain unallocated cost for hospital administration; and the very purpose of the cost allocation process would be defeated.

Following completion of the statistics worksheet, the overhead costs are allocated in the same proportion as the statistics. Thus, if general accounting represents 8 percent of the total direct costs indicated in the statistics worksheet (665.0 ÷ 8,296.2 = 0.0802 = 0.08 = 8%), general accounting will be allocated 8% of the cost of hospital administration: $950.0 × 8% = $76.1. This same math logic applies until the entire $950.0 has been allocated (Table 3-9).

Following the allocation of hospital administration, both the direct and allocated overhead costs associated with general accounting are ready to be "stepped down" to the remaining departments. In this example, $741.1 ($665.0 of direct cost plus $76.1 of allocated overhead cost) is allocated. The denominator in this case is also direct cost, but no longer the $8,296.2; rather, it is $7,631.2 ($8,296.2 − $665.0), the new sum of direct cost exclusive of hospital administration *and* general accounting. Thus, the billing department receives 5.2 percent ($395.0 ÷ $7,631.2), dietary receives 8.6 percent ($655.8 ÷ $7,631.2), and so on until the entire $741.1 is fully allocated.

The allocation process continues until all the costs in the overhead departments have been fully allocated to recipient revenue-producing departments (Table 3-10). It is then possible to develop rates for these revenue centers so that all of the hospital's direct and overhead costs will be recouped.

Now the total costs of operating each direct patient care revenue center is known. Note that the total cost before the allocations were made ($9,246.2) is the same as the total cost after the allocations.

Ever since the first dollar of overhead cost was allocated years ago, one thing has remained constant despite the passage of time and the increase, thanks in large part to computers, in sophistication of allocation methodologies: regardless of what the basis or dollar amount of the allocation is, the manager of the department receiving the allocation will believe the amount is too high.

PRICE DETERMINATION

The determination of the price to be charged for a service must include some recognition of the underlying cost associated with the service. All things being equal, any business, health care or otherwise, that adopts a pricing strategy that gives no consideration to cost will soon find itself out of business. This is not to say that a prudent business approach cannot include lower-than-cost prices. It means that cost must be understood and that management must always be aware of the difference between cost and price.

There are several widely recognized approaches to determining price. The first, cost-based pricing, has historically been the approach of choice among health care providers. The "lower of cost or charges (prices)" dictate of cost reimbursement mandated this approach. The second approach, competition-based pricing, has recently entered the health care marketplace. Finally, there is demand-based pricing. The greater the demand for a product or service, the higher the price. This has yet to make an appearance in the health care environment.

Cost-Based Pricing

In this method, the price charged for a service is a function of the costs associated with providing the service. These costs normally include the following.

- The direct expense of the department or departments (the revenue center or centers) associated with providing the service. Salaries, fringe benefits, supplies, and services are included.

- Overhead allocated to the revenue center from support departments (housekeeping, dietary, social work, accounting, and so on). Sometimes these are called indirect costs.

- If not included in the allocation of support department overhead costs, depreciation expense must be included.

- Financial requirements for debt retirement, achievement of profit goals, return on investment, and so on.

- The "cost" of bad debts and other uncollectible accounts, along with contractual allowances (discounts) associated with major third-party insurance payers. Although this is usually treated as a deduction from revenue on the operating statement, it is treated as a cost for purposes of determining price. Rather than a dollar amount, a percent is used to "gross-up" cost.

As an example of how this approach is used to determine a price for service, consider the following financial and service information for the SeaThru Imaging Center, Inc., a stand-alone imaging operation.

SeaThru offers three services for its clients. Single-organ Magnetic Resonance Imaging (MRI) scans have a workload value of 100 Relative Value Units (RVUs). The center performs 500 such scans each year. A second service is computerized tomographic (CT) scans. These are valued at 100 RVUs and 50 RVUs depending on complexity. Annual volume is 500 of each. Finally, mammography, at 25 RVUs per procedure, accounts for 400 procedures annually. The costs of operating the center are listed in Table 3-11.

The cost "pieces" are assembled in building-block fashion, beginning with the direct expense of operating the SeaThru Center (Table 3-12).

Gross-up. The term applied to the technique of determining a gross amount or value (before discounts, write-offs, and other deductions) from a net amount or value is called "gross-up." If, for example, it is known that net revenue must amount to $900,000 and that a 10 percent discount is given off of gross revenue, it would be necessary to "gross-up" the $900,000 to determine the necessary amount of gross revenue to charge and against which the 10 percent discount would apply. This is done by dividing net revenue by the percent of gross revenue

Table 3-11
SeaThru Imaging Center
Operating Facts

Salaries	$ 88,000
Fringe Benefits	18,000
Supplies & Services	210,000
Allocated Overhead	150,000
Depreciation	125,000
Profit Target	50,000
Collection Rate	90.5%
Service Volume (RVUs)	
MRI Procedures	50,000
Simple CT Scans	25,000
Complex CT Scans	50,000
Mammograms	10,000
Total RVUs	135,000

that it represents. In this example net revenue represents 90 percent (100 percent – 10 percent) of gross revenue. This proportion is often referred to as the collection rate. The "gross-up" resembles the following.

$$\text{Net Revenue} \div \text{Collection Rate} = \text{Gross Revenue}$$
$$\$90,000 \div .90 = \$1,000,000$$

Caution: The wrong answer will be obtained if an additive approach (simply adding 10 percent of net revenue to net revenue to determine gross revenue) is used. This would yield only $990,000 ($900,000 + $90,000 [.10 × $900,000]). The proper method to determine gross revenue from net revenue is the "gross-up" (division) method.

Price List. Having determined the price per relative value unit (RVU), the final step of determining the price to be charged for each procedure is a simple calculation. In the case of multiple-service operations like SeaThru, a series of calculations is used (Table 3-13).

Competition-Based Pricing

The competition-oriented pricing methodology bases the determination of price on factors in the competitive environment. Price is as much a function of the competition's price as it is a function of cost. In the extreme, this takes the form of sealed-bid price competition. But, for the most part, it involves setting prices at an industrywide or marketplace average. Although price competition is a recent phenomenon in the health care industry, abundant examples can now be found.

Table 3-12
SeaThru Imaging Center
Revenue Requirements

Pricing Elements	Total Dollars	Dollars per RVU
Total Revenue Requirements Summary:		
The revenue needed to cover the cost of the		
Center consists of the following:		
A. Direct Expenses	$316,000	$2.34
B. Allocated Overhead	150,000	$1.11
C. Depreciation	125,000	$0.93
D. Financial Requirements (Profit)	50,000	$0.37
E. Bad Debt Coverage	33,737	$0.25
Total Revenue Requirements	$674,737	$5.00

Total Revenue Requirements – Detailed Explanations:
A. Direct Expenses:

Only the direct expenses of the revenue centers		
Salaries	$88,000	
Fringe Benefits	18,000	
Supplies and Services	210,000	
Total Direct Expense	$316,000	$2.34

B. Allocated Overhead:

Using any of a number of cost allocation medhods, costs that cannot be billed to specific patients (accounting, housekeeping, etc.) are added to the direct expenses of the revenue center	$150,000	$1.11

C. Depreciation (Facilities Requirements):

The dollar value of equipment and physical plant assets "consumed" as services are rendered	$125,000	$0.93

D. Financial Requirements (Profit):

An annual profit target is likely to be spelled out in the goals and objectives in the annual budget	$50,000	$0.37

E. Bad Debt Coverage

In order to make sure that the amounts collected are sufficient to cover:		
A. Direct Expenses	$316,000	
B. Allocated Overhead	150,000	
C. Depreciation	125,000	
D. Financial Requirements (Profit)	50,000	
It is necessary to divide the sum of those items	$641,000	
by the collection rate. The difference between this	0.95	
derived amount and the four items from which it	$674,737	
is derived is the amount to be provided to cover	−641,000	
bad debts. This process is called a "gross–up."	$33,737	$0.25

Table 3-13
SeaThru Imaging Center
Procedure Price Calculations

Service	Price per RVU	x	RVUs per Procedure	x	Price per Procedure
MRI Procedure	$5.00	x	100	x	$500.00
Simple CT Scan	5.00	x	50	x	250.00
Complex CT Scan	5.00	x	100	x	500.00
Mammogram	5.00	x	25	x	125.00

Sealed-bid pricing has found its way into the environment as a method for health maintenance organizations (HMOs) and similar providers to obtain the lowest-cost health services for their clients. Some state-run medical assistance programs have also used a bidding approach to obtain the lowest cost from providers.

Medicare's prospective payment system has brought marketplace average pricing into health care by establishing the average price itself. Rather than the providers' determining the price, Medicare has established the price it will pay and has, in effect, forced providers to achieve that marketplace average or lose money.

Private insurance companies have introduced indemnity polices for health care coverage that direct participating beneficiaries to those preferred providers whose prices are at or below the marketplace average. This directing of beneficiaries takes the form of disincentives for using nonpreferred providers. A visit to the "wrong" emergency room may require a copayment by the beneficiary that would have been covered by the insurance company had the patient used the preferred emergency room. The same kind of disincentive applies to inpatient hospitalization; higher copayments and deductibles are applied if a nonpreferred hospital is used.

Hospitals and other providers that have become nonpreferred are, theoretically, given an incentive to reduce their prices to the marketplace average or some other threshold in order to become "preferred."

The beauty of a solely competitive pricing environment for the health care industry is that it gives greater latitude to management in establishing prices, attracting patients, maneuvering for survival, and so on. On the down side, however, programs that benefit society but are not "paid in full" by society may be abandoned. Examples include medical education, care for the indigent, introduction of expensive, new technologies that provide better, but more expensive, outcomes, and the like.

Chapter 4

Budgeting: An Introduction

Budgeting is a key component in the management process. Understanding what a budget is and the role budgeting plays is essential to the proper exercise of a manager's responsibilities, which include planning, organizing and staffing, directing or leading, and controlling.

DEFINITION

A budget is, simply stated, a plan for the future, any plan for any future period. A vacation itinerary and a meeting agenda, too, are budgets. A more suitable definition for the study of budgets in the context of financial management is that a budget is a detailed plan showing how resources will be acquired and used during a specific time period. It represents a plan for the future expressed in formal, measurable terms.

The Detailed Plan

To be helpful, a budget must be prepared in sufficient detail to inform all levels of management of the exact expectations. It is not sufficient to establish a personnel budget for an institution and limit the detail to a statement of the overall number of employees. This serves no purpose except, perhaps, as part of a summary. Rather, a personnel budget should detail the quantities and types of full-time equivalents by department or cost center, perhaps by shift or by workstation. It should detail the salaries to be paid and the components, including routine, overtime, shift pay, cost of living or merit increases, and so on. All positions—vacant and otherwise—should be included in the budget. To assemble the quantity of data necessary to support a detailed plan, a matrix organization of rows and columns is essential. The matrix allows a significant amount of information to be displayed in an orderly manner and a limited amount of space. If organized properly, interrelationships can easily be seen, the data can be viewed and understood quickly, and the chance of arithmetic error can be reduced or eliminated. Figures 4-1 and 4-2 display two such matrix-style worksheets for a nursing department's personnel budget in computer spreadsheet form.

One other advantage of a matrix-style worksheet is that it can help guard against errors of omission by specifying certain data to be collected in a particular set of columns or rows. Rather than calculate a salary budget and mistakenly omit "charge pay" or other premium payments, the worksheet can be set up in advance and require that information about these premiums be included for use in the calculations. In order to minimize the chance of leaving something out, it is best to set up budget spreadsheets well in advance of the actual budget preparation schedule and carefully consider actual data requirements. Remember that because computer spreadsheets can hold so much data, it is better to err on the side of collecting too much, rather than too little, data.

Personnel resources that pose a particular problem in terms of recruitment and/or retention can also be dealt with in the budget by inclusion of a recruitment plan, a budgetary emphasis on human resource development and training, or

Figure 4-1
XYZ Memorial Hospital Nursing Budget – Salaries, Fiscal Year 19XX

Personnel Class	2 North	2 South	3 North	3 South	4 North	Total
Head Nurse						
Charge Nurse						
Clinical Specialist						
RN - II						
RN - I						
LPN						
Nursing Aide						
Unit Clerk						
Total						

This matrix organization allows the salary data for five nursing units to be aggregated and displayed in such a way that the dollar amounts by type for each nursing unit can be compared easily with those for the other four units. The dollar values are added both down and across; and since the total from the rows must equal the total from the columns, the chance of arithmetic error is reduced or eliminated.

Figure 4-2
XYZ Memorial Hospital Nursing Budget – FTEs and Salaries,
Fiscal Year 19XX

Personnel Class	2 North		2 South		3 North		3 South		4 North		Total	
	FTEs	$$	FTEs	$$	FTEs	$$	FTEs	$$	FTEs	$$	FTEs	$$
Head Nurse												
Charge Nurse												
Clinical Specialist												
RN - II												
RN - I												
LPN												
Nursing Aide												
Unit Clerk												
Total												

A variation on the previous matrix, this worksheet includes a column for the FTE (full-time equivalent employee) values for each of the five nursing units. Again, the down and across totals for FTEs reduce the chance for arithmetic error. Using this matrix, one can easily compare both FTEs and dollars from one unit to the next. It is possible to add other information to the matrix (patient days, addmissions/discharges, length-of-stay, and so on) to yield a more comprehensive picture.

simply the diversion or addition of budget dollars to support a wage enhancement program.

Supply and service resources (medical/surgical supplies, radiology film, pharmaceuticals, rentals, professional fees, and so on) are also handled in great detail. In the pharmacy, for example, there may be a line item in the budget for every drug in the hospital's formulary; a separate complementary budget may plan for drug utilization on a user-by-user basis. Equipment resources are handled via a separate complementary capital equipment budget. The capital budget is described in greater length in Chapter 6.

The detail of the budget will also indicate where and how resources will be used (which departments will be supported and the level of that support).

The Resources

When thinking of resources, the natural tendency is to concentrate on equipment, supplies, and facilities—the material aspects. But in the health care environment, the single most important resource is people—both staff and patients. The budget must therefore indicate the kinds and quantities of both.

For a nursing unit, this may take the form of a budget document that specifies the number of patients to be treated (admissions), along with the necessary accompanying detail (patient days, average length of stay, breakdown by DRG, patient acuity, and so on). For the hospital as a whole, this may be a marketing plan indicating sources of current patients as well as areas of future efforts designed to modify referral patterns, enhance patient mix, and the like.

The Time Period

The hospital budget represents a plan for the coming fiscal year—a 12-month period; however, it also contains, as a subset, 12 individual monthly plans. The plan for the 12-month period is referred to as the *annual plan*. Some institutions prepare multiyear business plans covering from three to five years. Each year as the annual plan is prepared, the multiyear business plan is modified and extended.

The technique of establishing the detail of the 12 monthly plans is called *seasonalization*. The lazy man's method is to divide the annual plan values by 12 and assign 1/12th to each month. In the real world, however, do patients arrive evenly throughout the year? Are fewer patients admitted in December than in October? If this is expected to happen, the budget seasonalization should reflect it. Seasonalizing by simple division creates impressions of doing better or worse than budget when, in fact, the opposite may be the case. Figure 4-3 shows the comparison of actual results to an improperly seasonalized budget.

Figure 4-3
Budget Seasonalization

Amount

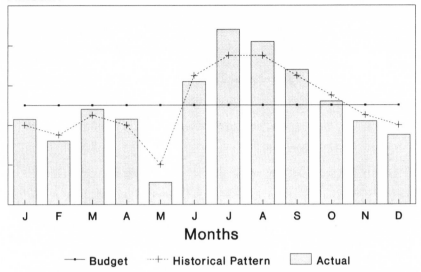

Months

⎯•⎯ **Budget**   ┄┼┄ **Historical Pattern**   ☐ **Actual**

If a budget is seasonalized by dividing it into 12 equal monthly amounts, the results approximate those shown here. Rather than follow the pattern of historical monthly activity and, thus, provide a reasonable monthly yardstick, the improperly seasonalized budget gives the impression that many months deviate significantly from the budget. The time saved by this lazy man's seasonalizing is more than lost during the year in determining why actual is so far off plan.

The Future

The budget is the formalization of a hospital's action plan for the future. Making it a formal document, publishing it, and presenting it to a governance group for review and approval establish an upper-level commitment to the actions, events, and values contained in it. In this regard, Appendix 3 presents a timetable that may be useful in preparing a budget for governing body review.

In exercising its responsibility to control, management uses the budget as a yardstick to measure actual performance. To accomplish this, the data contained in the budget must be expressed in the proper terms or units of measure. In managing the clinical labs, for example, management will be handicapped if the actual output is expressed in CAP workload units while the budgeted output is expressed in terms of tests performed or specimens processed.

WHY HAVE A BUDGET?

There are four purposes for a budget: (1) to increase awareness, (2) to determine resource needs, (3) to measure performance, and (4) to control. The budget process itself serves to increase awareness because the interaction between staff and management facilitates and enhances communication. Communication in turn serves to increase awareness and knowledge. Managers who isolate themselves from the people and events for which they are budgetarily responsible have little chance of success. In most cases they will be unaware of what is happening or why.

As the information needed to prepare a budget properly is gathered, a clear picture will develop of the resources at hand and the added resources that will be required to achieve stated objectives. This resource "shopping list" becomes the topic of discussion and/or negotiation during the budgeting process. It can result in a reallocation of available resources or modification of the underlying goals and objectives.

The budget provides an objective determination of success in measuring the performance of both the organization, by comparing its actual results with those budgeted, and individual managers, by comparing the results of their actions with the expectations agreed upon in the budget.

Finally, the budget functions as a control technique—not just for costs, but for all resources—by establishing limits and holding managers accountable for resource use consistent with those limits.

TYPES OF BUDGETS

There are several kinds of budgets. The operating budget consists of volume (patient days, admissions, discharges, RVUs, and so on), revenue, deductions from revenue, other operating revenues, and expenses. The capital budget is used to plan for new and replacement equipment and other additions to the hospital's fixed assets. The cash budget flows from, and supports, both of these budgets; it deals with cash flowing into and out of the organization. While department heads, managers, and supervisors throughout an institution are involved in the operating and capital budgets, they generally are not involved in the cash budget except to provide input regarding the pace and timing of spending related to operating expenses and capital budget items. Figure 4-4 demonstrates the relationships among these budgets.

The Operating Budget

Rather than treat the operating budget as a single large document, it is possible to break it into four separate but related segments, which can be recombined later. This can facilitate understanding and simplify budget preparation.

The cornerstone of budgeting, without which it is difficult to prepare the annual plan, is the volume budget. This defines the volume of business for the year.

Figure 4-4
Budget Relationships

OPERATING BUDGET		CAPITAL BUDGET
Volume Budget		Replacement Equipment
Revenue Budget	**Expense Budget**	
		New/Modified Equipment
Gross Charges	Personnel— Fixed Variable	
		Installation Costs
Deductions from Revenue	Supplies & Services— Fixed Variable	Construction Projects
Other Operating Revenue	Interest	Renovations
	Depreciation	Other Costs
CASH BUDGET		

Shown here are the relationships among the three types of budgets—operating, capital, and cash. They must complement and support each other.

It is expressed in terms such as patient days, admissions, visits, and so on. Usually, the terms used to express units of service or volume are the same terms that are used for billing purposes. If there is a charge rate for each relative value unit in radiology, it makes very little sense to express the budget for volume of business in radiology only in terms of procedures. The best way may be to express several statistics: (1) the number of visits, (2) the number of procedures, (3) the number of relative value units, (4) the number of relative value units per visit, (5) the number of relative value units per procedure, and (6) the number of procedures per visit. In this way a great deal of information has been developed that will be extremely valuable during the course of the year. Instead of just knowing how many people will be coming into the department, budget information is available on the number of procedures so management can tell if patients are having more or less procedures per visit. Since both relative value units and procedure counts are budgeted, it may be possible to construct a service or acuity profile for the patient population being served. If the actual results reported during the budget period indicate more procedures per visit or more relative value units per visit than expressed in the budget, it may mean that a more acutely ill group of patients is being served. It is also important to have these data for longer-range planning, since machines generally wear out not on the basis of RVUs or visits but on the basis of the number of procedures performed or, for that matter, the number of operating hours of service. As stated earlier, it is important in preparing any budget (volume, revenue, or expense) to include as much detail as possible to help management during the budget year. Once the volume budget has defined how busy the institution will be during the budget year, all other budgets can be prepared.

The revenue budget is a straightforward set of calculations that determines the gross amounts to be generated by charging patients for the institution's services. Simply stated, units of services (from the volume budget) are multiplied by the appropriate charge rates (prices) to arrive at gross revenue. As an adjunct, budgets are prepared for discounts to insurance companies, free care, and bad debts. A separate budget is prepared for other operating revenue like coffee and gift shop proceeds, parking lot profits, and so on.

The personnel budget accounts for the quantities and types of workers needed to achieve the objectives of the plan. Again, the budget should be as detailed as possible. On a department or cost center level, this means budgeting for each position. The key pieces of data are the number of staff, the kinds (clerical, nursing, supervisory, and so on), pay rates for each, the number of full-time equivalent employees that the staff complement equals, and the total salary cost associated with this staff. The personnel budget should not be prepared until and unless the volume budget is completed. How can managers properly determine the staffing size for a department if they do not know the expected workload?

The operating expense budget preparation continues with a compilation of supply and service budget amounts. This involves a listing of the various types or categories of supplies to be consumed and services to be utilized during the budget year, along with the dollar amounts to be expended for each category. Again, it is important to build as much detail as possible to aid in controlling costs. Budgeting of more than token amounts for "miscellaneous" or "other expenses" is unwise.

The list of supply categories would include such designations as medical/surgical supplies, intravenous (IV) solutions, stock drugs, office supplies, uniforms, instruments, books, and so on. Service categories would include equipment rental, contracted personnel, travel, professional fees, and the like. Usually the institution's chart of accounts contains a well-defined list of supply and service categories that can be supplemented on an as-needed basis.

The Cash Budget

At this point, one of the most important budgets, the cash budget, is prepared. It is a composite of several budgets. The revenue budget, the subbudgets for free work, bad debts, and discounts to insurance companies, and the budget for other operating revenue tell how much cash will be flowing into the hospital. The operating expense budget tells how much cash will be flowing out of the hospital. The difference between what flows in and what flows out tells whether the institution can afford to buy another CT scanner, whether it must go to the bank for additional short-term funds, or whether because of frugal management it has excess cash available to be invested.

The cash budget can be thought of like an individual's personal budget. It equals the revenues an institution generates minus the deductions for discounts and so on and is the same as one's weekly paycheck: it is the cash *inflow*. The expense budget is analogous to personal expenses for gas and electricity, telephone, food, and so on: it is the cash *outflow*. One of the first lessons we learn in life is that the cash inflow should be higher than the cash outflow. The importance of this budget is underscored by the amount of emphasis placed on it by personal financial advisers. One very simple question must be asked: if it is so important for the smallest of all companies (an individual) to have a cash flow budget, is it not important for the largest of all companies (hospitals, nursing homes, and so on) to have such a budget?

The Capital Budget

Often the capital budget is prepared concurrently with the operating budget but is not finalized until last because of the need to understand the cash budget and constraints, if any, it places on the size of the budget.

The capital budget deals with pieces of equipment and their installation costs, short-term building programs like renovations and modernization, and perhaps the budget year's portion of a long-term capital project such as a hospital rebuilding program. Sometimes the budget for long-term capital projects is handled separately because of differences in scope and duration of time. While the annual capital budget may involve such building projects as the renovation of a nursing station to improve staff efficiency and effectiveness or the remodeling of an outpatient pharmacy waiting area to provide a private patient/pharmacist counseling area, the long-term capital budget would typically include projects that would be completed over a multiyear period and that would involve significant program planning, acquisition of a certificate of need (CON), funding considerations (cash from operations, borrowing, fund-raising, and so on), scheduling and staging, and the like. A project designed to transform a hospital's image by converting most of its four-bed rooms to private and semiprivate accommodations is an example of a project to be included in the long-term capital budget. That portion of the project to be undertaken during the budget year could be included in the annual capital budget.

FIXED VERSUS VARIABLE BUDGETING

After all of these budgets are put together, the question arises whether to use a fixed or variable budgeting system for the operating budget. The essential difference is that a fixed budget is not changed during the year, while a variable budget takes into account changes in the volume of service and adjusts the revenue and expense budgets up or down accordingly. This provides a better management yardstick under all operating circumstances.

It is far easier to prepare and implement a fixed budgeting system. After determining the values for all items in the budget, they are locked in place and used to measure performance. Any significant deviations from the budget, any actual values significantly higher or lower than the budgeted values, must be examined to find the cause. One of the reasons may be volume. Perhaps the institution was busier than planned. With a variable budget, the values are determined; but instead of being locked into place, they are adjusted from time to time so that the actual performance at a given level of volume can be compared with a derived budgeted value consistent with the actual level of volume.

Table 4-1 provides an example of a fixed budget situation. In this example two things have changed: (1) the volume of activity has increased (110 patient days versus 100 in the budget) and (2) the revenue rate per patient day has decreased ($190/day versus $200/day in the budget). The financial report, however, indicates that revenue performance is favorable by $900, and the first assumption, not knowing the details behind it, might be that the hospital was busier. This is certainly true, but it gives only part of the answer. The 10 percent increase in volume (a good performance outcome) was offset by a 5 percent decrease in the revenue rate (a bad performance outcome).

A variable budget (Table 4-2) portrays a very different situation. An unfavorable variance results because the actual revenue generated was $1,100 worse than the variable budget revenue (the original revenue budget flexed to reflect the actual volume) was expected to be. Because management need not look at volume at all, it automatically knows that the problem is undercharging. What has hap-

Table 4-1
Fixed Budget Example

	Revenue
Fixed Budget	
100 patient days x $200 per patient day	$20,000
Actual Performance	
110 patient days x $190 per patient day	20,900
Variance – Favorable	$900

Table 4-2
Variable Budget Example

	Revenue
Variable Budget	
110 patient days x $200 per patient day	$22,000
Actual Performance	
110 patient days x $190 per patient day	20,900
Variance − Unfavorable	($1,100)

pened is that the adjustment of the revenue budget to reflect actual volume has caused less confusion in examining the budget and determining the cause of the performance deviation.

When it comes to deciding between a fixed budgeting system and a variable budgeting system, it should be remembered that a fixed system is by far simpler to implement and maintain. The downside of it is that it sometimes is more difficult to explain variances. The variable budgeting system, on the other hand, is much more difficult to implement and maintain, but its benefit is that it makes the understanding of performance easier.

DOCUMENTS TO EXAMINE BEFORE STARTING

Before preparing the budget, one should study a number of documents. All contain information that will be helpful to the preparation of the budget. Failure to consult these documents can result in an embarrassing omission, the use of incorrect data, the missing of an important deadline, and so on.

Budget Guidelines

As part of the budgeting exercise, institutions distribute budget guidelines. These differ from place to place but usually contain the paper budget forms (or, in some cases, computer spreadsheets − sometimes distributed on floppy disks in addition to, or in place of, the paper versions), information about rates of inflation and salary adjustments, the timetable for submission of the budget, the budgeting rules (including information about resource limits and budget constraints), and so on. The budget guidelines document is the most important of all, representing the minimum amount of information a department manager would need in order to prepare a workable budget.

In essence, these guidelines represent a "formula" approach to preparing a budget. The manager preparing the budget must know the absolute (or "real") need and compare it with what will likely be provided by a formula approach. If the difference is significant, the manager may need to "fight" for additional resources not provided by the formula approach.

The Mission Statement

A second document to be examined is the mission statement. It states the institution's reason for being. It follows that the budget must be in harmony with the institution's mission. If the mission is limited to serving the frail elderly of the surrounding community, the budgets of the various departments and cost centers should support this. Resources should, therefore, not be diverted to a new program designed to deal with, for example, adolescent substance abuse.

The Strategic Plan

This document should be reviewed to ensure that the current year's operating and capital budgets are appropriately integrated with subsequent years. The strategic plan will tell the direction of the institution for the next several years. It is likely to highlight strengths, weaknesses, threats, and opportunities that should be considered in preparing the operating and capital budgets each year. If, for example, the strategic plan calls for an abandonment of the obstetrics service in two years, this year's plan could be inconsistent if it devoted resources to an expansion of the labor and delivery suite. Further, given the current environment of scarce resources, the allocation of any resources to an endeavor that runs counter to the long-range plan prevents management from using those resources in a more appropriate or more opportunistic way.

As can be seen in Figure 4-5, even as straightforward a plan as the opening of a new MRI suite requires the orchestration of operating and capital budgets over a multiyear time frame. In order to begin operation in 19X3, the order must be placed in 19X1. Facility design and construction must begin early enough to assure completion of the physical plant facility not only in time to begin operations but early enough to allow equipment installation in a time frame that supports staff training in advance of the 19X3 operational date.

Market Analysis

If focused on market share rather than the more traditional zip code analysis, market analysis can be helpful in determining which service lines should be emphasized or de-emphasized during the budgeting process.

Resources might be diverted, for example, from a service line with low market share and low profitability to bolster a highly profitable service line that is suffering from a decline in market share. Figure 4-6 uses the major diagnostic categories (MDCs) to display several hospital service lines that have been ranked on the basis of their individual profitability and market share.

If the institution learned via market analysis of a potential to attract a younger, more affluent patient population, a decision could be made to market a sports medicine program more aggressively. The physical therapy department's manager, having read the marketing plan, may include a new initiative linking the department with the local community's youth recreation programs.

Figure 4-5
Schedule of Events – New MRI Suite

	Fiscal Years		
Actions/Events	19X1	19X2	19X3
Review Technologies	xx		
Select Vendor	xx		
Place Order	xx		
Obtain Certificate of Need	xx		
Design MRI Facility	xx		
Facility Construction	xx	xx	xx
Equipment Installation		xx	xx
Recruit MRI Staff		xx	
Staff Training		xx	
Begin Operations			xx

Any Other Budgets

Last, it is important to keep in mind any other budgets being prepared simultaneously so that proper communication can take place and the budgets can be integrated appropriately. If the clinic's budget for the upcoming year calls for new and expanded evening and weekend hours, there should be communication with the housekeeping department so its budget can reflect the need to plan for additional resources to cover the cost of the necessary supplies, equipment, and staff to support the clinic's expanded operation. Similarly, if significant amounts of new high-technology patient equipment are planned in the capital budget, the operating budget should address the need for additional staff in clinical engineering to maintain the new equipment, comply with medical device regulations, perform preventive maintenance in accordance with JCAHO (Joint Commission on the Accreditation of Healthcare Organizations) guidelines, and so on.

Problems can arise if management of the budgeting process is divided either by timetable (some budgets prepared, reviewed, and approved at an earlier or later date than others) or by responsibility (the chief financial officer responsible for the operating budget and the chief operating officer responsible for the capital budget). If the budgets are not properly coordinated, it is possible for the expense and capital elements of a program to be improperly, and quite embarrassingly, budgeted. Consider a patient transportation program that funds two drivers in the expense budget but, because of faulty budget coordination and control, fails to fund the purchase of an ambulance via the capital equipment budget.

SETTING GOALS AND OBJECTIVES

Budgets are the formalization or quantification of goals and objectives, but not in vague terms like "to increase the quality of care." There must be more quantifi-

Figure 4-6
Market Position of Hospital Services

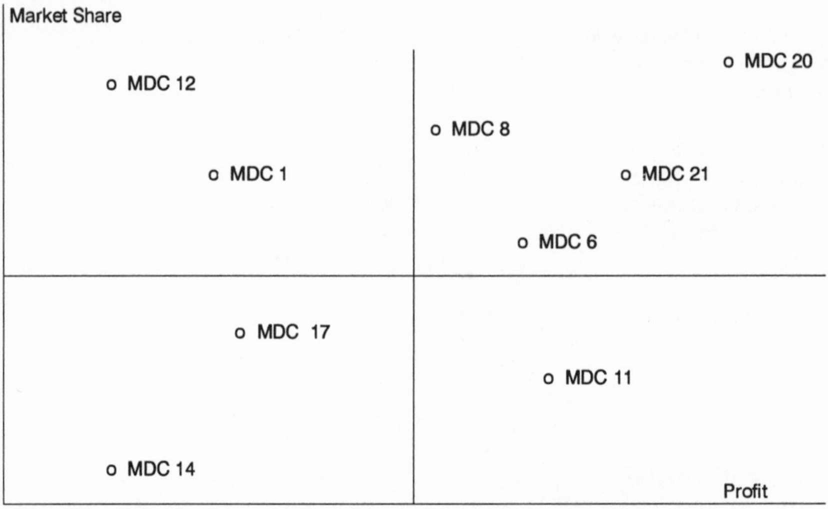

| Market Share |

o MDC 12		o MDC 20
	o MDC 8	
o MDC 1		o MDC 21
	o MDC 6	

o MDC 17	
	o MDC 11
o MDC 14	Profit

This matrix is divided into four quadrants (clockwise from upper right): high market share/high profit, low share/high profit, low share/low profit, and high share/
low profit. From a business standpoint, the preference would be for those MDCs
located in the most appealing quadrant—high market share/high profit (top right).
From a strategic planning point of view, attempts might be made to increase the
profitability of MDC 1 and MDC 12 in order to reposition them to the high share,
high profit quadrant. The performance of MDC 14—pregancy and childbirth—
might be tolerated and even subsidized, perhaps because of a desire to care for an
underserved population or because the service is required if the hospital wished to
market itself as a "full-service" hospital. It is also possible that a business decision
could be made to abandon MDC 14 because of its market share and profit position
and divert its resources to MDC 11 in order to increase market share in that product
line.

MDC #	Description
1	Diseases and Disorders of the Nervous System
6	Diseases and Disorders of the Digestive System
8	Diseases and Disorders of the Musculoskeletal System and Connective Tissue
11	Diseases and Disorders of the Kidney and Urinary Tract
12	Diseases and Disorders of the Male Reproductive System
14	Pregnancy, Childbirth, and the Puerperium
17	Myeloproliferative Disorders
20	Substance Use and Substance-Induced Organic Mental Disorders
21	Injuries, Poisoning, and Toxic Effects of Drugs

cation, such as "4.5 nursing hours of care per patient day on general acute units, 6+ hours on the more acute units, 12 hours of care in the ICU [Intensive Care Unit] and CCU [Coronary Care Unit], and 18 hours of care per day in the transplant unit." This level of quantification leads to better budgets and more successful management.

There are two levels of goals and objectives—corporate and departmental. At the corporate level, the hospital's goal may be to remain financially viable despite constraints in the reimbursement environment. Consequently, one of its objectives for the budget year may be to reduce patient length of stay by one day. That is the overall objective. The departmental goals and objectives form a subset. In the pharmacy, for example, it may translate to a goal of establishing a clinical pharmacist program. This goal, in turn, would be supported by objectives like (1) achieving a staffing ratio of one clinical pharmacist for each 40-bed nursing unit and (2) increasing the number of pharmacy technicians to a specific level to allow the clinical pharmacists to spend more time on the nursing units as opposed to in the pharmacy. But if the corporate objective is to reduce length of stay by a day anᵈ all the different departmental objectives call for an increase in length of stay by a half day, the objectives are out of step. They must be harmonious. They must tie back and forth to each other. They must be complementary and supportive.

Goals and objectives also possess a temporal quality; that is, some are short-term and others are long-term, and they, too, must complement and support each other. If the long-term goal is to increase the market share in obstetrics, the short-term goal must support that. In the short term, a recruitment program to increase the ratio of registered nurses (RNs) on the obstetrics unit may be in order, or perhaps a program to renovate the labor and delivery suite is desirable. The point is that whatever actions are taken in the short term must be complementary and supportive of the long-term goals.

Sometimes departmental objectives get out of step with corporate objectives. Whether caused by lack of understanding in the department, poor communication, or some other flaw, the situation must be discovered and corrected very quickly. Generally speaking, the flow of information in an organization is from the bottom to the top: supervisors to managers, managers to administrators, administrators to directors, and so on, until the information gets to the top of the organizational pyramid. When dealing with corporate goals and objectives, however, the flow is in the opposite direction. The board sets the goals and objectives for the hospital in concert with hospital executive leadership. This information is communicated down through the organization. In many organizations the goals and objectives are communicated along with the packet of forms to be filled out and completed as part of the budget preparation process. Managers throughout the hospital therefore understand clearly what is expected from the outset of the budget process. Department objectives can then be developed that are complementary, supportive, and expressed very clearly.

Just as the organizational pyramid broadens as one moves from the executive level to the first-line supervisory level, so, too, do the objectives that form the initial point for budgeting. Consider, for example, an executive-level objective of a break-even financial outcome for the budget year. At the senior level of the pyramid, this may translate into total dollar spending limits, a cap on the number of full-time equivalents (FTEs) employed, and so on. At the mid-level, the cap on FTEs may become specific limits on a department-by-department basis. At the department management level, this would produce objectives dealing with the types and quantities of workers (supervisors, lead workers, clerical, service, and so on), shift coverages, and so on. Table 4-3 presents a display of this interrelationship and level of detail.

One of the most important attributes of goals and objectives is that they must be attainable. Do not write an objective of reducing length of stay by three days on the Obstetrics (OB) Unit because it is not going to happen. Give a sense of ownership to the staff involved in achieving the objectives. Involve them and make them feel that they have been part of the process. Sit down with the staff and talk about the overall goals and objectives and the departmental objectives. Give everybody a sense of ownership and participation. Why? Because they will take pride in what they are doing; therefore, the probability of achieving the desired objectives will be higher. Convince the staff that they "own" it, and they will appreciate it and work hard for it. But if it is just a document that somebody else "dreamed up," they will not care about it. So, encourage the sense of ownership when building objectives.

Well-written objectives, regardless of their level of difficulty, are far easier for managers to deal with than poorly written ones. Well-written objectives spell out in great detail the full set of measurements necessary to determine if they have

Table 4-3
Goals and Objectives

Organization Level	Goals and Objectives
Senior (Operations)	Spending limit of $31.8 million in those departments comprising the Operations component and a cap of 560.5 FTEs

Middle (Support Services)	FTE Limits by department	
	Housekeeping	100.8
	Dietary	74.5
	Security	21.4
	All Others	363.8
	Total	560.5

Departmental (Housekeeping)	Staff Deployment by Shift:			
		Day	Evening	Night
	Mon.-Fri.	60.8	20.0	4.0
	Saturday	4.0	2.0	2.0
	Sunday	4.0	2.0	2.0

been achieved and, if not, by how much they have been missed. Well-written objectives, therefore, must be well defined, devoid of the "I'll know it when I see it" mentality. It is virtually impossible to work for the boss who says, "I'll know it when I see it" because the subordinates, lacking the appropriate "vision," are left to guess what will please the boss. Well-written objectives must be measurable.

Consider an objective that reads, "Our institution will provide the highest quality of care among the community hospitals in our city." As a goal, this is a fine statement, but as an objective, it is poorly written, lacking the detail and measurability necessary to determine what resources are needed to achieve it or whether it has, in fact, been achieved. The reason is that "the highest quality of care" is too vague. Is it measured by physician or staff perception? By patient satisfaction? Or by the impression given to a visitor?

Has the institution achieved its objective if a patient's hip replacement surgery was performed flawlessly, but the evening meal was usually served late and cold? Probably not. It must be remembered that quality, per se, is often judged subjectively, not objectively. Further, the caregiver's view of quality may not necessarily be shared by patients or visitors.

A well-written objective, supportive of the goal of providing "the highest quality of care," would specify measurable criteria: nursing hours per patient day, the number of "acceptable" medication errors, the number of patient complaints, and so on. These represent surrogates for quality. In other words, if the predetermined number of nursing hours is provided each patient day, and there are fewer than a certain number of medication errors and fewer than a tolerable number of patient complaints, the institution will have achieved the "highest quality" of care as it defines it. Moving forward in time and in keeping with the principles of continuous quality improvement, the institution can tighten its objectives and measure achievement against reduced numerical targets for medication errors or patient complaints.

Poorly written objectives often lack this level of specificity because "we don't want to pin ourselves down" or because of the mistaken belief that too much specificity stifles creativity.

THE ITERATIVE PROCESS

The preparation of a budget, be it at the departmental or institutional level, is iterative in nature. Rarely, if ever, can a manager at any level begin with a blank page, make the series of budget calculations only one time, and produce the finished budget. As can be seen in Figure 4-7, the process of budgeting begins and ends with the goals and objectives but may make several loops through the calculations of revenues, expenses, new programs, capital expenditures, and so on until all of the goals and objectives are attained.

The process begins with a conversion of the overall institutional objectives to the objectives the individual department will budget to achieve. Next, the objectives are converted from words to numbers—the workload to be performed dur-

Figure 4-7
The Iterative Process

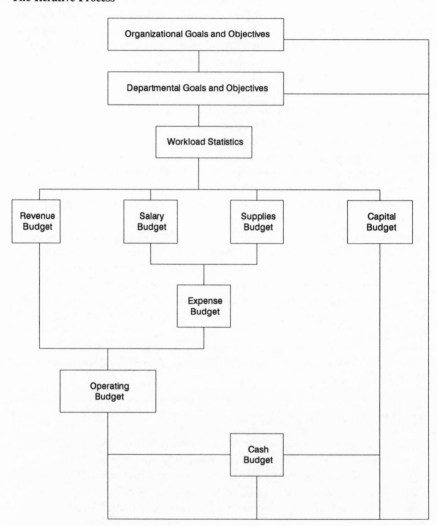

ing the period of time being budgeted. In turn, the amount of work forms the basis of calculations for revenues, staffing, salaries and supply expenses, capital equipment needs, and so on.

Often, however, managers new to the budgeting process approach the work to be done with the false expectation that a single pass at the calculations will suffice. When a second, third, or fourth iteration is required, such a manager can be unprepared for the additional workload or feel that the original set of calculations was inferior when such is not necessarily the case. In some respects, the preparation of a successful budget is like the firing of an old artillery piece: hitting the target on the first attempt is rare indeed. The first shot may sail beyond the target; the second may land short. By process of adjustment, the third or fourth is likely to be a hit. So it is with budgeting.

IMPORTANT POINTS TO REMEMBER

Preparing a budget requires an orderly progression through a series of calculations. But these calculations involve only four simple arithmetic functions: addition, subtraction, multiplication, and division. These will be done over and over again, perhaps hundreds, even thousands, of times before the budget is completed. But they are only simple arithmetic functions and should not be feared.

The use of computerized spreadsheets in making budget calculations greatly reduces the number of manual calculations and makes the iterative process less burdensome. In setting up spreadsheets, the formulas that will automatically make the calculations should be tested with known data to assure accuracy. From time to time, almost everyone is tempted to take a shortcut. On the backpacking trail, for example, taking a shortcut can mean arriving in camp sooner, but it can also mean getting lost in the woods and arriving late. The reward of an early arrival must be balanced against the risk of getting lost. Budgeting is no different. Here, too, there are risks associated with shortcuts. Errors of omission can occur, and a manager can be left with insufficient detail to support decision making later in the year.

An audit trail showing how budget amounts were calculated can be helpful when questions arise months after the calculations were prepared. How, for instance, was an $11,024 salary calculated? Was an assumption made that someone would be hired to work a full 40 hours per week at $5.30 per hour? Maybe a half-time person earning $10.60? Or perhaps a full-time person earning $10.60 per hour, but not hired until the halfway point in the budget year? An audit trail eliminates such speculation. The trail can be as simple as the paper tapes from a calculator annotated with simple notes and filed in an envelope labeled "Budget Year 19XX Calculations."

The more detailed information the budget contains, the easier it is to understand what went right and what went wrong as the actual results are reported and to know what was expected and what action is necessary. Consequently, the more detail the better. Given the ability of modern computers and spreadsheet software, there is really no excuse for insufficient budget data. Consider the situation in which the manager of Department A prepares a budget with limited information and takes an enormous shortcut, budgeting just a single line for supplies. This manager is unable to determine what went wrong and what corrective action must be taken when the monthly report, as displayed in Table 4-4, is examined. Another manager puts more effort into the preparation of the budget and is better served when the monthly report arrives. In the case of Department B, it is clear that the identical spending variance as in Department A is concentrated in a single account, stock drugs, and managerial action can be determined more easily.

Finally, as mentioned earlier, there is usually a difference between a budget derived strictly by "formula" and real need. Managers must be aware of the need to balance their roles as advocates for their departments with their roles as members of the management team. Sometimes, need prevails over formula, but keep in mind that sometimes the formula wins. Sometimes the formula *must* win for the good of the institution.

RESULTS OF GOOD AND BAD BUDGETING

Putting the necessary time and effort into budgeting will help achieve compliance with desired constraints; a sense of ownership will be instilled among

Table 4-4
Monthly Financial Performance Reports

Operating Department A

Description	Actual	Budget	Variance (Unfavorable)
Office Supplies	$5,000		($5,000)
Med/Surg Supplies	15,000		(15,000)
Stock Drugs	20,000		(20,000)
Miscellaneous	150	$35,000	34,850
Total	$40,150	$35,000	($5,150)

Operating Department B

Description	Actual	Budget	Variance (Unfavorable)
Office Supplies	$5,000	$5,000	
Med/Surg Supplies	15,000	15,100	$100
Stock Drugs	20,000	14,800	(5,200)
Miscellaneous	150	100	(50)
Total	$40,150	$35,000	($5,150)

As these two performance reports from similar departments demonstrate, preparing a budget with limited information and taking shortcuts can hamper a manager's ability to determine what went wrong and what corrective action must be taken.

employees; credibility will be built among subordinates and superiors; the coordination of long-term and short-term goals will be facilitated; and there will be a better understanding of the ways in which the hospital operates, and thus better management decisions will be made. All of this results in better resource management, which in turn results in success.

On the other hand, a poor budgeting effort will likely result in the failure to achieve objectives and the loss of credibility. Employees will give up and "throw in the towel." One will have difficulty in determining what corrective action to take. In fact, there will be difficulty deciding whether to take corrective action or not.

The roles of a manager are to plan, organize and staff, direct or lead, and control. Budgeting supports all of these. To budget is to plan. The budget allows a manager to understand expectations, to organize resources and staff accordingly, and to decide which management style (directing or leading) best fits the circumstances.

The way a manager controls is by knowing what was expected (the budget), by knowing what actually happened (results reporting), by examining the difference, and by taking appropriate supportive or corrective action.

Chapter 5

Operations Budgeting

One of the first impressions to be dealt with in preparing a budget, either for a department or for the entire institution, is that it is an overwhelming task involving millions of dollars, hundreds of people, expensive equipment, outside environmental threats and opportunities, third-party reimbursement mechanisms, patients' ability to pay, and so on. Putting together a budget, however, is really as elementary as multiplying some numbers, adding other numbers, and so on. It is a mechanical process that expresses the goals and objectives that form the foundation of the budget, in numerical terms.

INTERRELATIONSHIPS

If the elements of the annual plan are arrayed using a matrix format (Figure 5-1), the interrelationships can be seen more easily. Notice the relationship between the volume budget and all of the elements of revenue and expense. Similarly, the revenue budget affects all other elements and acts as a constraint on all budgets by establishing the "affordability" of all of the other elements.

As the process of putting the budget together begins, these interrelationships must be kept in mind; otherwise, costly and embarrassing errors can creep into the budget. All of the elements must blend together. They must complement and support each other.

If there is one key in dealing with the interrelationships of the budget elements, it is orchestration. Just as orchestration is responsible for the rich, full sound of a symphony orchestra so, too, orchestration brings out the best in budgeting. Consider, for example, the symphony orchestra. Each section plays different instruments and different notes at different times. Orchestration makes the difference between the din one hears during warm-up and the recognizable sounds that come forth once the conductor taps his or her baton.

Figure 5-1
Interrelationships

	Volume	Rates	Revenue	Personnel	Supplies and Other	Equipment and Renovations	New Programs	Cash Budget
Volume	▨	O	O	O	O	O	O	
Rates	O	▨	O					
Revenue (including Deductions)	O	O	▨	O	O	O	O	O
Personnel (including Salaries)	O		O	▨	O	O	O	O
Supplies and Other	O		O	O	▨	O	O	O
Equipment and Renovations	O		O	O	O	▨	O	O
New Programs	O		O	O	O	O	▨	O
Cash Budget			O	O	O	O	O	▨

A matrix format can be used visually to point out the interrelationships of annual plan elements. A dot at the intersection of a row and column signifies an interrelationship.

It is vital that the same information used to prepare one element be used to prepare all others. It is clear that operating expense and capital budgets based on an 80 percent occupancy and a revenue budget based on an 85 percent occupancy rate are disconsonant. If the 85 percent occupancy is not achievable, the plan for cash management during the year will likely be wrong before the year even starts. Further, plans for new program implementations, expansion of existing programs, and the enhancement of older (but still viable) services may fall by the wayside. Beyond that, there is a very real embarrassment associated with putting together a budget that does not make sense. Finally, since the budget is an important management tool, faulty budgeting leads to faulty management, which in turn leads to the wasting of valuable resources.

SOURCES OF INFORMATION

The question that confronts many managers is, Where does one find all the information needed to prepare the budget? The best answer is that the information is available throughout the environment. When preparing the personnel budget, for example, ask the personnel department about salary rates, any planned general increases in the wage rates, rules for merit increases, the potential for hiring new staff during the upcoming budget period, training programs, and so on.

When it comes to supplies and other consumable items, the purchasing department or storeroom may be able to help with information on cost and usage patterns. The accounting department may be a source of information about inflation. Table 5-1 indicates some of the factors that influence the various elements of the budget and sources to which managers can look for helpful information in preparing the budget.

Often, the best source of information necessary to the budget process is overlooked. Managers and supervisors are probably the most knowledgeable about department performance because of their day-to-day involvement. They possess the hands-on understanding of how and why a department functions. Their input in preparing the budget can be invaluable.

Finally, the best way to gather information is to ask questions—the more, the better. Do not worry about asking a "dumb" question; in reality, a "dumb" question is often one that no one has the nerve to ask but that everyone has thought about asking. The uncomfortable feeling sometimes associated with asking a lot of questions can almost always be mitigated by prefacing the questions with such statements as "Let me play devil's advocate" or "We'll need to answer a lot of questions from higher up in the organization, and we should prepare our answers now. How will we answer these questions?" In this way the onus shifts to an unidentified someone else. It makes it easier to ask the tough, pointed questions that must be asked.

AN ORDERLY APPROACH

After the raw data have been gathered from outside sources and from within the department, it is time to put pencil to paper and prepare the department bud-

Table 5-1
Sources of Information

Budget Element	Influencing Factors & Sources of Information
Hospital Goals and Objectives*	o Board of Trustees or Directors o Upper Management o External Environment
Departmental Goals and Objectives	o Hospital goals and objectives o Department management
Volume	o Upper management o Accounting Department (for historical information) o Past relationships of one department's volume to another department's o New program influences o Physician practice patterns o Historical trends o Regulatory/competitive influences o Technology effect o Process improvements (which increase capacity) o Marketing results o Reimbursement changes that alter demand patterns
Revenue**	o Volume projections o Prices (rates) o Regulatory/competitive influences o Marketing strategies (pricing strategies) o Mix of third-party payers
Deductions from Revenue*	o Third-party payer discount arrangements o Accounts receivable collection information o Hospital and department goals and objectives o Patient insurance information o Reimbursement changes o Hill-Burton Act requirements o Charity care targets o Discount and collection policies
Other Operating Revenue**	o Activities related to

Table 5.1 (continued)

	"nonhospital" lines of business such as gift shop, snack bar, parking lot, etc.
Personnel	o Volume
	o Productivity acuity data
	o Targeted staffing ratios and patterns
	o Payroll department (for pay rates)
	o Personnel (for data on planned salary and benefits changes)
	o Accounting Department (for information on fringe benefits cost per employee)
	o labor contracts
	o Hospital and departmental goals and objectives
	o New program needs
	o Technology effect
	o Process improvements (which increase productivity)
	o Budgetary constraints
Supplies and Other Expenses	o Volume
	o Usage trends
	o Fixed/variable expense profile
	o Accounting or Materials Management Department (for inflation information)
	o Budgetary constraints
	o Hospital and departmental goals and objectives
	o New program needs
	o Technology effect
Interest Expense*	o Existing level of debt
	o Interest rates
	o Projected cash inflows and outflows
	o Fixed asset values
	o Depreciation method (straight line, declining balance, etc.)
	o Capital budget

* Not normally prepared by department level personnel.
** May be prepared by department level personnel but customarily are prepared at a central point in the organization.

get. The best way to approach this is by following an orderly progression from one element to the next. After reviewing the appropriate documents as explained in Chapter 4, the recommended sequence is as follows.

- Statement of goals and objectives
- Volume budget
- Revenue budget (if prepared departmentally)
- Personnel budget (sometimes including fringe benefits)
- Supplies and services budget

Logic plays a major role in determining this sequence. A budget cannot be prepared until two questions have been answered: (1) what is to be accomplished? and (2) what are the expectations? Thus, the statement of goals and objectives is logically the first step in the process. This tells what the department hopes to accomplish (its own goals and objectives for the budget year) and what upper management expects from the department (its departmentalization of the institution's goals and objectives). Because budgeting is mainly a mathematical exercise and because goals and objectives are customarily expressed using words, it is necessary to provide a transition from words to numbers. This is the role of the volume budget. It provides the translation of goals and objectives into usable mathematical statements of what the department will be doing (patient days, visits, tests, meals to serve, RVUs, and so on). The remaining budgets are based on these numbers.

The revenue budget comes next. Of the budgets that involve money, this should be the first because it sets a boundary—an upper spending limit—that constrains the size of the personnel budget and the supplies and services budget, which are the last to be prepared.

Statement of Goals and Objectives

Whether for the entire hospital or a single department, this should be a tightly written document spelling out all of the planned actions for the budget year in clear, precise language. To use an analogy, it is the music to which the entire department will march.

The Volume Budget

Two kinds of situations can be encountered in preparing the volume budget. Either a department's volumes are dependent on another department (as in the case of ancillary services), or they are independent of other departments' volumes.

Independent Volumes. The simplest situation is the one involving independent volumes—perhaps a clinic or an inpatient nursing unit. Volumes for these kinds of operations are generally established as part of the overall institutional objectives or by estimating the demand for service.

Case #1

The 25-bed newborn special care unit is expecting an average occupancy rate of 85 percent in the fiscal year being budgeted. The volume budget is calculated as follows.

Beds	25
Calendar Days	× 365
Bed Days	9,125
Occupancy Rate	× 85%
Patient Days Budget	7,756

or

Beds	25
Occupancy Rate	× 85%
Average Daily Census	21.25
Calendar Days	× 365
Patient Days Budget	7,756

It is important to know the capacity of the unit for which the budget is being prepared. In some cases occupancy targets are expressed in terms of patient days, not occupancy percent. In the example of the newborn unit, if someone had inadvertently assigned a target of 9,756 (perhaps as the result of a typographical error) instead of 7,756, the budget for the entire unit could be significantly misstated unless it was known that the unit capacity is 9,125 (25 beds × 365 days).

Understanding unit capacity is also important when basing the volume budget on an estimate of demand.

Case #2

The outpatient clinic at Alphabet General has experienced the visit counts shown in Table 5-2 for the past five fiscal years.

The budget for fiscal 19X6 is arrived at in two steps. The visit counts are examined to see if there is a trend and to determine if it will continue as is, increase, or decrease. At Alphabet General, the trend is an upward growth of 10 percent per year. If it is expected to continue, the volume budget would be calculated by adding 10 percent to the 19X5 estimated volume. Assuming there was no capacity limit, the visits budget for 19X6 would be set at 19,360 visits.

Fiscal Year 19X5	17,600	
Annual Growth	+1,760	(10% × 17,600)
Fiscal Year 19X6	19,360	

Table 5-2
Outpatient Visits

Year	Visits
19X1	12,000
19X2	13,200
19X3	14,520
19X4	16,000
19X5	17,600
19X6	? ? ?

Consider some additional information about the clinic. It includes five exam rooms, which can handle a maximum of two exams per hour during a five-day-a-week (eight-hour day) schedule with 10 holidays. This translates into a capacity of 20,000 visits.

Weeks in the year	52	Exam Rooms	5
	× 5	Exams/hours	× 2
Weekdays	260		10
Holidays	−10	Clinic Hours/days	× 8
Clinic Days	250	Exams/day	80
Clinic Days	250		
Exams/day	× 8		
Visit capacity	20,000		

Assuming the trend in visit growth (10% per year) continued into fiscal 19X6, the maximum 19X7 budget would be 20,000 visits.

Fiscal Year 19X6	19,360	
Annual Growth	+1,936	(10% × 19,360)
	21,296	
Capacity	20,000	

If no trend was apparent, one might set the volume budget at the level of visits experienced during the most recent 12-month period. This may be influenced by the overall goals and objectives of the institution, if, for example, it was the institution's goal to do more or less outpatient business.

Dependent Volumes. More complex is the situation involving a department whose volume of business is dependent on another department. Consider the clinical laboratories whose demand is created by nursing units, clinics, and so on. To prepare the volume budget for labs, it is necessary to establish or document these relationships and then project the budget based on the volume budgets of the other departments. As an example, consider the volume relationships shown in Table 5-3.

Table 5-3
Ancillary Services

	Patient Days	Lab Tests	Tests per Patient Day
19X1	19,500	72,150	3.7
19X2	20,000	72,000	3.6
19X3	19,900	75,620	3.8
Three Year Average	19,800	73,257	3.7
19X4	20,300	? ? ? ?	? ? ? ?

The volume budget for 19X3 could be 77,140 tests (20,300 patient days × 3.8 tests per day) or 75,110 tests (20,300 patient days × 3.7 tests per day) depending on whether the most recent experience (19X2) or the three-year average was used.

In reality, the volume budget for the laboratory will be the sum of many pieces (chemistry, hematology, bacteriology, and so on), each of which is dependent on the volumes in a number of areas (a variety of medical/surgical nursing units, special care units, clinics, and so on), each of which will have a slightly different relationship with the laboratories. Table 5-4 displays, in simple form, the tests per patient day relationships that can be used to develop the volume budget for the laboratory. Using these data, the bottom half of the table would be prepared. The number of tests is calculated by multiplying the number of applicable patient days by the tests per patient day ratios. For example, the 12,880 tests chemistry will perform for pediatrics is a function of 9,200 patient days and 1.4 tests per patient day (9,200 × 1.4 = 12,880).

Table 5-4
Lab Test Volumes

Lab Tests per Patient Day and Clinic Visit by Lab and Location

	2 North	Peds	I C U	O P D
Patient Days/Visit Budget	19,800	9,200	3,600	20,000
Chemistry	1.2	1.4	2.9	1.0
Hematology	1.2	1.2	1.4	1.1
Bacteriology	1.2	1.2	1.6	0.5

Test Budget by Lab and Location

	2 North	Peds	I C U	O P D
Chemistry	23,760	12,880	10,440	20,000
Hematology	23,760	11,040	5,040	22,000
Bacteriology	23,760	11,040	5,760	10,000
Total	71,280	34,960	21,240	52,000
Grand Total	179,480			

The volume budget is now complete; and since it was prepared in such detail, any changes in occupancy levels, ratios of tests to patient days, and so on that impact on actual volume can be examined and better understood.

The Revenue Budget

This budget represents the product of two pieces or groups of data—volume and prices. The formula is as follows: Units of Service × Charge Rate = Revenue.

Thus, assuming a charge rate of $850 per day, the revenue budget for the neonatal special care unit described in Case #1 would be: 7,756 × $850 = $6,592,600.

In departments with more than one billable unit of service, the revenue budget is produced by multiplying each unit of service by the appropriate charge rate and summing the results. Consider, for example, a department with five billable units of service. Its revenue budget would be calculated (Table 5-5) using the formula just listed.

For an entire hospital, the revenue budget would be the sum of all the department revenue budgets. Table 5-6 displays a typical hospital revenue budget.

The Personnel Budget

After the volume budget has been established, the personnel budget can be prepared. This involves planning for the types and qualities of personnel required, salaries to be paid, shift premiums, performance or cost-of-living raises, and so on. While guidelines can be used in determining staffing levels (e.g., one laboratory technologist for every 100,000 laboratory workload units), these differ from one unit to the next and from one institution to the next depending on patient acuity, geographic considerations, equipment sophistication, and so on. There are no hard-and-fast rules.

One useful technique in preparing the personnel budget is a matrix format with positions and the names of personnel running vertically down the form and the categories of information (hourly pay rate, FTE values, and so on) across the top.

Table 5-5
Department XYZ Revenue Budget

	Quantity	Charge Rate	Revenue
Procedure # 1	1,000	$100.00	$100,000
Procedure # 2	1,500	90.00	135,000
Procedure # 3	400	50.00	20,000
Procedure # 4	5,000	30.00	150,000
Procedure # 5	100	200.00	20,000
Revenue Budget			$425,000

Table 5-6
Insitutional Revenue Budget

Revenue Center	Units	Volume	Rate	Revenue
Adult Med/Surg	Patient Days	20,500	$364.00	$7,462,000
Pediatrics	Patient Days	5,500	404.00	2,222,000
Acute Psychiatric	Patient Days	6,800	502.00	3,413,600
Intensive Care	Patient Days	2,900	900.00	2,610,000
Coronary Care	Patient Days	2,100	900.00	1,890,000
Emergency Services	Visits	36,500	150.00	5,475,000
Clinics	Visits	52,000	60.00	3,120,000
Operating Room	Minutes	203,700	10.00	2,037,000
Anesthesiology	Minutes	180,800	2.00	361,600
Medical Supplies	Cost + 10%			2,718,000
Pharmacy	Cost + 10%			2,135,100
Laboratory	CAP Units	2,374,600	1.65	3,918,090
Blood Bank	500cc Units	2,000	175.00	350,000
Radiology	RVUs	79,500	20.00	1,590,000
Nuclear Medicine	RVUs	12,000	19.00	228,000
Respiratory Therapy	RVUs	251,000	4.00	1,004,000
Physical Therapy	RVUs	69,100	8.00	552,800
Occupational Therapy	Hours	6,400	16.00	102,400
Total				$41,189,590

Figure 5-2 displays such a matrix that has been set up to run on a computerized spreadsheet. It provides spaces for rank or type of employee (Column A) and the name of the incumbent (Column B). This ensures that no employee or labor category is inadvertently and embarrassingly omitted. The FTE value is provided for in Column C and is used later in the matrix as part of the individual salary calculations. A full-time person who works 2,080 hours (a full 40-hour week) per year is 1.0 FTE. A half-time employee works 1,040 hours and is expressed in the worksheet as 0.5 FTE. In organizations working a 37.5 hour week, a full-time person would work 1,950 hours (37.5 × 52 weeks). The current hourly pay rate (Column D) is included to establish an audit trail from the current period to the future. The next columns (E and F) provide a way to adjust the current hourly pay rate for any increase scheduled to take effect before the budget year begins. In this way, the budget calculations will begin with the pay rate in effect on the first day of the new fiscal year (Column G). Column H is the location of the base salary budget for each employee. It is the product of 2,080 hours, the annual number of hours associated with a full-time employee (40 hours per week × 52 weeks = 2,080 hours) and the data from columns C and G. If no wage increases were planned during the budget year, the worksheet would stop at this point. However, since wages are usually adjusted for one or more reasons during the course of a budget year, space is provided in this worksheet (in Columns I through N) for two increases. The total salary budget (Column O) is the sum of the salary and salary increase amounts found in Columns H, M, and N.

It would be possible to add columns to provide for a variety of additional budget information, including premium pays that each employee could earn; or

Figure 5-2
Salary Budget Worksheet

	A	B	C	D	E	F	G	H	I	J	K	L	M	N	O
	POSN or RANK	INCUMBENT	FTE VALUE	CURRENT HOURLY PAY RATE	INCREASE SCHEDULED BEFORE START OF FY XX AMOUNT	DATE	RATE AT START OF FY 19XX	BASE SALARY BUDGET FY 19XX	INCREASES SCHEDULED AFTER START OF FY 19XX AMOUNT #1	DATE #1	AMOUNT #2	DATE #2	SALARY INCREASE #1	SALARY INCREASE #2	TOTAL SALARY BUDGET FY 19XX
1															
2															
3															
4															
5															
6															
7															
8															
9															
10															
11															
12															
13															
14															
15															
16															
17															
18															
19															
20															

this information could be recorded on separate lines in the matrix if such information as overtime and shift premium payments are not identified with specific employees. A matrix similar to this is used in developing the salary budget in Case #5.

Using Computer Spreadsheets. Be advised that computer spreadsheets can be set to display the result of a calculation with, for example, two decimal places (e.g., an hourly pay rate of $15.57). In reality, the software will calculate the rate to six or seven decimal places and merely round it off to two places for display purposes. For example, an hourly pay rate calculated by dividing annual earnings of $32,380 by 2,080 hours ($32,380 ÷ 2,080 = $15.5673076923) could be displayed as $15.57 if limited to a two-decimal-place display. It should be noted, however, that 2,080 times $15.57 does not equal $32,380, but $32,385. Small differences like this are possible in computer spreadsheets and should not be cause for alarm. In the example cited, the five-dollar difference is immaterial.

How to Calculate Staffing Needs. Since staff costs represent the largest single expense item in health care, determining the right staff size is a critical element in budgeting. It involves the merging of productivity data with volume data. In essence, the amount of work to be done is divided by the work output of each worker to determine staffing needs. Care should be exercised to make sure both productivity and FTE data are expressed consistently during the calculations and that a provision is made for routine nonproductive time. If productivity is expressed in terms of output per FTE, no adjustment is needed for non-productive time. If, on the other hand, productivity is expressed in terms of output per hour (worked), an adjustment, called a "gross-up," will be necessary.

Case #3

A department has annual volume of 442,000 tests. The workers performing these tests can produce 100 tests each day. Each worker uses an average of 10 holidays, four weeks of vacation, and nine sick days per year. How many FTEs must the department manager include in the budget?

Step #1
Output required: 442,000 tests

Step #2
Productivity per worker = 100 tests × 5 days × 52 weeks = 26,000 tests/year

Step #3
Workers needed = 442,000 tests ÷ 26,000 tests/year
                        = 17 workers

At this point, it is known that 17 workers are needed. The calculations so far, however, have not recognized the fact that each worker will take time off for vacation, holidays, and so on, meaning more will be needed to produce the 442,000 tests. In order to complete the calculations, productive time as a percentage of total time must be calculated and then used to adjust the number of workers from 17 to a larger work force.

Total Paid time = 40 hours/week
                  × 52 weeks/year
                  2,080 hours/year

Nonproductive time = 10 holidays
                     20 vacation days (4 weeks × 5)
                     +9 sick days
                     39 days off
                     × 8 hours/day
                     312 hours/year

Productive time = 1,768 hours (2,080 − 312)

Productivity Rate = .85 = (1768 ÷ 2080)

Step #4
FTEs Needed = Workers Needed ÷ Productivity Rate
            = 17 ÷ 85%
            = 20 FTEs

Now the staffing budget is correct. The 20 FTEs will provide enough manpower to accomplish the 442,000 tests. Had only 17 FTEs been provided, staff shortages would have resulted, and the test output would not have been achieved.

In professions such as physical therapy and nursing, it should be noted that there is a difference between "hands-on" time and productive time. This is because a nurse, for example, may be on the unit and productive (charting, giving report, ordering medications, and so on) while not providing "hands-on" care. In this profession, total time is greater than productive time, which, in turn, is greater than "hands-on" time. These distinctions should be recognized in making staffing calculations in these and similar departments.

Case #4

Volume in the budget year is planned to be 9,125 patient days. The plan is to provide six hours of "hands-on" RN care per patient day. Nurses spend an average of 25 percent of work time doing charting, ordering medications, and so on. Productive time is 80 percent of total paid time. How many FTEs must be budgeted?

Step #1
Output required: 54,750 "hands-on" hours (9,125 × 6)

Step #2
Productivity per worker
    = 8 hours × 5 days × 52 weeks × 75% "hands-on" (100% − 25% lost to charting, etc. = 75%)
    = 1,560 "hands-on" hours/year

Step #3
Workers needed
    = 54,750 tests ÷ 1,560 "hands-on" hours/year/nurse
    = 35.096 nurses

Step #4
FTEs Needed = Workers Needed ÷ Productivity Rate
              = 35.096 ÷ 80% (given in the case)
              = 43.87 FTEs

It is possible that the staffing budget would be set at 44 FTEs because, depending on the institution and job market circumstances, it may be possible to hire nurses only in half or whole FTE increments.

Case #5

It has been determined that Department XYZ requires one FTE manager, 12 FTEs of Technician I's, six FTEs of Technician II's, and two FTEs of clerks for the July 1, 19X1, to June 30, 19X2, budget year. Each FTE works 2,080 hours each year. Hourly pay rates are $30.00 for the manager, $20.00 for Technician II's, $15.00 for Technician I's, and $10.00 for clerks. A raise of 10 percent will be given before the budget year begins, and another of 8 percent halfway through the budget year. Table 5-7 displays the personnel budget for the budget year.

The Technician II's will be used to trace the data through the worksheet. The first column shows the rank. The name of the incumbent or the notation "vacant" is shown in the second column. The third column contains the full-time equivalent factor. Some, it is noted work only half-time (Paker and Hull), and the appropriate value (0.5) is recorded in the FTE column. Since all vacant positions will be paid the same hourly rate, their accumulated value is listed only once in the FTE column (2.0 FTEs resulting from the difference between the named 4.0 FTEs and the six FTEs required).

The hourly rate column shows the budget year base hourly pay rate. This is the rate that will be in effect on the first day of the budget year. In the case of the Technician II's, that is $22.00 (the present rate of $20.00 plus the 10 percent increase given before the budget year begins). This rate is multiplied by 2,080 hours and then by the FTE value to determine the base salary budget (Column G).

The salary increase columns (Columns H, I, and J) record the amount of any salary raise that applies to the budget fiscal year. In this case the staff is to receive an 8 percent raise halfway through the year (January 1, 19X2). The salary increase is calculated by multiplying percent of increase (8 percent) by the annual salary amount and then by the applicable portion of the budget year to which the increase applies. Johnson's raise of $1,830 is calculated as follows: $45,760 × 8% × 1/2 year = $1,830.40, rounded to $1,830.

If Johnson was given a salary increase of 12 percent after 12 weeks (thus being

Table 5-7
Salary Budget Worksheet

	A POSN or RANK	B INCUMBENT	C FTE VALUE	D CURRENT HOURLY PAY RATE	E INCREASE BEFORE START OF FY 19X2	F RATE AT START OF FY 19X2	G BASE SALARY BUDGET FY 19X2	H INCREASE SCHEDULED DURING FY 19X2 AMOUNT	I INCREASE SCHEDULED DURING FY 19X2 EFFECTIVE DATE	J SALARY INCREASE	K TOTAL SALARY BUDGET FY 19X2
1											
2	Mgr.	Mercado	1.0	30.00	10.0%	33.00	68,640	8.0%	1/1/X2	2,746	71,386
3											
4	Tech II	Johnson	1.0	20.00	10.0%	22.00	45,760	8.0%	1/1/X2	1,830	47,590
5		Robinson	1.0	20.00	10.0%	22.00	45,760	8.0%	1/1/X2	1,830	47,590
6		Page	1.0	20.00	10.0%	22.00	45,760	8.0%	1/1/X2	1,830	47,590
7		Parker	0.5	20.00	10.0%	22.00	22,880	8.0%	1/1/X2	915	23,795
8		Hull	0.5	20.00	10.0%	22.00	22,880	8.0%	1/1/X2	915	23,795
9		Vacant	2.0	20.00	10.0%	22.00	91,520	8.0%	1/1/X2	3,661	95,181
10		Total	6.0				274,560			10,982	285,542
11											
12	Tech I	Naylor	1.0	15.00	10.0%	16.50	34,320	8.0%	1/1/X2	1,373	35,693
13		Shilling	1.0	15.00	10.0%	16.50	34,320	8.0%	1/1/X2	1,373	35,693
14		Bridgeford	0.5	15.00	10.0%	16.50	17,160	8.0%	1/1/X2	686	17,846
15		Frasier	0.5	15.00	10.0%	16.50	17,160	8.0%	1/1/X2	686	17,846
16		Vacant	9.0	15.00	10.0%	16.50	308,880	8.0%	1/1/X2	12,355	321,235
17		Total	12.0				411,840			16,474	428,314
18											
19	Clerks	Jones	1.0	10.00	10.0%	11.00	22,880	8.0%	1/1/X2	915	23,795
20		Kelley	1.0	10.00	10.0%	11.00	22,880	8.0%	1/1/X2	915	23,795
21		Total	2.0				45,760			1,830	47,590
22											
23		Grand Total	21.0				800,800			32,032	832,832

in effect for 40 of the budget year's 52 weeks), the calculation would look like this: $45,760 × 12% × 40/52 of a year = $4,224.

Column K is merely a sum of the previous two. There could be other columns (for shift differential, on-call pay, additional planned raises, and so on) added to the matrix and also summed in the total column.

This may seem to be a great deal of detail. In fact, the budget could be prepared with much less detail, but the information developed using this matrix approach will be valuable later when comparing actual performance with the budget. As a rule, the more budget information available, the easier it is to understand any differences in performance and take corrective management action. Computer spreadsheet software programs are capable of storing enormous amounts of data. The more data, the better is a good rule of thumb.

If fringe benefits are included in the personnel budget, the calculation is usually a simple case of multiplying total salaries by a benefits percent.

Supplies and Services Budget

The final calculations relate to the budget for supplies and services. An account-by-account workup provides a good level of detail, but it is possible to budget down to the detail of IV tubing, solutions, and the like.

The first step in preparing this budget is to segregate into a minimum of two categories: (1) fixed expenses (those that are not related to the volume of business) and (2) variable expenses (those that fluctuate as a result of changes in volume). A third category, semivariable, could be used, but it is difficult to work with and as a result produces less precise results. After the expenses have been segregated, the mechanics of formulating budget amounts begin.

Figure 5-3 displays a matrix worksheet for calculating a supplies and services budget. It has been set up as it might appear on a computer screen as a spreadsheet program.

An appropriate base period should be selected. Data from this period will be helpful in calculating the budget amounts. This may be the year-to-date values in the current fiscal year, the latest 12-month period (which would be part of the prior fiscal year and part of the current fiscal year), or some similar period of time. In the case of a new program, data may be developed via consultation with other institutions or "experts," reference to "market basket" data for similar services, or estimation on an item-by-item basis.

The budget amounts are arrived at via a step-by-step conversion of base period amounts to budget period amounts. Fixed expense amounts in the base period are first divided by the number of months in the base period to arrive at an amount per month. This monthly amount is then multiplied by the number of months in the budget period to arrive at a preliminary budget amount. The same procedure is used for variable expenses, but volume (patient days, test counts, RVUs, and so on) is substituted for months.

The budget amounts may also be arrived at by developing a ratio of the budget

Figure 5-3
Supplies and Services Budget Worksheet

	A	B	C	D	E	F	G	H	I
1	EXPENSE ACCOUNT	BASE PER AMOUNT	BASE PERIOD UNITS	AMOUNT PER UNIT	BUDGET PERIOD UNITS	BASIC BUDGET AMOUNT	INFLATION RATE	INFLATION AMOUNT	TOTAL BUDGET AMOUNT
2									
3									
4									
5									
6									
7									
8									
9									
10									
11									
12									
13									
14									
15									
16									

volume (for variable expenses) to the base period volume and (for fixed expenses) a ratio of the duration of the budget period, usually 12 months, to the duration of the base period (3 months, 5 months, and so on). The base period dollar amounts are then multiplied by the appropriate ratio.

Variable Expense Ratio = Budget Volume ÷ Based Period Volume

Variable Budget Amount = Actual Variable Expense × Variable Expense Ratio

Fixed Expense Ratio = Budget Duration ÷ Base Period Duration

Fixed Budget Amount = Actual Fixed Expense × Fixed Expense Ratio

Both of these methodologies will be used to determine the supplies and services budget in Case #6

Case #6.

The supplies and services budget for the ABC Department must be prepared. The budget period is the upcoming fiscal year, in which volume is budgeted at 17,500 units of service. The data available after the first four months of the current fiscal year are.

Office Supplies	$ 2,000
Billing Supplies	140
Med/Surg Supplies	112,000
IV Solutions	38,500
Stock Drugs	28,000
Maintenance Contracts	5,000
Total	$185,640
Patient Days	7,000

The budget calculation begins by segregating the six expense categories into fixed and variable categories and applying a step-by-step conversion of the base period amounts to budget amounts (Table 5-8). The budget may also be arrived at using the ratio method as shown in Table 5-9.

BASE PERIOD ADJUSTMENTS

Exercise caution in selecting data from a base period. Guard against situations that could invalidate the data and cause budget calculations to be inaccurate. An adjustment to the base period data may be necessary before using the data for budget calculations. Thus, it is important to examine the actual expenditure amounts in the base period to make sure they are representative. This is particularly important in those accounts that are charged with an expense only once a year. An example of this would be the maintenance contracts account from Case #6. The budget was based on the assumption that the $5,000 was an amount rep-

Table 5-8
Supplies and Services Budget Worksheet

	A	B	C	D	E	F	G	H	I
1	EXPENSE ACCOUNT	BASE PERIOD AMOUNT	BASE PERIOD UNITS	AMOUNT PER UNIT	BUDGET PERIOD UNITS	BASIC BUDGET AMOUNT	INFLATION RATE	INFLATION AMOUNT	TOTAL BUDGET AMOUNT
2	Office Supplies	2,000	4 (months)	500.00	12 (Months)	6,000	5.0%	300	6,300
3	Maintenance Contracts	5,000	4 (months)	1,250.00	12 (Months)	15,000	5.0%	750	15,750
4									
5	Billing Supplies	140	7,000	0.02	17,500	350	5.0%	18	368
6	Med/Surg Supplies	112,000	7,000	16.00	17,500	280,000	7.5%	21,000	301,000
7	IV Solutions	38,500	7,000	5.50	17,500	96,250	6.0%	5,775	102,025
8	Stock Drugs	28,000	7,000	4.00	17,500	70,000	8.0%	5,600	75,600
9									
10	Total	185,640				467,600		33,443	501,043
11									
12									
13									
14									
15									
16									

Table 5-9
Supplies and Services Budget Worksheet – Ratio Approach

	A EXPENSE ACCOUNT	B BASE PERIOD AMOUNT	C BASE PERIOD UNITS	D BUDGET PERIOD UNITS	E BUDGET DIVIDED BY BASE	F BASIC BUDGET AMOUNT	G INFLATION RATE	H INFLATION AMOUNT	I TOTAL BUDGET AMOUNT
1									
2	Office Supplies	2,000	4 (months)	12 (Months)	3.00000	6,000	5.0%	300	6,300
3	Maintenance Contracts	5,000	4 (months)	12 (Months)	3.00000	15,000	5.0%	750	15,750
4									
5	Billing Supplies	140	7,000	17,500	2.50000	350	5.0%	18	368
6	Med/Surg Supplies	112,000	7,000	17,500	2.50000	280,000	7.5%	21,000	301,000
7	IV Solutions	38,500	7,000	17,500	2.50000	96,250	6.0%	5,775	102,025
8	Stock Drugs	28,000	7,000	17,500	2.50000	70,000	8.0%	5,600	75,600
9									
10	Total	185,640				467,600		33,443	501,043
11									
12									
13									
14									
15									
16									

resentative of the four-month base period. If this were not the case and the $5,000 represented the expense for the entire year (but paid in a single lump sum payment at the start of the fiscal year), the budget of $15,000 would be overstated by $10,000 since only $5,000 would be necessary. Three situations can be particularly troublesome.

The Unusual Month

The base period may contain one or more months in which events occurred that are not likely to be repeated in the budget year. Start-up expenses, items billed and paid once a year, a onetime expenditure, or a onetime cost avoidance are examples of financial events that could be reflected in a base period.

Normalization

Occasionally, a base period is selected that does not fully reflect the current, ongoing operation. Perhaps the prior 12-month base period was absent the full effect of a newly instituted program that has added or reduced expenses on an ongoing basis. The base period may not reflect staff that have yet to be brought on or other changes that will be instituted between the time budget calculations are made and the new budget year begins.

Seasonal Patterns

Be careful in selecting a base period for any expense category that is affected by seasonal patterns. Utility costs, for example, are particularly vulnerable to seasonal highs and lows. Institutions that air-condition their facilities using electrical centrifugal chillers will have higher electric bills in the summer than in winter. Use of a base period heavily weighted toward the summer months will result in too high an electricity budget. Conversely, use of a base period heavily weighted toward the winter months will result in too low an electricity budget.

Resource needs should be budgeted as accurately as possible. A calculation resulting in too high a budget is just as bad as one resulting in too low a budget. In both cases, resource allocation decisions elsewhere in the organization are influenced by the erroneous calculations. Consider the effect on an institution that overstates its electricity budget by $200,000. Elsewhere in the institution, a needed program may be deferred because sufficient budget resources are not available. Then, months into the budget year, when actual electricity use is running well below budget and the error becomes apparent, it may be too late to implement the new program.

REVIEW PROBLEMS

Problem 1

Using the information provided, prepare a salary budget for FYX2 (7/1/X1 to 6/30/X2). Volume in the budget year is planned to be 5,400 patient days, and staff needs are for six hours of hands-on RN care per patient day. Productive time is 85 percent of total paid time. For purposes of this solution, the assumption is that nurses can be hired only in half FTE increments (e.g., if you calculate a need for 12.8 FTEs, 13 FTEs must be budgeted).

A pay raise will be given to all staff on May 1 of each year at a rate of 6 percent. The July 1, 19X1, rate of pay for new hires is set at $13.00/hour regardless of the date of hire.

The following are the current staff with FTE values and hourly rates of pay as of November 4, 19X0:

Abelein	1.0	$14.30
Brenchley	1.0	13.80
Brownstein	0.5	13.50
Colson	1.0	14.00
Cottingham	0.5	12.75
Cyr	1.0	14.20

Problem 2

Prepare a salary budget for the fiscal year 7/1/X1 to 6/30/X2. Staffing levels are based on the need for six hours of hands-on work per patient day. Volume in the budget year is to be 3,600 patient days. Productive time is 80 percent of total paid time. For purposes of this solution, staff can be hired only in half FTE increments; thus if there is a need for 7.4 FTEs, 7.5 must be budgeted. The following are the current staff with FTE values and hourly rates of pay as of 4/1/X1:

King	1.0	$14.00
Law	1.0	13.80
Rogers	1.0	13.50
Ruby	1.0	14.00
Russell	0.5	12.75

A pay raise will be given to all staff on May 1 of each year at a rate of 6 percent. The starting rate of pay for new hires is $13.00 regardless of hire date.

Problem 3

Using the information provided, prepare a salary budget for FYX3 (7/1/X2 to 6/30/X3). Volume in the budget year will be 3,000 units of service, and staff needs are for five hours of hands-on work per unit of service. Productive time is 85 percent of total paid time. For purposes of this solution, the assumption is that staff can be hired only in half FTE increments. A pay raise will be given to all staff (and to the starting rate of pay) on June 1 and December 1 of each year at a rate of 6 percent.

The following are the current staff with FTE values and hourly rates of pay as of March 8, 19X2:

Critz	1.0	$14.50
Zeri	0.4	13.50
Goel	1.0	15.00
Taft	0.5	13.75
Freeman	0.6	14.60
Starting Rate		13.00

Problem 4

You must prepare a budget for fiscal year 19X2 for your 75-bed nursing unit. Target occupancy rate is 80 percent. You have determined that the staffing pattern needed to support this level of occupancy is 50 FTEs of RNs managed by a single head nurse. The fiscal year begins on July 1, 19X1. The existing rates of pay as of November 30, 19X0, are $15/hour for RNs and $20/hour for the head nurse. These rates will be increased on January 1, 19X1 by 10 percent and on January 1, 19X2, by 8 percent. Benefits are 20 percent of salaries for all employees. Inflation on nonsalary items is 10 percent for the budget year. The budget you are to prepare should include patient days, salaries, benefits, and supplies. The following data are available for consumable supplies.

Departmental Expense Report
July 1 −− November 30, 19X0

Description	Amount
Office Supplies (F)	$500
Med/Surg Supplies (V)	18,000
Stock Drugs (V)	13,500
Books & Periodicals (F)	50
Miscellaneous (F)	1,000
Total	$33,050
Partient Days	9,000

(V) = variable expense items
(F) = fixed expense items

Problem 5

You have been asked to prepare your unit's salary budget for the next fiscal year, which begins on July 1, 19X6. You have the following data. A total of 10 Tech I FTEs are required along with 4 Tech II FTEs. The rates of pay shown below are those in effect on 10/5/X5. A salary increase is given on May 1 every year to all Tech I's at a rate of 4 percent. Tech II's receive an increase of 2 percent on the first day of each fiscal year. The starting rates of pay for newly hired staff for the budget year are $8.50 for Tech II's and $9.40 for Tech I's.

Name & Rank	FTE Value	Hourly Rate
Tech I – –		
Bull	1.0	$9.80
Jones	1.0	9.80
Carroll	1.0	10.00
Kulis	0.8	9.70
Condon	1.0	9.40
Kennedy	0.2	9.90
Lewiston	0.5	9.50
Smith	0.5	9.60
Tech II – –		
Swartz	0.8	8.60
Johansson	1.0	8.70

Problem 6

Prepare the salary budget needed to achieve the indicated staffing pattern shown below. Staff are paid $8.00 per hour plus $1.00 per hour shift premium for evening, night, and all weekend hours worked. Vacation, holiday, sick, and other nonproductive time amounts to 20 percent of paid time.

	Sun	Mon	Tue	Wed	Thu	Fri	Sat
Day Shift	2	2	2	2	2	2	2
Evening Shift	1	1	1	1	1	1	1
Night Shift		1	1	1	1	1	

Problem 7

To prepare the salary budget for your department, you have the following information. The budget calls for a volume of 21,000 procedures. You have determined that staffing should be based on 1 FTE for each 2,000 procedures. Staff receive a 6 percent salary increase on their anniversary dates. The budget year is July 1, 19X1, to June 30, 19X2, and today is April 20, 19X1. The staff will also receive a $0.50/hour general increase on January 1. The anniversary date for all staff hired from today forward will be July 1. The starting rate of pay is $9.00 The current staff is as follows:

Name	FTE	Current Rates	Anniversary Dates
Milligan	1.0	$10.00	May 1
Gomez	0.5	9.60	June 1
Ripken,B.	1.0	9.80	July 1
Worthington	1.0	9.20	December 1
Anderson	0.8	9.60	December 1
Davis,G.	0.2	9.00	December 1
Dempsey	0.5	9.50	April 1
Ripken,C.	1.0	9.75	April 1
Horn	0.7	9.00	October 1
Evans	0.3	9.10	October 1

Premium pay, for hours worked on all three weekend shifts and weekday evening and night shifts, is $1.00 per hour. Productive time is 80% of total paid time. How many FTEs and dollars should the budget cover?
dollars should the budget cover?

Problem 8

You have been asked to prepare your unit's salary budget for the next fiscal year, which begins on July 1, 19X8. You have the following data. A total of 12 FTEs of RNs are required along with 5 FTEs of nursing aides. The rates of pay shown below are those in effect on 12/20/X7. A 4 percent salary increase is given to all RNs each year on April 1. Aides receive an increase of 2 percent on the first day of each fiscal year. The starting rates of pay for newly hired staff for the budget year are $8.50 for aides and $11.40 for RNs.

In addition, you have determined that 16 hours of agency RN time and 24 hours of staff overtime will be used each week during June, July, and August to cover for staff vacation leave. You must also budget for charge pay. One RN on each evening and night shift Monday through Friday and all three shifts on Saturdays, Sundays, and holidays is assigned charge responsibility. The individual selected is paid a premium of $2.50 per hour.

Rank & Name	FTE Value	Hourly Rate
R.N.s – –		
Arnold	1.0	$11.80
Balog	1.0	11.80
Chalmers	1.0	12.00
Coffey	0.8	11.70
Davila	1.0	11.40
DeMeester	0.2	11.90
Escobar	0.5	11.50
Heaton	0.5	11.60
L.P.N.s – –		
Baker	0.8	$8.60
Caldwell	1.0	8.70

Problem 9

Given the following information, calculate the test volume for the upcoming budget year.

	Base Year (6 Months)	Budget Year
Patient Days	150,000	250,000
Outpatient Visits	100,000	210,000
Inpatient Tests	450,000	
Outpatient Tests	400,000	

Problem 10

You are the manager of the Clinical Laboratory Department and must submit a detailed budget for your department showing salary, fringe benefits, supplies, and other costs for the new fiscal year by this afternoon. Resources are extremely tight; thus no budget adjustments will be made during the course of the year. Consequently, you must prepare a budget that gets the necessary operating dollars without being excessive and that does not cut short your true need. The data available are presented below. What is your budget for the coming fiscal year for test volume, salaries, benefits, supplies, and total expense?

For the first five months of the current fiscal year, your expenses have been as follows:

Technician Salaries	$458,255
Manager Salaries	24,400
Clerical Salaries	15,550
Fringe Benefits	64,400
Office Supplies	5,000
Billing Forms	12,555
Solutions	1,843,600
Uniforms	630
Maintenance Contracts	48,000
Laboratory Supplies	10,000
Education Expense	1,260
Dues and Subscriptions	350
	$2,484,000

The statistics provided by the central budget office for these same five months and for the coming fiscal year are

This Year (to date):		
Patient Days	45,000	
Outpatient Visits	72,000	
Lab Tests −−		
Inpatient Tests	2,025,000	
Outpatient Tests	2,160,000	
Quality Control	5,000	(1,000 per month)
Total Lab Tests	4,190,000	
Next Year:		
Patient Days	108,000	
Outpatient Visits	192,000	

You know the following about your operation:

1. You pay equal monthly amounts for maintenance contracts.
2. Your staff is composed of
   10 Technician I's ($25,000 annual salary each)

22 Technician II's ($27,500 annual salary each)
10 Technician III's ($30,000 annual salary each)
2 Billing Clerks ($19,600 annual salary each)
3. You are paid $58,700 for managing the department.
4. Fringe benefits are 20% of salaries.

In the upcoming fiscal year, each person will receive a 5 percent salary increase at the end of six months. Inflation on nonsalary items is planned at 10 percent.

Problem 11

Your pharmacy is able to produce up to 30,000 unit doses each month. The trend in unit doses over the years has been as shown below. What amount of unit doses will you budget for in 19X4?

19X1	312,000	Unit Doses
19X2	327,600	Unit Doses
19X3	343,890	Unit Doses

Problem 12

You manage a Therapeutic Radiation Department with five machines. These machines have a maximum total capacity of 600 treatments per month, each valued at 50 RVUs. What number of RVUs will you budget in 19X8, given the following RVU trend over time?

19X1	––	190,000	19X5 ––	278,180
19X2	––	209,000	19X6 ––	306,000
19X3	–––	229,900	19X7 ––	336,000
19X4	––	252,890		

Chapter 6

Capital Budgeting

Capital budgeting, the planning for capital equipment acquisition and renovations, customarily takes place as part of the annual budgeting process. It involves integration of the short- and long-term operating needs of the institution with equipment and renovations. In this way only those pieces of equipment and those renovations that are needed to achieve the goals and objectives specified in the annual plan and the three-to-five–year business plan are acquired, and resources are not consumed in acquiring equipment that is not consistent with goals and objectives.

By definition, capital equipment has an acquisition cost in excess of a stated dollar amount (usually $300 to $500), has a useful life of more than one year, and is large enough to be identified with a tag of some kind. The cost of this equipment is not charged to an expense account; it is carried on the balance sheet and depreciated over the course of its useful life.

CAPITAL ACQUISITION

The acquisition of capital equipment and renovation projects should occur via one of three possible methods: (1) as part of the annual plan, (2) as part of a multiyear plan, or (3) as a response to a business opportunity.

Part of the Annual Plan

This is applicable to replacement equipment (which replaces older, worn-out pieces or pieces that have become technologically obsolescent) and renovations to the physical plant. Renovations can result from a need to refresh cosmetically or modernize space, improve functionality, or provide for a new or expanded function. Acquisitions and renovations made as part of the annual plan must be consistent with the multiyear plan. If the multiyear plan envisions the replacement of monitoring systems throughout the critical care units in 19X3 and 19X4 with Brand A equipment, the short-term goal must support that. In 19X2, it would be imprudent to acquire monitors that are incompatible with Brand A. Whatever actions are taken in the short-term must be complementary and supportive of the long-term plan.

Table 6-1 displays a capital equipment budget that integrates the short- and long-term thinking necessary to budget successfully. Note that the first call on dollars goes to programmed replacements. Rather than replace all the anesthesia machines in 19X1, all the dialysis machines in 19X2, ventilators in 19X3, and so on, a predetermined number of each are replaced each year — as part of an ongoing renewal program. Next come minor acquisitions, those costing less than an institution-specific amount (in this case, $50,000). Major acquisitions, costing more than the institution-specific amount, are listed on an item-by-item basis. These are followed by a small amount of contingency dollars to allow some latitude to the institution's leadership in taking advantage of developing opportunities that may not wait for the next year's budget or to provide "insurance" in the event that a piece of equipment must be replaced on an emergency basis. Last in this example, a department with high-priced equipment needs, radiology, is listed. Two lines are used. The first indicates the amounts needed in each of the five years covered by the plan. The second indicates that over the first three years of the plan, funds will be saved to ensure that enough cash will be available in year four, when the largest single-year outlay (greater than the entire year's budget) is scheduled. In this way, the excess funds that would otherwise be available in years one, two, and three are safeguarded, there are no surprises in 19X4, and all necessary equipment can be acquired.

Part of a Multiyear Plan

Certain pieces of high-cost, high-technology equipment lend themselves to a longer-range approach. Typically, these include pieces of equipment for radiology and laboratory departments. Major renovations to existing buildings or the construction of new ones are also covered here. Inclusion in the long-term business plan is consistent with the need for additional "up-front" work in the acquisition process, such as financial and regulatory feasibility studies, certificate of need (CON) acquisition in certain cases, architectural and engineering studies and planning, and the like.

Response to a Business Opportunity

Occasionally, an opportunity arises outside the normal planning process. This usually takes the form of an opportunity to improve financial performance by lowering the cost of operations or increasing the ability to generate and collect

Table 6-1
Annual Capital Spending Plan ($000s)

Description	FY 19X1	FY 19X2	FY 19X3	FY 19X4	FY 19X5
Programmed Replacements	$463	$463	$423	$423	$423
Minor Acquisitions (<$50,000 each)	407	410	432	440	450
Major Acquisitions (>$50,000 each)					
Unspecified		400	400	400	400
ICU Monitoring – Nursing	195				
Laser – Ophthalmology	125				
Pot Scrubber – Dietary	65				
Holter Monitors – Cardiology	100				
Surveillance System – Security	88				
Contingency	50	50	50	50	50
Radiology					
Multiyear Replacement Plan	280	350	1,095	3,136	1,477
Funding Set Aside	227	527		(1,849)	
Total	$2,000	$2,200	$2,400	$2,600	$2,800

Acquisitions and renovations made as part of the annual plan must be consistent with the multiyear plan. Actions taken in the short term must be complementary and supportive of the long-term plan.

revenue. Examples include pieces of equipment that reduce labor and supply costs (perhaps an automated chemistry analyzer) or that provide additional capacity to treat patients (perhaps an automated outpatient scheduling system that increases the number of patient visits to a clinic). In addition, the opportunity to acquire a major piece of equipment at a substantially reduced price occasionally presents itself; this, too, would be included in this business opportunity category.

QUESTIONING TECHNIQUE

The acquisition of capital equipment or the renovation of the physical plant involves the commitment of large sums of money—a resource that hospitals, nursing homes, and other health care providers are finding to be in scarce supply. Consequently, it is important that every piece of equipment and every renovation represent the best possible choice. One way to increase the likelihood of this is to ask questions, many questions, in order to develop as much understanding and factual information as possible as part of the decision-making process.

At the departmental level, where the request for a piece of equipment or a renovation is most likely to originate, questions should focus on the following: (1) the effect on volume (additions, reductions, or substitutions); (2) the likely changes to revenue and collections (payment caps like PPS, experimental technologies, and so on must be taken into account); (3) the impact on operating costs (more or fewer staff, changes in supply type and cost, maintenance requirements, and so on); and (4) the profile of installation costs (special electrical requirements, possible heating, ventilating, and air conditioning (HVAC) modifications, and so on). A more detailed list of questions to be considered as part of the original decision and justification process at the department level is presented in Table 6-2.

Questions should also be asked regarding the availability of the equipment and any supportive pieces, along with the amount of lead time to be built into an acquisition schedule. Delivery and installation should be dovetailed with the time schedule of any associated renovations in order to avoid the delivery of equipment before its physical environment is prepared. Depending on the particular piece of equipment, it is possible that significant costs could be incurred for storage while construction progresses. It is also possible that the unavailability of a particular brand in time to meet a program deadline could result in a decision to pursue a different manufacturer's offering.

A number of tough questions need to be asked throughout the process. Will it "work"? Are the projections and assumptions about cost and revenue performance sound? Does the new piece of equipment or the renovation represent a genuine improvement or simply the latest fad? Does this represent merely the addition of "bells and whistles"? Can the institution afford not to proceed with acquisition? What are the intangibles (image, marketability, mission, and so on) that can influence the decision-making process? Occasionally, the decision to proceed or not may rest on the answer to one or more of these questions.

Table 6-2
Questions in Search of Answers

1. Volume
   - o What is the effect on units of service volume?
   - o Will there be additional units of service?
   - o Will there be fewer units of service?
   - o Will there be increases in some and decreases in others?
   - o Will there be volume changes in departments other than the one requesting the equipment or renovation?
   - o Will any incremental volume attributable to the new equipment be more than the department can physically handle?

2. Revenue and Collections
   - o What is the effect of the change in volume on gross revenue?
   - o How much change will there be to inpatient revenue? Outpatient revenue? Ancillary revenue?
   - o What changes will there be to revenues in departments other than the requesting department?
   - o How much of any incremental revenue will actually be collected?
   - o What is the effect on the generation of additional, incremental revenue of such arrangements as PPOs, HMOs, PPS, etc.?
   - o Will charge rates be modified because of a change in volume?
   - o Will charge rates need to be modified in order to afford the requested acquisition?
   - o In a cost reimbursement environment, how much of any incremental revenue will find its way through the reimbursement formulas to the per diem reimbursement rate?
   - o In a rate control environment, how much of any incremental revenue will be lost because the regulator reduces charge rates because of the increased volume?
   - o Will the new equipment improve the collection of revenue? (This question is applicable to automated systems for collection of patient data faster, more accurately, and so on.)
   - o Will any incremental revenues be generated by procedures deemed to be "experimental" by third party payers? If not covered by insurance, how will the incremental revenues be collected?

Table 6-2
Questions in Search of Answers (Continued)

3. Operating Costs
    o   What additions, reductions, or changes to the staff complement will be needed to support the new piece of equipment?
    o   What kinds of skills must incremental staff possess?
    o   Are staff available internally or must they be recruited from outside the institution?
    o   Must staff be specially trained? If so, on site or at the factory?
    o   If a reduction in staff is involved, because of an equipment related productivity increase, will attrition or a layoff be used to reduce the workforce?
    o   In a unionized environment, what will be the effect of contractually guaranteed layoff "bumping" rights (for staff reductions) or the promotional bid system (for staff additions)?
    o   If a layoff "bump" is involved, what will the likely effect be on other departments?
    o   What will happen to supply costs (increase, decrease, or remain the same)?
    o   Are replacement/maintenance parts readily available?

Sometimes, asking the tough questions can be difficult. Often, they appear to challenge authority, but they must be asked. The process can be facilitated by prefacing the questions, as described previously, with a phrase such as "Let me play devil's advocate." In this way the "bad guy" onus shifts away from the questioner to an unnamed third party.

Finally, at the department level, there should be postacquisition questioning to see if the decision process can be improved in the future. This closes the loop in the process of planning, implementing, and assessing. In this capital "postmortem," questions should center on an assessment of the process. Were the original assumptions correct? Were projections achieved? Could anything have been done better? Where could improvements have been made? Last, the most difficult question to ask: Where did we go wrong? It is similarly important to understand the positive aspects of the process and repeat them in subsequent years.

By following up after the fact, it is possible to learn from the mistakes of the past and avoid them in the future. Mistakes can be a valuable learning tool, but only if people learn from them.

REVIEW COMMITTEE

Many institutions use a committee structure to review all requests for equipment and renovations. Separate committees may review equipment and renovations, or a single committee may review both. Regardless, this group reviews each request and attempts to match available resources with department requests. But this is more than a simple matching exercise. The committee reviews each request to determine the following: (1) the level of need, (2) the "fit" of the request as compared with departmental or institutional objectives, (3) applicability to the capital budget (some requests should more appropriately be charged to the operating budget), and (4) priority for funding.

The budgeting process begins with a departmental request. It then proceeds to a review by the committee. If a decision is made to approve the request, a recommendation will be made to the upper level of the institution's administration. Finally, approval is sought from the board of trustees. This can be seen more clearly by referring to Figure 6-1, which highlights the process.

Decisions are usually based on a review of information supplied by the request-

Figure 6-1
Approval Process

The flow of the capital budgeting approval process can be traced by following this simple chart.

ing department and the knowledge of the institution the committee members bring with them to the review process.

While the structure of the review committee or committees differs from institution to institution, one thing is certain: its membership should be broad-based and include, as a minimum, a representative of administration, nursing, the medical staff, and engineering and materials management. It should be large enough so there are enough hands to get the job done, but not so large as to be ineffective. Every discipline need not be represented; rather, internal "consultants" can be used for certain pieces or classes of equipment. The committee should be charged with the responsibility to review all requests and the authority to reject those that it feels are not deserving of funding via the capital budget.

This committee, too, should ask the "tough" questions and should complete the process with a follow-up to determine what aspects of its review should be strengthened, modified, or eliminated in future years.

THE REVIEW PROCESS

While each piece of equipment requested by the various departments is likely to be different, all will possess certain attributes that can be used by the review committee to facilitate the decision-making process. These attributes include the following:

1. Sphere of use
   a. patient care
   b. administrative
2. Financial effect
   a. cost improvement
   b. revenue enhancement
3. Service effect
   a. replacement
   b. service expansion
   c. quality or service improvement
   d. new service

Knowledge of these attributes is helpful in determining priorities for funding, especially when the demand for available budget dollars exceeds supply. Given limited resources, a review committee might opt to fund only replacement and patient care items, or equipment requested to support a new service that had been approved in the operating budget might receive automatic approval.

Remember that, in essence, this is a competitive environment. Each department is competing against all the others for limited resource dollars. Thus, the justification accompanying each request is important to the decision-making process. This information "sells" the review committee and convinces it that this request, more so than many others, is deserving of inclusion in the budget. Consequently, the justification must present the most compelling reason or reasons to allocate scarce resources.

Of all the information provided in the justification, the most important may be the financial information, such as a marginal profit-and-loss statement, benefit/cost ratio, payback period, and the like. Chapter 8 describes these decision-making and investment analysis techniques.

HOW TO PACKAGE THE REQUEST

For equipment, many institutions use a multiform request procedure to collect the detailed information about each piece of equipment requested and provide departmental summarization. The basic equipment request form varies from one institution to the next; but the information it seeks to collect is, for the most part, standard to all institutions and includes the following:

1. Requesting department
2. Cost center or department number
3. Location
4. Requested by
5. Priority (as compared with all other requests from a particular department)
6. Quantity
7. Model number
8. Description
9. Unit cost
10. Sphere of use
    a. patient care
    b. administrative
11. Financial effect
    a. cost improvement
    b. revenue enhancement
12. Service effect
    a. replacement
    b. service expansion
    c. quality or service improvement
    d. new service
13. Operating budget needs
    a. staff
    b. supplies
    c. training and orientation
    d. routine maintenance
    e. other
14. Manufacturer (including name of contact, address, and phone number)
15. Equipment evaluated?   yes/no   (If yes, by whom and when?)
16. Periodic maintenance?   yes/no   (If yes, in-house or vendor?)
17. High-technology equipment?   yes/no   (If yes, acceptance tested by whom and when?)
18. Installation requires
    a. electrical
    b. mechanical
    c. HVAC

     d. plumbing
     e. carpentry
     f. other (specify)
19 Special installation requirements
20. If replacement, provide the following information about the piece to be replaced: model number, description, serial number, asset tag number, location.
21. Justification

A second form summarizes all the requests from a single department and contains only summary information about each request.

1. Department name
2. Priority
3. Description
4. Sphere of use
     a. patient care
     b. administrative
5. Financial effect
     a. cost improvement
     b. revenue enhancement
6. Service effect
     a. replacement
     b. service expansion
     c. quality or service improvement
     d. new service
7. Cost
8. Expected acquisition date (for cash flow planning purposes)

These documents are then sent to the review committee in accordance with a predetermined budget timetable.

SELECTION PROCESS

The selection of make and model often depends on the equipment or systems already present in a department. New infusion pumps must be compatible with existing ones. Additions to monitoring systems should be of the same make as the system already in place.

Sometimes, the brand (the manufacturer) can be predetermined, but the model or size has yet to be determined. For example, a hospital may have decided that all of its computers will be IBM or Digital or Data General, but the model to be acquired still has to be determined by the application (the project or function) to be supported.

On other occasions nothing is predetermined. In selecting an automated chemistry analyzer, for instance, there may be no predisposition to make or model, no reason to require compatibility. In a situation like this, effort must be placed on selecting the "right" piece of equipment. The following step-by-step approach is vital to achieving success.

1. Begin with the development of a detailed, objective set of specifications outlining what is expected of the equipment. This includes specifications and expectations not only for the equipment but also for its environment, cost performance, personnel impact, and so on. An acquisition cost target should be included.

2. A review of the literature (trade publications, professional journals, and sales brochures) will facilitate the development of a list of potential vendors and pieces of equipment for further consideration.

3. A detailed comparison of product features with predetermined specifications should serve to trim the list of candidates. Only those pieces of equipment that meet all, or substantially all, the specifications should remain in the running.

4. Site visits to see a similar product in operation in a similar environment (same size operation, same operating constraints and challenges, and so on) should be arranged. In many cases, equipment manufacturers will assist with this. In addition, interviews with current users and with colleagues at other institutions can be most helpful.

5. An in-house demonstration or trial period can sometimes be arranged. This is one of the best methods of determining if a product will "work" in the institution. Product acceptance can be tied to meeting certain performance criteria (number of tests per hour and so on) as a way of guaranteeing that the equipment meets the institution's specifications and the manufacturer's claims.

Finally, buy only what is truly needed. Do not consume scarce resources by acquiring the latest bells and whistles that may never be used. Remember to buy what is necessary, not what the salesman wants to sell.

Integration with the Operating Budget

The capital budget and the operating budget should be thoroughly integrated so that the staff and supplies needed to operate a piece of equipment acquired in the capital budget are provided in the operating budget and the equipment needed for staff to be effective is provided in the capital budget. How embarrassing would it be to acquire a new MRI unit only to find that the radiology department's expense budget provided no incremental staff to operate it? While integration of these budgets may seem simple, occasionally they are prepared separately with separate timetables that make integration difficult. It is also important to make sure that the items in the capital budget complement and support each other. Including new carpet in the main halls of a hospital but omitting the necessary carpet-cleaning equipment to maintain it would be imprudent.

SOURCES OF FUNDS

Once the decision to proceed has been made, the issue of paying for the acquisition must be addressed. A source of funds must be identified. Some obvious ones include cash from operations, borrowing, leasing, endowments and philan-thropy, the new piece of equipment itself, or any combination of these.

Cash from Operations

Cash is generated by the normal profits of the institution. Generally, this amounts to the gain from operations (the "bottom line") plus depreciation and any other extraordinary cash items. Table 6-3 demonstrates this calculation for the Real General Hospital.

Borrowing Cash

When deemed necessary, cash can be borrowed from a bank at approximately the prime interest rate. Important here is the ability to repay the borrowed funds using "tomorrow's" cash from operations. Borrowing has an effect on the institution's financial ratios; this, too, must be taken into account. It is possible that this option cannot be used because the institution has exhausted its debt capacity (the ability to borrow based on the demonstrated ability to repay) or because debt ca-pacity is being reserved for a more important need.

Table 6-3
Cash Generated from Operations

| | For the 12 Months Ended June 30, | |
	19X2	19X1
Gross Patient Service Revenue	$92,805,908	$77,185,080
Less Deductions		
Contractual Allowances	$5,907,416	$4,755,060
Provision for Bad Debts	2,342,708	1,505,041
Provision for Charity Care	676,844	690,246
Total Deductions	$8,926,968	$6,950,347
Net Patient Service Revenue	$83,878,940	$70,234,733
Other Operating Revenue	3,342,121	3,615,015
Total Operating Revenue	$87,221,061	$73,849,748
Operating Expenses		
Salaries and Wages	$38,204,953	$34,436,411
Fringe Benefits	7,517,926	6,460,602
Supplies and Purchased Services	29,916,553	25,573,883
Interest Expense	1,867,590	1,491,970
Depreciation	3,390,416	2,419,783
Cost of Operations	$80,897,438	$70,382,649
Excess of Revenue over Expenses	$6,323,623	$3,467,099
Add Back Non-Cash Expense: Depreciation	3,390,416	2,419,783
Cash Generated from Operations	$9,714,039	$5,886,882

Leasing

Often an attractive funding alternative for equipment acquisition, leases can be entered into with the equipment manufacturer or a subsidiary company or via a third-party leasing company. Many issues must be examined when selecting this funding option, not the least of which are changing technologies and equipment obsolescence, ownership at the conclusion of the lease, tax benefits, and so on. Leases should not be entered into without a thorough legal and financial review.

Caution should be exercised before entering into a lease because of the effect lease payments can have on future periods. It is possible to benefit the current year at the expense of the future. Table 6-4 displays an example of leasing as a constraint on the future. With a limited capital equipment budget in 19X1, the institution turned to capital leasing to "stretch" its available capital dollars. In effect, it acquired a million-dollar piece of equipment for a much smaller annual lease payment. It did the same in 19X2 and 19X3. By the time 19X4 arrives, however, the capital funds are nearly exhausted. Capital leases can also constrain the institution's ability to borrow money because a capital lease is a form of borrowing.

Department managers should understand whether a lease is a capital lease or an expense lease. The capital lease implies an ownership interest at the termination of the lease. The payments would come from the capital budget, as shown in Table 6-4, and the value of the asset, as well as the lease liability, would be displayed on the balance sheet. No ownership interest is present in the expense lease. In essence, it is merely an equipment rental arrangement, but for a long term. The lease payments are charged to expense, and an appropriate amount should be provided in the operating budget to cover the lease expense.

Cash from Endowments and Philanthropy

Because of the generosity of others, funds may have been donated to the institution to be set aside to purchase equipment, to fund renovations, or to support

Table 6-4
Effect of Leasing on the Future

	– – – – – Fiscal Years – – – – –			
	19X1	19X2	19X3	19X4
Maximum Available Capital Budget Funds	$2,000	$2,000	$2,000	$2,000
Deductions:				
Amounts Committed to Lease #1	−300	−300	−300	−300
Amounts Committed to Lease #2		−400	−400	−400
Amounts Committed to Lease #3			−500	−500
Amounts Committed to Lease #4				−600
Remaining Available Capital Budget Funds	$1,700	$1,300	$800	$200

(While leases do assist in stretching limited capital equipment resources, it should be remembered that they can compromise management's latitude in the future.)

capital needs of a specific department. Occasionally, charitable and civic organizations will "adopt" an institution and provide funding. It may be possible to borrow from the institution's own endowment fund. In this way the interest paid is kept "in the family."

Cash Generated by the Equipment

It is possible that a new piece of equipment will generate the sufficient incremental revenues and associated cash flows to "pay its own way."

CONSTRAINTS

There are always constraints on any process or venture. In capital budgeting, one major constraint is the availability of funds. This determines the upper dollar limit for the budget. Throughout the process it is vital to success that everyone involved be aware of these limits. It is also essential that as many people as practical be involved so that a sense of participation in, ownership of, and support for, the decision-making process will result. The objective is to give everyone a fair hearing. The true test of whether the process is working is if a manager who has had his request denied can say: "I told them what I needed. I understood the constraints they were operating under, and I feel they treated me fairly. Maybe next year I will have better results."

Never, as a reviewer, put people off or ignore them. Always listen. Remember, a piece of equipment that a reviewer thinks is unimportant may be the most important to the person requesting it. Listen to people. Give them 15 or 20 minutes. At least extend them the courtesy of hearing their problems and concerns. It may turn out that they foresee a real opportunity for the institution that no one previously recognized. Consider that it is easier to tame a wild horse than to ride a dead one. Dead horses have a tendency just to lie there, going nowhere. Wild horses, on the other hand, have a high energy level. They do a lot of wrong things but are very much alive, and they perform really well once they have been trained.

When someone has a way-out idea about equipment or renovations, listen to it. It may turn out to be the wild horse that will outperform someone else's dead one.

Chapter 7

Departmental Performance Reports

A manager's responsibilities include planning, organizing and staffing, directing or leading, and controlling. Controlling requires information, specifically, the kind of performance information contained in periodic departmental performance reports. Typically, these are monthly, occasionally quarterly, reports that provide managers with information about departmental volume (units of service), revenue, salaries and man-hours, fringe benefits, consumable supplies, purchased services, and so on. These reports show the results—in dollars and other numbers—of what managers did and *did not do*. While managers may not appreciate the "messages" contained in the reports, it is important to remember that accountants only report—managers made it happen.

Generally, certain characteristics apply to these reports. They are usually tabular in format and provide some comparative information, such as budget amounts, prior month data, or values from the same period in the prior year. This comparative information helps put the current period data in perspective. These reports are usually prepared centrally by the accounting or information systems department on a frequent enough basis to help managers, but not so frequently as to confuse.

Some reports may be prepared in the department to provide a slightly different perspective or to report data not gathered and reported by others. Many of these department-specific reports are prepared using personal computers (PCs) and can be arranged in any format and at whatever frequency is most desirable. Given currently available software, it is possible to combine tabular data with a graphic display to produce a comprehensive yet easy-to-understand report. It is also possible with today's technology to "download" data from the centrally prepared reports to a PC to allow for easier analysis, report customizing, or the combination of centrally and departmentally prepared data.

The timing of performance reports is critical if they are to be helpful in managing. If a report for March that highlights an unfavorable trend does not arrive until late April, it could be well into May before the problem is fully understood and corrective action is taken. It could be June or even July before the results of the corrective action plan can be seen in the reports. It is, thus, essential that performance reports be received as soon after the end of the reporting period as possible; timeliness is critical.

WHAT DO ALL THESE NUMBERS MEAN?

Basically, there are two kinds of reports—transaction listings and summary reports. Transaction listings (e.g., inventory distribution reports, payroll journals, and accounts payable listings), as the name implies, list transactions charged to a specified cost center or department and a specific account number (occasionally referred to as an expense code or natural expense category). Summary reports summarize data from one or more tabular reports and combine them with any comparative data to be reported.

The technique of summarizing data as part of the reporting process is known as data reduction. Figure 7-1 illustrates this technique. It is important to understand

Figure 7-1
Data Reduction

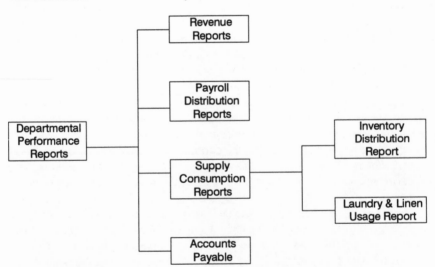

An inventory distribution report would typically tell the quantities and prices of items withdrawn from inventory. A laundry report would tell the same about our use of laundry. They may be summarized into a single line, "supply consumption." Whatever the organization, it is important to understand the level of detail reports and the way they are summarized.

the reductions that are taking place in the performance reports in order to be able to trace information backward from the final summary report to the most thorough level of detail if the need arises. If, for example, the medical/surgical supply line of a summary report indicates that more was spent than was budgeted, it is necessary to backtrack through the data reduction in order to find the cause.

In most cases the summary report of the actual results of operations will be reported using a multicolumn format. Also in most cases, there will be an "actual" column and a "budget" column (Table 7-1). In many cases the report will also provide a "variance" column indicating, in the most basic, arithmetic way, the difference between "actual" and "budget" (Table 7-2). A dual set of dollar value columns would be used to provide data about the year to date as well as the current period, which is usually a single month.

Centrally prepared reports vary from institution to institution, even when the same software package or shared management information system is employed, because of the ability to customize these packages and systems. In effect, the same system in two institutions can appear to be completely different. It is a manager's duty to understand the performance reporting system and process.

Do not be afraid of all the numbers displayed in the tabular and summary reports. Look through the report slowly and note column headings and row titles.

Table 7-1
Operating Expenses

Description	Actual	Budget
Office Supplies	$1,000	$900
Med/Surg Supplies	5,500	5,600
Nutrition Supplies	6,231	6,000
Stock Drugs	4,365	4,500
IV Solutions	5,346	5,300
Miscellaneous	52	100
Total	$22,494	$22,400

Table 7-2
Operating Expenses with Variances

Description	Actual	Budget	Variance (Unfavorable)
Office Supplies	$1,000	$900	($100)
Med/Surg Supplies	5,500	5,600	100
Nutrition Supplies	6,231	6,000	(231)
Stock Drugs	4,365	4,500	135
IV Solutions	5,346	5,300	(46)
Miscellaneous	52	100	48
Total	$22,494	$22,400	($94)

Generally, the title of each row defines the name of the data elements while the column heading provides a further definition/explanation. Do not be afraid of calling on the accounting or finance department to provide an explanation of the reports (their content, source, timing, and so on). Just as department managers have an obligation to examine and act based on the data reported, the accounting or finance department has an obligation to make certain that the reports are understandable, useful for the task at hand, and accurate.

HOW TO EXAMINE A REPORT

One reaction, especially among new managers, is to be put off by the sheer volume of numbers contained in some departmental performance reports. But a methodical approach can be helpful. Consider the departmental performance report displayed in Figure 7-2. Like many tabular reports, it is arranged in a series of columns and rows. Begin by reading the titles and other narrative data to develop a rudimentary understanding. The title tells the reviewer that it is a departmental performance report for December 31, 19XX. Descriptive information contained in the middle of the report identifies two kinds of revenues, several kinds of expenses, which are displayed in summary form, and something, which will be discussed later in this chapter, called "income contribution." Financial data are presented on either side of the descriptions; the current month's numbers on the left and the year to date's on the right. The financial data are presented in a comparative format that compares actual with budget and spells out the variance, which is marked with brackets when unfavorable. While the titles and other descriptive headings tell a good deal about the report, some interpretation must be done. A methodical approach is helpful here as well. Even though the fiscal year that Makebelieve Medical Center uses is unknown, it is possible to determine the amount of time covered by the report. The amounts reported suggest the year-to-date values are for six months. This can be implied by examining the budget column. The year-to-date values are six times the current month values, suggesting that the budget was probably seasonalized by division into 12 equal monthly amounts.

By comparing actual with budget, one can glean certain other information from the report. Inpatient revenues are worse than budget for the month but even with budget for the first six months. Outpatient revenues are at the budgeted level for the month but are better than budget on a year-to-date basis. Since the current month is December, would revenues be expected to be lower than in other months? Given the effect of a holiday season stretching from Thanksgiving to just after New Year's, one would expect to see fewer patients and consequently have a lower revenue expectation during this period. If the budget is seasonalized by 12ths, comparison will automatically create the impression that revenue performance was worse than planned, when in reality it may be tracking exactly as expected based on historical usage patterns. Since total revenue on a year-to-date basis is slightly better than budget, there may be no revenue problem at all. Vari-

Figure 7-2
A Typical Departmental Financial Performance Report

MAKEBELIEVE MEDICAL CENTER
DEPARTMENTAL PERFORMANCE REPORT
DECEMBER 31, 19XX

	------ CURRENT MONTH ------			DESCRIPTION	------ YEAR TO DATE ------		
ACTUAL	BUDGET	VARIANCE			ACTUAL	BUDGET	VARIANCE
				DEPARTMENTAL REVENUES			
$70,000	$100,000	($30,000)		TOTAL INPATIENT	$600,000	$600,000	$0
50,000	50,000	0		TOTAL OUTPATIENT	320,000	300,000	20,000
$120,000	$150,000	($30,000)		TOTAL PATIENT REVENUES	$920,000	$900,000	$20,000
				DIRECT EXPENSES			
$70,000	$70,000	$0		TOTAL SALARIES	$428,000	$420,000	($8,000)
10,000	10,000	0		TOTAL EMPLOYEE BENEFITS	62,000	60,000	(2,000)
17,000	20,000	3,000		TOTAL SUPPLIES	125,000	120,000	(5,000)
16,000	20,000	4,000		TOTAL PURCHASED SERVICES	118,000	120,000	2,000
13,000	15,000	2,000		TOTAL REPAIRS	88,000	90,000	2,000
4,000	5,000	1,000		TOTAL OTHER EXPENSES	29,000	30,000	1,000
$130,000	$140,000	$10,000		TOTAL DIRECT EXPENSES	$850,000	$840,000	($10,000)
($10,000)	$10,000	($20,000)		INCOME CONTRIBUTION	$70,000	$60,000	$10,000

ance analysis (Chapter 8), however, would be necessary to determine this precisely. Salaries appear to be a problem, both now and for the future. Since salaries usually are higher in the second half of the year because of raises given during the year, the year-to-date unfavorable variance is likely to worsen over time. Supplies are about 4 percent higher than budget (the $5,000 variance divided by the $120,000 budget), but volume, using revenue as a surrogate, is only higher than budget by about 2 percent ($20,000 ÷ $900,000).

The "income contribution" line refers to the difference between the direct revenues and direct expenses of the department, the amount it contributes to the income of the organization. Granted, the departmental performance report as shown is not a full and complete departmental profit-and-loss statement because it does not include deductions from revenues or overhead allocations. It is, nonetheless, a useful expression of the department's contribution to the organization's overall success. It can be used over time to gauge a department's overall performance. Because it combines revenues and expenses in a single yardstick, it allows managers to avoid a preoccupation on expense as the only element of financial performance to be managed.

ACCRUAL ACCOUNTING

There are two methods or bases for recording financial transactions. The "cash basis" recognizes an event when cash changes hands. Most individuals operate their personal lives on a cash basis, recognizing debt when the bill arrives, income when the paycheck is received, and so on. The "accrual basis" recognizes events when they happen, regardless of when the cash changes hands. In business, debt is recognized when a liability is incurred, income when it is earned. Managers must exercise caution because the natural tendency is to manage with the same cash basis mentality used in their personal lives. The following illustrates the concept of accrual accounting.

On March 15, an order is placed for $1,000 of supplies. The vendor delivers $600 of the order to the department a week later. The balance is placed on "back order" and will be delivered at a future date. By month end, no additional deliveries have been made, and no invoice is sent by the supplier. In April, the remainder of the order, $400, is delivered. Again, no invoice is rendered by the supplier. The invoice is finally received in May.

To record the events properly, an accrual must be made in March, in place of the missing invoice, to reflect the $600 of supplies received. In April, the accrual is reversed, and a new accrual must be made, again in place of the missing invoice, to reflect the total of $1,000 of supplies received. In May, the $1,000 accrual is reversed, and the $1,000 invoice is recorded. The reversal of the accrual and the recording of the invoice net to zero. Table 7-3 reflects these transactions. Recording these events on an accrual accounting basis correctly records $600 of expense in March, $400 in April, and no expense in May.

Table 7-3
Accrual Accounting Transactions

	March	April	May
Amount Actually Received	$600	$400	$0
(A) Accounts Payable (Invoice Recorded)			$1,000
(B) Accrual Entry	$600	$1,000	
(C) Reversal of the Accrual Entry		600	1,000
Total Expense (A + B − C)	$600	$400	$0

If these events were recorded on a cash basis, no expense would be recorded in March or April, and $1,000 would be recorded in May. Clearly, this is incorrect.

Managers should pay attention to the effect of accrual accounting transactions on their departmental performance reports. Make sure that accruals are completely reversed the next month and that accrual amounts are calculated accurately and based on sound assumptions. Remember, the proof is in the invoice. Keep track of how accurately the accounting department records accruals. If need be, work with the accountants so the proper amounts are reported in the appropriate reporting period.

A DIFFERENT WAY TO LOOK AT DATA

Because computers have vastly expanded the amount of data that can be monitored and reported, it is possible to suffer from information overload—the presence of so much data that a clear picture is difficult to obtain. This often happens with summary reports as well. In situations like this, another technique may be helpful in synthesizing the message contained in the data. Consider the volume and cost data contained in Table 7-4.

Table 7-4
Monthly Volume and Supply Data

Month	Volume	Supplies
January	864	$3,591
February	809	2,869
March	889	2,721
April	864	5,487
May	883	5,406
June	856	3,692
July	880	4,549
August	872	6,481
September	865	5,336
October	904	4,190
November	873	6,140
December	771	4,463
Total	10,330	$54,925

What message or picture does this table convey? Is there a pattern, a trend, a relationship between or among the values reported? It is possible to make observations based on the data. January volume was 864. Supply costs in July amounted to $4,549. March volume was higher than February. The number of such possible observations is quite high. A technique that may prove to be helpful is to graph the data, thereby converting it to a visual form and taking advantage of the human mind's ability to assimilate data and see patterns more rapidly if presented visually. Recall the old adage "A picture is worth a thousand words." The "picture" of volume is shown in Figure 7-3. Note the message: volume falls off sharply in February (the data are from a hospital in the northeastern United States) when the snow and cold force many people to stay indoors. The pattern "sawtooths" along until October when it rises (are elective admissions being taken care of before the holidays?). Volume falls sharply in November and fairly evaporates in December (who wants to be admitted during the holiday season?). It also appears that despite the peaks and valleys, volume is relatively stable over time.

What about supply consumption; does it follow a similar pattern? The pattern displayed in Figure 7-4 is very different; essentially, consumption is up one month and down the next. One trend does, however, appear: supply consumption is growing. Note the rough trend line, the slope of which is about 3 percent per month.

Figure 7-3
Monthly Volume

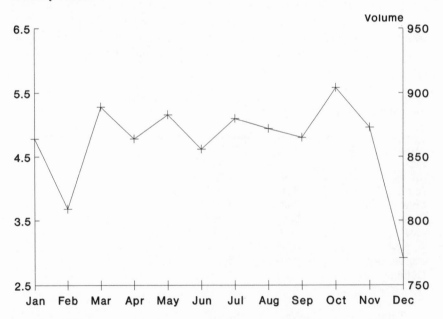

The monthly volume information that is included in Table 7-4 can be easily translated into graph form.

Figure 7-4
Monthly Supply Consumption

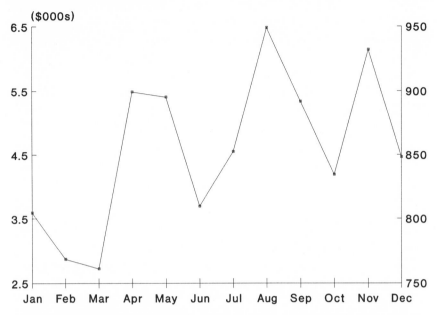

The monthly supply consumption included in Table 7-4 can also easily be transferred to graphic data.

From the combined graph of volume and supply consumption (Figure 7-5), there appears to be no relationship. But, remember that data reported too frequently can be confusing. Perhaps quarterly data (Table 7-5) would provide a better indication.

Again, the question of pattern or relationship is difficult to answer using only the tabular information. There still are not strikingly apparent trends or relationships. But as the graph displayed in Figure 7-6 demonstrates, a strong relationship does exist between volume and supply consumption. The effect of inflation can be seen in the slightly steeper slope of the supply line. The gulf between volume and supplies in the fourth quarter can likely be attributed to the sharp vol-

Table 7-5
Quarterly Volume and Supply Data

Calendar Quarter	Volume	Supplies
Quarter # 1	2,562	$9,181
Quarter # 2	2,603	14,585
Quarter # 3	2,614	16,366
Quarter # 4	2,545	14,793
Total	10,324	$54,925

Figure 7-5
Monthly Volume and Supply Consumption

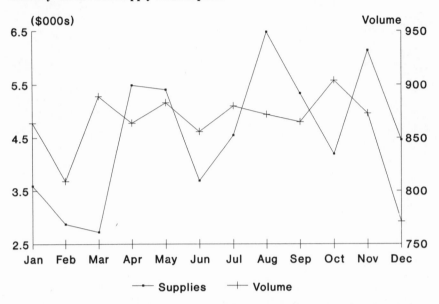

This graph represents the combination of Figures 7-3 and 7-4. There is not an obvious relationship between volume and supply consumption.

Figure 7-6
Quarterly Volume and Supply Consumption

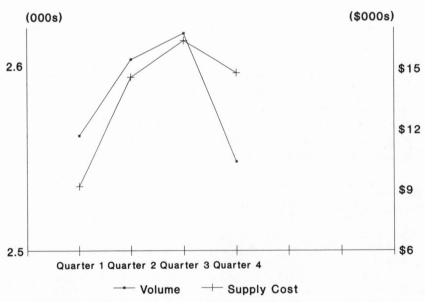

The strong relationship between volume and supply consumption becomes evident when viewed on a quarterly basis.

ume drop in the last month of the quarter; this may have happened so rapidly that there was little time to reduce properly supply par levels. As a result unneeded supplies may have been delivered to, and stored in, the department. If this is a pattern that repeats from year to year, it may be possible to establish seasonally adjusted supply par levels.

Reporting data in both tabular and graphic fashions is made easy by using a PC with spreadsheet and graphics software. Statistical software packages are widely available so that even the novice PC user can analyze trends; seek out and measure patterns and relationships; and make predictions of volume, staffing needs, and so on.

While graphs are easier to comprehend, managers must never lose sight of the hard tabular data. Graphs are only representations of data – tools to facilitate comprehension and understanding. They are not meant to replace data.

CHAPTER 8

Analytical Tools for Managers

Whether trying to determine the cause of a performance variance, forecast future business results, or make a decision about equipment acquisition or program viability, there are a number of financial analysis techniques available to assist managers throughout an organization.

VARIANCE ANALYSIS

Simply stated, a variance is the difference between actual performance and planned performance. In examining performance reports, do not worry about whether actual is more or less than budget; concentrate on better or worse. If actual is *better* than budget, the variance, regardless of how it is marked, is favorable. If actual is *worse* than budget, the variance is unfavorable.

Given the manager's responsibility to control the use of resources, variance analysis is one of the most important tools a manager can use. It is the only way to understand the real cause of a variance so that appropriate action can be taken. If the reason pharmaceutical spending is worse than budget is drug utilization, the solution may lie in physician education, clinical pharmacist interaction, and so on. But if the real reason for the unfavorable variance is the price of the drugs, a different set of actions will be necessary. Guessing the cause can send the pharmacy director off in the wrong direction and yield no improvement despite a great deal of activity. Variance analysis will assist the pharmacy director in determining if the cause is price, drug utilization, or a combination of the two. Do not confuse variance reporting with variance analysis. Reporting merely lists the elements that sum up to the variance while variance analysis determines the underlying cause.

Table 8-1
Departmental Performance Report
(Period Ended January 31, 19XX)

	Actual	Budget	Variance	Percent Variance	
Printing	$19,820	$20,000	$180	0.9 %	
Office Supplies	10,080	10,000	(80)	−0.8	
Uniforms	1,980	2,000	20	1.0	
Books & Periodicals	890	900	10	1.1	
Equipment − Non Capital	2,880	300	(2,580) **	−860.0	++
Instruments	5,820	6,000	180	3.0	++
Linens	18,300	10,400	(7,900) **	−76.0	++
Chemicals	3,820	560	(3,260) **	−582.1	++
IV Supplies	43,750	43,000	(750) **	−1.7	
IV Solutions	9,280	9,300	20	0.2	
Stock Drugs	13,516	3,620	(9,896) **	−273.4	++
Medical Gas	9,030	9,000	(30)	−0.3	
	$139,166	$115,080	($24,086)	−20.9 %	

When to Look

Many departmental performance reports list dozens and dozens of line items, and the thought of analyzing each variance can be daunting. Should every line item variance be examined using variance analysis? To answer this question, consider the performance report shown in Table 8-1. A responsible manager must perform enough variance analysis to understand the underlying causes of the total unfavorable variance of $24,086. The best approach to reducing the amount of analytical work is the establishment of a performance corridor. This approach recognizes that there will always be variances. Only those significant enough to fall outside the predetermined corridor need be analyzed. There are two ways to establish the corridor.

The first is to base it on a dollar amount, say $200. All variances greater than $200, whether favorable or unfavorable, would be examined. Had this $200 corridor been used with the data in Table 8-1, only 5 of the 12 variances (those marked **) would be analyzed. The problem with a dollar corridor is that in some cases, it can mislead. A $200 variance against a $35,000 budget is not worth the effort, but a $200 variance against a $500 budget item should be examined.

A better approach is to establish a percentage corridor. If a 2 percent corridor had been established in approaching Table 8-1's data, 5 variances (those marked ++) would be analyzed. The advantage of a percentage corridor is that it establishes the limit in terms relative to the size of the budget. Thus, the $200 variance against the $500 budget, which missed the dollar cut, would now be included because it is a 40 percent variance.

As important as when to look is when not to look. Do not confuse variance analysis with simple spending analysis that merely identifies how funds were used. Although large expense amounts may yield savings, they may not involve a *variance* from budget. Again, consider the data in Table 8-1. To determine why the budget is overspent by more than $24,000, the manager's time and effort should be directed at the major variances, in this case, those with a greater than 2 percent deviation from budget. The account with the greatest amount of spending (IV supplies) had very little variance, and based on a 2 percent corridor, it need not be examined. If, on the other hand, the manager wished to develop a corrective action plan to reduce spending, an analysis of spending on IV solutions may be helpful in identifying some future spending that could be deferred.

How to Look

Two methods can be used to analyze a variance. These can be used when dealing with either revenue or expense variances. One is an unsophisticated method that accounts for differing volumes as part of the explanation. The other is a sophisticated method that accounts for volume before any analysis is prepared. Using the unsophisticated method, variance analysis would resemble the following.

Case #1

Table 8-2 reports the supply consumption for the first month of the fiscal year. From the budget preparation worksheets, it is known that the plan was to spend $3,200 on supplies, broken down as shown in Table 8-3. The variance to be accounted for is $600 favorable; actual spending was better than budgeted spending. The unsophisticated method will account for two variances—usage and purchase price (or price).

Table 8-2
Supply Consumption

Items	Quantity	Unit Price	Total
500cc Syringes	1,000	$0.50	$500
4x4 Gauze Pads	2,000	0.05	100
IV Sets	1,000	2.00	2,000
Total			$2,600

Table 8-3
Planned Consumption

Items	Quantity	Unit Price	Total
500cc Syringes	2,000	$0.50	$1,000
4x4 Gauze Pads	2,000	0.05	100
IV Sets	1,000	2.10	2,100
Total			$3,200

The usage variance is developed by examining the quantities of planned consumption and the actual consumption.

Budgeted Use	2,000	syringes
Actual Use	−1,000	
Better Consumption	1,000	
Price	× $.50	
Usage Variance	$500	favorable

Next, a review of prices reveals that the price paid for IV sets was different (better); therefore, there is a purchase price variance (also referred to as a price variance) that can be accounted for as follows:

Budgeted Price	$ 2.10	
Actual Price	−2.00	
Better by	$ .10	
Quantity	× 1,000	
Price Variance	$ 100	favorable

Thus, the variance of $600 is now completely accounted for as follows:

Usage Variance	$ 500	favorable
Price Variance	100	favorable
Total Variance	$ 600	favorable

Case #2

Sometimes these variances may go in opposite directions (some favorable, some unfavorable), with a total variance that may be either. Using the same budget data as in Case #1, the variance to be accounted for is $400 unfavorable; actual spending (Table 8-4) is worse than budget ($3,600 − $3,200 = $400). Again, the unsophisticated method will account for the usage and price elements.

Table 8-4
Actual Consumption

Items	Quantity	Unit Price	Total
500cc Syringes	3,000	$0.50	$1,500
4x4 Gauze Pads	2,000	0.05	100
IV Sets	1,000	2.00	2,000
Total			$3,600

Budgeted Use	2,000	syringes
Actual Use	−3,000	
Worse Use	1,000	
Price	× $.50	
Usage Variance	($500)	unfavorable

Note that the unfavorable variance is shown in brackets or parentheses to indicate that it is unfavorable. Next comes the price variance calculation.

Budget Price	$ 2.10	(for IV sets)
Actual Price	−2.00	
Better By	$ .10	
Quantity	× 1,000	
Price Variance	$ 100	favorable

Now the unfavorable variance of $400 is accounted for as follows.

Usage Variance	$(500)	unfavorable
Price Variance	100	favorable
Total	$(400)	unfavorable

Note that instead of being added, the smaller amount is subtracted from the larger to arrive at the total. This is because like variances are combined (added), and unlike variance are netted, with the sign of the largest (bracketed or unbracketed) carried forward to the total.

In determining if a variance is favorable or unfavorable, the simplest and most accurate method is to disregard the mathematics of whether actual performance is higher or lower or more or less than plan. If the actual performance is better than budget, the variance is favorable. If the actual performance is worse than budget, the variance is unfavorable.

Better = Favorable
Worse = Unfavorable

Case #3

One can also examine revenue variances (Table 8-5) using the same unsophisticated method. The inpatient revenue variance is favorable because actual revenue is better than budget, and the ancillary revenue variance is unfavorable because revenue is worse than budget. Because the variances are not alike, they are netted to arrive at a total of ($10,000), which is in parentheses because it is worse than budget. The detailed accounting for this variance begins by examining the elements contributing to the inpatient revenue variance. The analysis (Table 8-6) will use a three-column format to make it easier to comprehend.

Table 8-5
Revenue Data

	Actual	Budget	Variance
Inpatient Revenue	$100,000	$90,000	$10,000
Outpatient Revenue	50,000	50,000	
Ancillary Revenue	90,000	110,000	(20,000)
Total	$240,000	$250,000	($10,000)

Table 8-6
Inpatient Revenue Data

	Actual	Budget	Variance
Patient Days	500	450	50
Room & Board Rate	$200.00	$200.00	
Total Revenue	$100,000	$90,000	$10,000

There is a volume variance in inpatient revenue of $10,000, calculated as before.

Actual Volume	500	patient days
Budget Volume	–400	
Better Volume	50	
Rate	× $200	
Volume Variance	$10,000	favorable

The analysis would continue by examining the ancillary revenue variance of ($20,000) and, again, breaking it down into its component pieces (Table 8-7). In this case, for simplification, it is assumed that the ancillary revenue is composed of only radiology and laboratory revenue. In the "real world," there would be many more pieces (drugs, nuclear medicine, EKG, blood charges, EEG, anesthesia, and so on).

Now it appears that a rate variance is involved in radiology; the plan was to

Table 8-7
Ancillary Revenue Data

	Actual	Budget	Variance
Radiology Procedures	5,000	5,000	
Procedure Rate	$10.00	$14.00	($4.00)
Radiology Revenue	$50,000	$70,000	($20,000)
Laboratory Tests	5,000	5,000	
Test Rate	$8.00	$8.00	
Laboratory Revenue	$40,000	$40,000	
Total Revenue	$90,000	$110,000	($20,000)

charge $14.00 for each procedure, but actually only $10.00 was charged. The calculation of that variance is as follows:

Budgeted Rate	$14.00	
Actual Rate	× 10.00	
Worse Rate	$ 4.00	
Procedures	× 5,000	
Rate Variance	($20,000)	unfavorable

Thus, the revenue variance is accounted for as follows:

Volume Variance (Inpatient)	$10,000
Rate Variance (Ancillary)	(20,000)
Total	($10,000)

Other variances that can be identified similarly are the labor rate variance, which is the result of paying higher or lower rates of pay than were budgeted, and the efficiency variance, which is caused by the use of more or less labor than was contemplated in the budget.

Up to this point, the unsophisticated method has been used to examine simple and straightforward variances; each variance (syringes, inpatient revenue, ancillary revenue) was the result of a single cause—usage, price, rate, or volume. Often, however, a combination of factors contribute to the variance.

Case #4

The details for this case are introduced by the information contained in Table 8-8. The unfavorable variance of $10,000 is composed of a favorable volume variance (patient days were better than budget) and an unfavorable rate variance (the rate charged was worse than budget). The pieces are calculated as follows:

$$\text{Volume Variance} = (\text{Actual Volume} - \text{Budget Volume}) \times \text{Actual Rate}$$
$$= (500 - 400) \times \$200$$
$$= \$20,000$$

Table 8-8
Revenue Data

	Actual	Budget	Variance
Patient Days	500	400	100
Room & Board Rate	$200.00	$275.00	($75.00)
Total Revenue	$100,000	$110,000	($10,000)

$$\text{Rate Variance} = (\text{Actual Rate} - \text{Budget Rate}) \times \text{Budget Volume}$$
$$= (\$200 - \$275) \times 400$$
$$= (\$30,000)$$

The elements are then combined with the $20,000 favorable volume variance netted against the $30,000 unfavorable rate variance to account for the $10,000 total unfavorable variance. This analysis tells management that there are two different causes of the performance variance.

The unsophisticated method has now been helpful in accounting for the following variances: revenue, usage, price (or purchase price), volume, rate, labor rate, efficiency, or combinations of the others.

The sophisticated method differs from the unsophisticated method in that it adjusts the budget for the actual level of activity before any variance analysis is performed. Unlike the calculation of the unsophisticated volume variance, the adjustment to the budget is based on a recognition that not all costs vary with volume. This is called volume adjusted variance analysis. An example will help clarify the differences.

Case #5

The monthly departmental financial report for the 2-West nursing unit has just been received. In abbreviated form it contains the information listed in Table 8-9. At first glance, there is a $115,250 unfavorable variance. Using the sophisticated method, the budget is adjusted to the actual level of activity (10,000 actual patient days versus 7,500 in the budget); then the comparison is made. Those portions of the budget that are related to patient day volumes, in this case, are salaries, medical/surgical supplies, and IV solutions. The adjustment of the budget to the actual volume is accomplished as shown in Table 8-10.

The amounts indicated in the adjustment column are arrived at by multiplying the appropriate amounts in the original budget column by the amount of change in volume (expressed as a decimal):

Change in Volume $= (10,000 - 7,500) \div 7,500$
$= 2,500 \div 7,500$
$= .3333333$

Adjustment Amount $=$ Original Budget Amount $\times$ Change in Volume

Salaries $= \$300,000 \times .33333$
$= \$99,999.999 = \$100,000$

Med/Surg Supplies $= \$37,500 \times .33333$
$= \$12,499.875 = \$12,500$

IV Solutions $= 11,250 \times .33333$
$= \$3,749.963 = \$3,750$

Table 8-9
Expense Data

	Actual	Budget	Variance
Nursing Salaries	$400,000	$300,000	($100,000)
Med/Surg Supplies	50,000	37,500	(12,500)
IV Solutions	15,000	11,250	(3,750)
Office Supplies	2,000	3,000	1,000
Total	$467,000	$351,750	($115,250)
Patient Days	10,000	7,500	(2,500)

Table 8-10
Expense Budget Adjustments

	Original Budget	Adjustments	Volume Adjusted Budget
Nursing Salaries	$300,000	$100,000	$400,000
Med/Surg Supplies	37,500	12,500	50,000
IV Solutions	11,250	3,750	15,000
Office Supplies	3,000		3,000
Total	$351,750	$116,250	$468,000

No adjustment is made to office supplies, which are presumed, at least in this example, not to be related to volume. Now, the comparison of actual and volume adjusted budget can be seen (Table 8-11).

The situation has changed dramatically, and the volume adjusted variance is $1,000 *favorable*—a turnaround of over $116,000. Management now knows to direct its efforts only in the area of office supply consumption to determine why the budgeted amount was underspent.

In most cases, however, it would be impossible to adjust the entire budget on an account-by-account or line-by-line basis. Instead, an average variability approach

Table 8-11
Expense Data

	Actual	Volume Adjusted Budget	Variance
Nursing Salaries	$400,000	$400,000	
Med/Surg Supplies	50,000	50,000	
IV Solutions	15,000	15,000	
Office Supplies	2,000	3,000	$1,000
Total	$467,000	$468,000	$1,000
Patient Days	10,000	10,000	

is used to adjust budgets with the adjustment made to the budget total rather than the pieces.

Case #6

For the cost center in Table 8-12, it has been determined that expenses are 60 percent variable with volume; 60 percent of the budget total would be adjusted for the increase (or decrease, if that were the case) in volume. This percent, expressed as a decimal, is called the variable expense factor. In instances where this has not been determined previously, it is possible to assume a 50 percent variability until proven otherwise. The rate of change associated with volume is the volume change factor. It is calculated as follows:

$$\text{Volume Change Factor} = (\text{Actual Volume} - \text{Budget Volume}) \div \text{Budget Volume}$$
$$= (10,000 - 8,000) \div 8,000$$
$$= .25$$

The formula for the budget adjustment is as follows.

Original Budget Amount
× Variable Expense Factor
× Volume Change Factor

Budget Adjustment Amount

Using the information from above, the budget adjustment would be an addition of $52,065, calculated as follows:

Original Budget Amount	$347,100
Variable Expense Factor	× .6
	$208,260
Volume Change Factor	× .25
Budget Adjustment	$52,065

Table 8-12
Expense Data

	Actual	Budget	Variance
Salaries	$350,600	$300,000	($50,600)
Med/Surg Supplies	15,400	14,000	(1,400)
Stock Drugs	12,500	10,000	(2,500)
Solutions	24,500	17,500	(7,000)
Unit Supplies	1,000	2,500	1,500
Miscellaneous		100	100
Office Supplies	2,000	3,000	1,000
Total	$406,000	$347,100	($58,900)
Patient Days	10,000	7,500	(2,500)

The adjustment is added to the original budget amount to arrive at the volume adjusted budget. The volume adjusted variance is calculated as follows:

Original Budget	$347,100
Volume Adjustment	$ 52,065
Volume Adjusted Budget	$399,165
Actual Expense	$406,000
Volume Adjusted Variance	($6,835)

The variance is unfavorable because expenditures are worse than budget. Another way to display this variance is shown in Table 8-13. To account for the elements composing the ($6,835) variance, the individual cost center manager could adjust the individual account budgets and then make a determination as to why the variance occurred (price, labor rate, efficiency, and so on).

Case #7

The monthly departmental financial report for another unit has been received, and the budget has been adjusted to reflect the level of actual volume. As a result only one account—salaries—still shows a variance. The following information (Table 8-14) from the financial reports and the worksheets used in preparing the budget is available.

Before analyzing the variance, the budget must be adjusted for volume. In this cost center, expenses are considered 80 percent variable with volume (the variable expense factor). The volume change factor is calculated as follows:

$$\text{Volume Change Factor} = (\text{Actual Volume} - \text{Budget Volume}) \div \text{Budget Volume}$$
$$= (10,000 - 8,000) \div 8,000$$
$$= .25$$

Table 8-13
Volume Adjustment

	Actual	Budget	Variance
Total Expenditures	$406,000	$347,100	($58,900)
Volume Adjustment		52,065	52,065
Total	$406,000	$399,165	($6,835)

Table 8-14
Salary Data

	Actual	Budget	Variance
Salaries	$456,750	$320,000	($136,750)
Total Paid Hours	45,000	32,000	
Hourly Pay Rate	$10.15	$10.00	
Patient Days	10,000	8,000	

The adjustment to the salary budget is calculated as follows:

Original Budget	$320,000
Variable Expense Factor	× .80
	$256,000
Volume Change Factor	× .25
Volume Adjustment	$ 64,000

The same adjustment is made to the budget for nursing hours:

Original Budget	32,000
Variable Expense Factor	× .80
	25,600
Volume Change Factor	× .25
Volume Adjustment	6,400

Now the comparisons of actual and budget yield a different result as seen in Table 8-15. Since volume is better than budget, the adjustment is positive (funds are added to the budget). Had actual volume been worse than budget, the adjustment would have been negative and the budget would have been reduced. The volume adjusted variance to be accounted for is $72,750 unfavorable rather than the $136,750 unfavorable originally reported. At this point the question, Why? must be answered. From the data, it is known that the labor rate is different ($10.15 versus $10.00), indicating a labor rate variance. Since the actual rate is worse than budget, the variance is unfavorable.

It is also apparent that more staff hours were consumed than planned; therefore, there is an unfavorable efficiency variance. The calculations are the same as used with the unsophisticated methodology. The two variances are calculated and then combined.

Labor Rate Variance = (Actual Rate – Budget Rate) × Adjusted Budget Hours
= ($10.15 – $10.00) × 38,400 hours

Table 8-15
Salary and Hours Budget Adjustments

	Actual	Budget	Variance
Salaries	$456,750	$320,000	($136,750)
Volume Adjustment		64,000	64,000
	$456,750	$384,000	($72,750)
Total Paid Hours	45,000	32,000	(13,000)
Volume Adjustment		6,400	6,400
	45,000	38,400	(6,600)
Hourly Pay Rate	$10.15	$10.00	($0.15)

$$= \$0.15 \times 38,400$$
$$= (\$5,760)$$

Efficiency Variance = (Actual Hours – Adjusted Budget Hours) $\times$ Actual Rate
$$= (45,000 - 38,400) \times \$10.15$$
$$= 6,600 \times \$10.15$$
$$= (\$66,990)$$

Combination   = ($72,750)

Thus, it can be reported that the unfavorable variance results from two different factors.

Labor Rate	($ 5,760)
Efficiency	($66,990)
Total Variance	($72,750)

It is important to know the factors contributing to the variance because management actions will be different in each case. This is especially true if the variance is composed of both a favorable portion and an unfavorable portion. Without examining the variance in detail, management action could be misdirected.

Case #8

The departmental performance report for the pharmacy (Table 8-16) indicates that $296,433 was spent for drugs for the period ended September 30 versus a budget of $255,620. Volume for the period was 10 percent higher than budget. Drug expense is considered 100 percent variable with volume, and so the drug budget is increased by 10 percent. This results in a volume adjusted unfavorable variance of $15,255.

The variance analysis (Table 8-17) begins with an adjustment to raise the drug usage budget (units, not dollars, at this point) to a level consistent with the higher level of volume. The analysis is done on a drug-by-drug basis for maximum impact. This presumes that the budget, against which actual performance is compared, was also prepared on a drug-by-drug basis. If it was not, if only a single line item budget was prepared for "drugs," it will be impossible to perform variance analysis on anything but total drug spending, and this may be of little or no value in controlling cost.

Once the volume adjusted budget (Column E) has been determined, the usage variance in units (Column F) is calculated by subtracting actual usage (Column B) from the adjusted budget usage (Column E). Attention is then turned to a comparison of prices, also on a drug-by-drug basis. No adjustment for volume is made to the prices. The price variance for each drug (Column I) is arrived at by subtracting actual price (Column G) from budget price (Column H). The final calculations derive the price and usage variances (Columns J and K) as follows, using Drug #6 as an example:

Table 8-16
Drug Expenditures
(Pharmacy Department, September 30, 19XX)

	Actual	Budget	Variance (Unfavorable)
Drug #1	$41,360	$17,625	($23,735)
Drug #2	60,540	64,536	3,996
Drug #3	45,405	46,131	726
Drug #4	17,355	8,294	(9,061)
Drug #5	38,200	40,683	2,483
Drug #6	27,765	20,560	(7,205)
Drug #7	2,176	2,655	479
Drug #8	22,918	8,707	(14,211)
Drug #9	1,197	2,245	1,048
Drug #10	16,990		(16,990)
Drug #11	14,735	5,795	(8,940)
Drug #12		19,978	19,978
Drug #13	4,750	14,355	9,605
Drug #14	3,042	4,056	1,014
Total	$296,433	$255,620	($40,813)
Volume Adjustment Add 10%		25,562	
Volume Adjusted Totals	$296,433	$281,182	($40,813)

Usage Variance = (Volume Adjusted Budgeted Usage
　　　　　　　　　　– Actual Usage) × Actual Price
　　　　　　　　= (198 – 236) × $117.65
　　　　　　　　= 38 × $117.65
　　　　　　　　= ($4,470.70) – rounded to ($4,471)

The variance is unfavorable because, for this drug, usage was worse than budget.

Price Variance = (Budgeted Price – Actual Price) × Volume Adjusted
　　　　　　　　　Budgeted Usage
　　　　　　　= ($117.65 – $114.22) × 198
　　　　　　　= $3.43 × 198
　　　　　　　= ($679.14) – rounded to ($679)

This variance is also unfavorable because price is worse than budget. The two variances are added together to arrive at the total variance for this drug (Column L). The sum of Columns J, K, and L provides an insight into the causes of the excess drug spending. Usage is the chief problem, accounting for about 85 percent of the unfavorable variance. Price contributes as well. This means that management's strategy should concentrate on usage but should devote some attention to price as well.

Table 8-17
Drug Expenditures Analysis
(Pharmacy Department, September 30, 19XX)

	A Drug	B Actual Usage	C Budgeted Usage	D Volume Adjustment	E Adjusted Budget	F Usage Variance (Unfav)	G Unit Price Actual	H Unit Price Budget	I Unit Price Variance (Unfav)	J Usage Variance (Unfav)	K Price Variance (Unfav)	L Total Variance (Unfav)
	Drug #1	1,760	750	75	825	(935)	$23.50	$23.50		($21,973)	$	($21,973)
	Drug #2	1,500	1,599	160	1,759	259	40.36	40.36		10,449		10,449
	Drug #3	1,500	1,524	152	1,676	176	30.27	30.27		5,340		5,340
	Drug #4	860	411	41	452	(408)	20.18	20.18		(8,231)		(8,231)
	Drug #5	400	426	43	469	69	95.50	95.50		6,551		6,551
	Drug #6	236	180	18	198	(38)	117.65	114.22	(3.43)	(4,471)	(679)	(5,150)
	Drug #7	74	93	9	102	28	29.41	28.55	(0.86)	832	(88)	~744
	Drug #8	916	348	35	383	(533)	25.02	25.02		(13,341)		(13,341)
	Drug #9	16	30	3	33	17	74.84	74.84		1,272		1,272
	Drug #10	81				(81)	209.75	209.75		(16,990)		(16,990)
	Drug #11	290	114	11	125	(165)	50.81	50.81		(8,363)		(8,363)
	Drug #12		18	2	20	20	1,109.90	1,109.90		21,976		21,976
	Drug #13	10	33	3	36	26	475.00	435.00	(40.00)	12,493	(1,452)	11,041
	Drug #14	9	12	1	13	4	338.02	338.02		1,420		1,420
	Total									($13,035)	($2,219)	($15,255)

Usage Variance: (Volume Adjusted Budgeted Usage − Actual Usage) x Actual Price

Price Variance: (Budgeted Price − Actual Price) x Volume Adjusted Budgeted Usage

The example of variance analysis in Table 8-17 dealt with only a handful of drugs. Analysis of a medical/surgical supply variance might include dozens of individual supply items from four-by-fours to catheters to infusion sets. The effort needed to perform a detailed variance analysis every month can be reduced significantly by using a computer spreadsheet that contains the budgeted values for usage and price for each line item (Columns C and H). The spreadsheet could be updated every month by adjusting the actual year-to-date usage and price (Columns B and G) and revising the formula used to adjust the budget (Column D). The "80-20 rule" can be applied to this kind of item-by-item variance analysis; 80 percent of the variance will likely be accounted for by 20 percent of the supply items. Thus, it is reasonable to limit the analysis to those items that consume the most expense. In a pharmacy, for example, a couple of dozen drugs may account for nearly all of the drug spending and most of the variance.

Shortcuts in Variance Analysis

The volume change factor and the variable expense factor can be combined before adjusting the budget for volume. Thus, using the data from Case #7, the two factors are combined by multiplying the volume change factor (.25) by the variable expense factor (.80) to arrive at a single adjustment factor, called the volume adjustment factor, (.25 × .80 = .20). This can be seen in Table 8-18.

A second shortcut bypasses the calculation of the volume adjustment amount and calculates the volume adjusted budget directly. This can be accomplished only if the volume adjustment factor shortcut method is used. It is achieved by adding 1.0 to the volume adjustment factor. In the example just given, the volume adjustment was added to the original budget to arrive at the volume adjusted budget ($320,000 + 64,000 = $384,000). The second shortcut multiplies the original budget amount by 1.00 plus the volume adjustment factor to arrive at the volume adjusted budget ($320,000 × 1.20 = $384,000).

A more structured format can be employed to determine the volume adjusted expense variance by using the worksheet shown in Table 8-19.

Table 8-18
Original and Shortcut Volume Adjustment Methods

	Original Method	Shortcut Method
Original Budget	$320,000	$320,000
Variable Expense Factor	x 0.80	
	$256,000	
Volume Change Factor	x 0.25	
Volume Adjustment Factor		x 0.20
Volume Adjustment	$64,000	$64,000

Table 8-19
Volume Adjustment Worksheet

A	Actual Amount	
B	Budget Amount	
C	Actual Volume	
D	Budget Volume	
E	Volume Change ((C / D) − 1.00)	
F	Variable Expense Factor	
G	Volume Adjustment Factor (F x E)	
H	Volume Adjustment (G x B)	
I	Volume Adjusted Budget (B + H)	
J	Volume Adjusted Variance (I − A)	

Some Cautions

Exercise caution when deciding not to analyze an account that has a small variance. Not doing variance analysis can result in a false sense of security and inappropriate management action. It is always possible that two variances, one strongly positive and one strongly negative, are balancing each other. If the favorable one deteriorates over time, as often is the case in the "real world," a manager can face a sudden financial performance "surprise" and not be able to recover. The best approach in situations like this is to analyze these small variance accounts periodically, but less frequently than monthly.

The best way to make variance analysis easier is to prepare the budget with sufficient detail. Budgeting only total amounts for large categories like supplies or purchased services makes variance analysis impossible.

With the information gained from variance analysis, there are three action steps for managers. The first is to communicate the facts of the situation to higher management. In this way everyone benefits from the analysis, increasing its value to the organization. The second step is the preparation of an action plan to remedy a bad situation or take advantage of a good situation. The last step is to maintain vigilance to avoid problems as time progresses. The knowledge gained from the variance analysis should be helpful in this regard.

FORECASTING

In the simplest sense, a forecast is merely a prediction of the future. In a more formal way, one would define a business or financial forecast as a prediction of the outcome of a specified future period based on historical data, current operating facts, and other information. It is expressed, just as a budget is, in formal and measurable terms.

Historical data provide the forecaster with an understanding of trends over time, relationships among various aspects of the business (volume and supply consumption, admissions and ancillary usage, acuity and staffing levels, and so on), and performance capabilities (both strengths and weaknesses). Just as with many other ventures, history provides a strong foundation for a forecast.

The incorporation of current operating facts provides a perspective from which to view the historical data and make a judgment regarding their relevance to the future period being forecast. Understanding the impact that current reimbursement pressures are having on historical inpatient utilization patterns, for instance, is necessary to achieve realism in forecasting patient volume.

Sources of information that can be useful in forecasting include departmental files, hospital financial reports, formal and informal records, and professional associates from outside the organization (about such marketplace matters as salary competition). Human intuition and plain old common sense play an important part as well.

Other information rounds out the series of inputs for a forecast. This input, sometimes entirely anecdotal in nature, includes such things as the ability of management to operate effectively in the period to be forecast. This may mean a sense of management's ability to continue favorable performance; rectify, or at least balance, poor performance; and respond to internal and external challenges.

Forecasts represent critical, upwardly directed information. They must be accurate, not conservative or protective. One manager overestimating the forecast for expenses can compromise others in the organization. Understating the forecast of bad news can delay remedial action until it is too late. As a forecaster, tell the boss what he or she needs to hear, not what he or she wants to hear.

Managers who are the recipients of forecasts should listen to what is being forecast, even if the message is an unpleasant one. Do not pressure subordinate managers to forecast only what they think the boss wants to hear. Do not "shoot the messenger," or the messenger will stop coming. Neither foster nor tolerate an environment in which differences cannot be dealt with openly. Always list the assumptions made in developing a forecast.

Forecasting is a tool managers can use to control operations. In serial form it blends with budgeting, results reporting, and variance analysis, as depicted in Figure 8-1. Actual results and variance analysis represent significant parts of the operating facts on which forecasts are based. Depending on the results of the forecast, management action planning (to ensure management's ability to operate effectively) may be necessary.

Figure 8-1
The Management Cycle

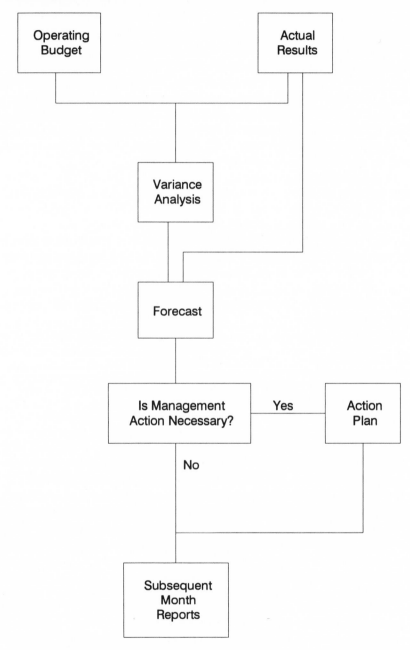

From this visualization, it is obvious how forecasting meshes with budgeting, results reporting, and variance analysis.

Table 8-20 demonstrates one method of preparing an expense forecast (a summary forecast) using six-month, year-to-date financial results as a starting point. The forecast is for the fiscal year ending on December 31, 19XX. The first step is to determine just how busy the department will be: what level of volume will have been achieved when the year is completed? This is important because variable expenses will be forecast using this volume estimation. The next step is to break the base period data into two components: fixed and variable. This division should be based on the forecaster's best understanding of the spending patterns in the department. Having done this, adjustments are made for "onetime" items. These represent events that occurred during the base period but that are not expected to repeat during the balance of the forecast period. Notes in the comments section of the worksheet describe three such events.

The data are then annualized using time and volume. The $60,000 of adjusted fixed expenses do not vary with volume but will be affected instead by time. Since $60,000 covered 6 months, $120,000 will be needed for the full 12-month forecast period. This is calculated by dividing the $60,000 by 6 (months) and then multiplying the result by 12 (months). The same logic applies to the variable expense component. The adjusted expense of $39,500 was consumed in delivering 395 units of service. These could be patient days, RVUs, patient meals, and so on. The $39,500, which covered 395 units of service, must be increased to $100,000 to cover the 1,000 units of service being forecast ($39,500 ÷ 395 × 1,000 = $100,000).

Next, adjust the annualized amounts for those onetime items that had been added or deducted previously. If an item was deducted, add it back in at this point. If it had been added, deduct it. This must be done because in the process of adjusting the base period data, these onetime items were removed. They must now be replaced in the forecast data.

The final adjustment is for events that will happen in the future and that, consequently, are not reflected in the base period data. In Table 8-20, the notation indicated that additional staff will be hired during the second half of the fiscal year.

The comments section should contain any other pertinent information the forecaster used in preparing the forecast. It is here that assumptions are listed.

If a manager must prepare a detailed forecast for every line item in a departmental performance report, the easiest way to approach the work is to convert the report containing the base period year-to-date data into a forecasting worksheet by making a photocopy of it and pasting over the current month financial data with plain paper (a sophisticated financial technique known as wallpapering). The necessary adjustments to the base period can be made right next to the particular account to which they relate. While fixed and variable expense accounts may not be aggregated, it is possible to apply the same formula approach used in annualizing the data in Table 8-20, on a line-by-line basis. It may be possible to download the details of the departmental performance report to a PC to make the job easier.

Table 8-20
Expense Forecast Worksheet

BASED ON YTD DATA AS OF: | 6/30/XX |

Description	Fixed	Variable	Total
Year to Date Expense	$57,000	$40,000	$97,000
Adjustments			
Add back "One Time" credits	4,000		4,000
Deduct "One Time" expenses	(1,000)	(500)	(1,500)
Adjusted Total	$60,000	$39,500	$99,500
Annualization			
Divide by days/months/etc	6 months		
Divide by volume		395	
Multiply by days/months/etc	12 months		
Multiply by volume		1000	
Annualized Amounts	$120,000	$100,000	$220,000
Adjustments			
Add back "One Time" expenses	1,000	500	1,500
Deduct "One Time" credits	(4,000)		(4,000)
Events thru year end (+/−)	25,000		25,000
Expense Forecast as of 12/31/XX	$142,000	$100,500	$242,500

Comments:

1 The one time credit of $4,000 resulted from supplies ordered last fiscal year
being returned last month for a credit from the vendor.
2 The one time expense of $1,000 resulted from paying for a maintenance contract
for the entire year during the 1st month of the fiscal year.
3 The one time expense of $500 was for probes used in procedures. This took
advantage of a one time price break.
4 Between now and year end, two new staff will be added.

DECISION ANALYSIS

Whether contemplating a new or replacement piece of equipment, a replacement facility, a program expansion, or a major change in operations, it is important to determine if a project is financially justified. A number of sophisticated and unsophisticated approaches can be used in this evaluation. Unsophisticated approaches include average rate of return, average payback period, and actual payback period. Net present value, benefit/cost ratio, and internal rate of return are sophisticated approaches.

Unsophisticated Approaches

Using an unsophisticated approach, an investment opportunity is examined in Case #9.

Case #9

A new laboratory machine will generate $15,000 per year in profits over current operating levels. The machine costs $120,000, has an eight-year life, and will be depreciated at a rate of $15,000 per year over that time period (Table 8-21).

The cash inflow in this case is the sum of profit and depreciation because depreciation is a noncash expense. The average investment is always equal to the total investment cost divided in half. In this case, the average investment is $60,000 ($120,000 ÷ 2). The calculation of average rate of return is:

$$\text{Average Rate of Return} = \text{Average Profit} \div \text{Average Investment}$$
$$= \$15,000 \div \$60,000$$
$$= .25 \text{ or } 25\%$$

Table 8-21
Profit, Depreciation, and Cash Inflow Data

Year	Profit	Depreciation	Cash Inflow
1	$15,000	$15,000	$30,000
2	15,000	15,000	30,000
3	15,000	15,000	30,000
4	15,000	15,000	30,000
5	15,000	15,000	30,000
6	15,000	15,000	30,000
7	15,000	15,000	30,000
8	15,000	15,000	30,000
Averages	$15,000	$15,000	$30,000

The average payback period is the amount of time it takes for the average annual cash inflow (the sum of annual profit and annual depreciation) to "repay" the investment. The formula for calculating it is as follows:

$$\text{Average Payback Period} = \text{Net Investment} \div \text{Average Annual Cash Inflow}$$
$$= \$120{,}000 \div \$30{,}000$$
$$= 4 \text{ years}$$

Case #10

In Case #9, the cash inflows were identical from year to year; however, in many investments they are different from year to year. Consider the example of three different investment possibilities with the annual cash inflows as shown in Table 8-22. If the net investment associated with each was identical at $120,000, the average payback period for all three projects is identical – four years ($120,000 ÷ 30,000); however, the actual payback period is different for each. Table 8-23 shows the calculation of the actual payback periods.

Table 8-22
Comparative Project Data

Year	Project #1	Project #2	Project #3
1	$30,000	$10,000	$50,000
2	30,000	20,000	40,000
3	30,000	30,000	30,000
4	30,000	40,000	20,000
5	30,000	50,000	10,000
Averages	$30,000	$30,000	$30,000

Table 8-23
Payback Period Calculations

	Project #1	Project #2	Project #3
Investment	$120,000	$120,000	$120,000
1st Year	(30,000)	(10,000)	(50,000)
	$90,000	$110,000	$70,000
2nd Year	(30,000)	(20,000)	(40,000)
	$60,000	$90,000	$30,000
3rd Year	(30,000)	(30,000)	(30,000)
	$30,000	$60,000	$0
4th Year	(30,000)	(40,000)	
	$0	$20,000	
5th Year		(50,000)	
		($30,000)	
Payback Period	4 Years	4–2/5 Years	3 Years

If all of these projects were equal in every other respect, the best selection would be project #3 because it has the shortest payback period. In effect, cash is tied up in a shorter-term investment and is, theoretically, available for another investment sooner than if invested in either project #1 or #2.

While the unsophisticated approaches of average and actual payback period take into account the cash flows associated with an investment, the sophisticated approaches consider the present value of those cash inflows.

Sophisticated Approaches

The first of the sophisticated approaches is the net present value, defined as the difference between the present value of the cash inflows and the present value of the investment. The present value of the cash inflows is arrived at by discounting the cash inflows from a project at a rate equal to the organization's "cost of capital" or "hurdle rate." In effect, this expresses the value of funds received in the future in current terms. Ten dollars received three years from now is not the same as ten dollars received today; in fact, it has a lower value.

Case #11

An investment costing $56,370 has a cash inflow of $20,000 each year. The company's cost of capital or hurdle rate is 15 percent. The net present value is calculated as shown in Table 8-24.

The decision to invest or not is based on this rule: if the net present value is equal to, or greater than, $0, the investment should be made; if the net present value is less than $0, the investment should be rejected. In this case the net present value is greater than $0, and the investment should be pursued.

Another way to think of present value is that it is the amount of cash in hand today that, if invested at the hurdle rate, would yield the same future cash flow. Referring back to Table 8-24, the data show that the future flow of $20,000 in the fifth year has a value in today's terms of $9,940. That $20,000 is worth only

Table 8-24
Present Value Data

Year	Cash Inflow	Present Value Factor	Present Value
1	$20,000	0.870	$17,400
2	20,000	0.756	15,120
3	20,000	0.658	13,160
4	20,000	0.572	11,440
5	20,000	0.497	9,940
Present Value of Inflows			$67,060
Present Value of Investment			56,370
Net Present Value			$10,690

$9,940. If the $9,940 was invested starting today at 15 percent (the same rate used to produce the present value discounting factor of 0.497), it would accumulate to a value of $20,000. Table 8-25 shows $19,994 (essentially $20,000) as the ending balance in the fifth year.

A similar methodology would be used if the investment was made over more than one year. In that instance, the cash outflows of the investment would also be discounted to the present value to arrive at the present value of the investment. In those instances in which the investment is made in a single year, the amount of the investment and its net present value are the same.

Case #12

An investment costing $56,370 is to be made in two installments – one of $25,000 upon delivery of the original equipment and the second 18 months later. The investment has a cash inflow of $20,000 each year, and the hurdle rate is 15 percent. The net present value, calculated as shown in Table 8-26, is much improved: $14,768 compared with $10,690 in the previous case. The only difference is the timing of the investment. The payment of the entire amount at the beginning (Case #11) results in a higher present value for the investment than the second example (in which the same amount is paid out, but a large part of the payment is shifted to the future, where it has a lower present value).

The present value factors used in discounting the cash flows can be derived via the following formula (where i stands for the hurdle rate expressed as a decimal, and n for the year):

$$\frac{1}{(1 + i)^n}$$

Using the 15 percent hurdle rate from the above example yields the following:

$$\text{Year 1} = \frac{1}{(1 + .15)^1} = .870$$

$$\text{Year 2} = \frac{1}{(1 + .15)^2} = .756$$

Table 8-25
Future Value of Today's Cash

Year	Starting Balance	Applicable Rate	Amount Earned	Ending Balance
1	$9,940	15.00%	$1,491	$11,431
2	11,431	15.00%	1,715	13,146
3	13,146	15.00%	1,972	15,118
4	15,118	15.00%	2,268	17,386
5	17,386	15.00%	2,608	19,994

Table 8-26
Net Present Value Analysis

Year	Cash Inflow	Present Value Factor	Present Value
1	$20,000	0.870	$17,400
2	20,000	0.756	15,120
3	20,000	0.658	13,160
4	20,000	0.572	11,440
5	20,000	0.497	9,940
Present Value of Inflows			$67,060

Year	Cash Outflow	Present Value Factor	Present Value
0	$25,000	1.000	$25,000
1	31,370	0.870	27,292
Present Value of Investment			$52,292
Net Present Value			$14,768

Alternatively, the factors can be obtained from a present value table like the one in Appendix 4. The present values are applied to the inflows and outflows differently. It is presumed that the investment's first year is year 0 and the inflows begin in year 1. If the investment takes place over a number of years, it is presumed to take place in years 0, 1, 2, and so on. This is a conservative approach, which is used in calculating the net present value as well as the other sophisticated approaches, including benefit cost ratio and internal rate of return.

Another of the sophisticated approaches is the benefit/cost ratio, also called the profitability index. It is a ratio of the number of dollars of benefit to the dollars invested. In effect, it tells how many dollars are gained for each dollar invested. It is arrived at by division rather than subtraction.

$$\text{Benefit/Cost Ratio} = \frac{\text{Present Value of Cash Inflows}}{\text{Present Value of Investment}}$$

Decisions are based on the rule that if the benefit/cost ratio is equal to, or greater than, 1.0, the investment should be made; if it is less than 1.0, the investment should not be pursued. The added value of the benefit/cost ratio in analyzing investment possibilities over the net present value method is that the benefit/cost ratio shows the dollar return for each dollar invested while the net present value method shows merely the amount of dollars returned on the total investment. This is important when faced with more than one investment decision.

Case #13

Two projects have identical net present values (based on 15 percent cost of capital). Only one investment can be pursued. Table 8-27 illustrates the approach to selecting the best investment based on the benefit/cost ratio of each. The benefit/cost ratio of Project #2 is higher, making it the investment of choice. This is be-

Table 8-27
Comparative Project Data

		– – – – Project #1 – – – –			– – – – Project #2 – – – –	
Year	Cash Inflow	Present Value Factor	Present Value	Cash Inflow	Present Value Factor	Present Value
1	$20,000	0.870	$17,400	$20,000	0.870	$17,400
2	20,000	0.756	15,120	20,000	0.756	15,120
3	20,000	0.658	13,160	20,000	0.658	13,160
4	20,000	0.572	11,440	19,895	0.572	11,380
5	20,000	0.497	9,940	– 0 –	0.497	– 0 –
Present Value of Inflows			$67,060			$57,060
Present Value of Investment			50,000			40,000
Net Present Value			$17,060			$17,060
Benefit/Cost Ratio			1.3412			1.4265

cause there is $1.43 of "benefit" for each $1.00 invested (the "cost") in Project #2 versus $1.34 with Project #1.

$$Project \#1 = \$67,067 \div \$50,000$$
$$= 1.3412$$
$$Project \#2 = \$57,060 \div \$40,000$$
$$= 1.4265$$

In benefit/cost ratio analysis, the terms *cash inflows, inflows,* and *benefit* may be used interchangeably. The terms *investment, cost, cost of the investment,* and *cash outflows* may similarly be used interchangeably.

The final sophisticated technique is internal rate of return, the discount rate that causes the present value of inflows to exactly equal the present value of the investment, resulting in a net present value of $0 and a benefit/cost ratio of exactly 1.0. The decision rule followed when using internal rate of return (IRR) is that if the IRR is equal to, or greater than, the cost of capital or hurdle rate, the investment should be accepted; if it is less than the hurdle rate, the investment should not be made. The internal rate of return must be calculated on a trial-and-error basis.

A number of elements should be considered in determining the financial impact that a potential investment will have on operations. Among these are additions, reductions, or substitutions of units of service, collections, staff, supplies, maintenance contracts, installation costs, and so on. The following case illustrates the interplay of some of these elements.

Case #14

A new computerized scheduling system will schedule patients more easily. As a result, an additional 30,000 relative value units (RVUs) of service can be delivered annually. A charge of $16.00 per RVU will be made. The collection rate is 70 percent. To install the system, a special room must be prepared at a cost of $50,000. Additionally, a maintenance contract will be required (annual cost =

$40,000) after the one-year warranty expires. The system itself costs $850,000, paid in two installments: $500,000 in the first year and $350,000 in the second.

Changes to department operations include an increase in supply consumption of $3,000 in computer supplies and $1 per RVU for films and solutions. A technician will be added to handle the increased business; however, two scheduling clerks will no longer be needed. Salaries in the department are $22,000 for clerks and $27,000 for technicians, annually. Fringe benefits are 20 percent of salaries. The hurdle rate is 7 percent.

Table 8-28 displays the accumulation of data needed to support the benefit/cost ratio analysis, which is displayed separately in Table 8-29. The extremely favorable benefit/cost ratio and the significant net present value mean the investment should be made.

In preparing benefit/cost ratio analysis, the cash inflows or "benefit" should be accumulated for the life of the project or the length of time the investment is to be continued. If a new piece of equipment will be kept in operation for seven years, the analysis would accumulate the benefit and value it over a seven-year stretch. If the plan was to abandon an investment in three years, only three years would be accumulated, and so on. Lacking specific knowledge, a five-year life should be assumed for the analysis.

BREAK-EVEN ANALYSIS

Break-even analysis is an analytic technique that helps determine the level of volume needed to reach the financial break-even point—the point at which net revenue exactly equals cost. At this point there is neither a loss nor a profit.

Under the principles of cost reimbursement, break-even analysis was unnecessary in hospitals. Since cost determined net revenue, even a single unit of volume constituted approximately a break-even point. However, as the health care industry has moved to the competitive model for reimbursement, with prices (and thus net revenue) determined as a function of marketplace forces rather than cost, break-even analysis takes on added importance.

The break-even point is expressed in units of volume and is a function of fixed cost, variable cost per unit of service, and net revenue per unit of service. The break-even point is displayed graphically in Figure 8-2. The formula is:

Break-even Point = Fixed Cost ÷ (Net Revenue per Unit – Variable
            Cost per Unit)

A hospital considering a new product line or service can use break-even analysis to determine if such a move is prudent.

Case #15

Hospital X is considering the addition of a radiation therapy unit. Net revenue per treatment is expected to be $80 while variable costs are targeted at $30 per

Table 8-28
Investment Opportunity Data

	1st Year	2nd Year	3rd Year	4th Year	5th Year
Investment Information					
System Cost	$500,000	$350,000			
Room Preparation	50,000				
Total	$550,000	$350,000			
Revenue Increase					
Relative Value Units	30,000	30,000	30,000	30,000	30,000
Price per RVU	$16.00	$16.00	$16.00	$16.00	$16.00
Incremental Gross Revenue	$480,000	$480,000	$480,000	$480,000	$480,000
Collection Rate	70.00%	70.00%	70.00%	70.00%	70.00%
Incremental Net Revenue	$336,000	$336,000	$336,000	$336,000	$336,000
Expense Increase					
Technician Salary	$27,000	$27,000	$27,000	$27,000	$27,000
Fringe Benefits (20%)	$5,400	$5,400	$5,400	$5,400	$5,400
	$32,400	$32,400	$32,400	$32,400	$32,400
Computer Supplies	$3,000	$3,000	$3,000	$3,000	$3,000
Films and Solutions	$30,000	$30,000	$30,000	$30,000	$30,000
Maintenance Contract		$40,000	$40,000	$40,000	$40,000
Total	$65,400	$105,400	$105,400	$105,400	$105,400
Expense Decrease					
Clerical Salaries	$44,000	$44,000	$44,000	$44,000	$44,000
Fringe Benefits (20%)	$8,800	$8,800	$8,800	$8,800	$8,800
Total	$52,800	$52,800	$52,800	$52,800	$52,800

Table 8-29
Benefit/Cost Ratio Analysis

Present Value of the Investment

Year	System	Room Preparation	Total Investment	Present Value Factors	Investment Present Value
0	$500,000	$50,000	$550,000	1.000	$550,000
1	350,000		350,000	0.935	327,250
2				0.873	
3				0.816	
4				0.763	
Total	$850,000	$50,000	$900,000		$877,250

Present Value of Inflows

Year	Revenue Increases	Revenue Decreases	Expense Increases	Expense Decreases	Total Inflows	Present Value Factors	Inflow Present Value
1	$336,000		$65,400	$52,800	$323,400	0.935	302,379
2	336,000		105,400	52,800	283,400	0.873	247,408
3	336,000		105,400	52,800	283,400	0.816	231,254
4	336,000		105,400	52,800	283,400	0.763	216,234
5	336,000		105,400	52,800	283,400	0.713	202,064
Total	$1,680,000		$487,000	$264,000	$1,457,000		$1,199,340

Net Present Value $322,090
Benefit/Cost Ratio 1.37

Figure 8-2
The Break-even Point

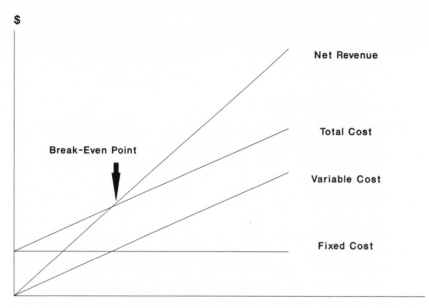

In this visual representation of the break-even point, as volume increases, so do profits. Break-even is located at the point at which the net revenue line crosses the total cost line.

treatment. Fixed costs are $200,000 annually. The calculation of the break-even point would be:

Break-even Point = Fixed Cost ÷ (Net Revenue per Unit – Variable Cost
           per RVU)
        = $200,000 ÷ ($80 – $30)
        = $200,000 ÷ $50
        = 4,000 (units or treatments)

In this instance, if Hospital X was unable to achieve 4,000 treatments annually, it should avoid the move.

Keep in mind that many new endeavors experience volume additions in steps: 2,000 visits in year #1, 3,000 in year #2, 4,500 in the year #3, and so on. Further, it is possible that the break-even point may not be achievable during the first year. The decision to proceed or not should be influenced by the length of time needed to reach the break-even point; the amount of losses accumulated during the initial, unprofitable stage; and the amount of profit and the pace at which it is generated after the break-even point. In a sense this is analogous to decision analysis using payback period calculations and benefit/cost ratio analysis. In a case such as this, the losses incurred during the period leading to the break-even point can be thought of as the cash outflow associated with an "investment," while the profits after the break-even point can be thought of as the cash inflow.

Gross Versus Net Revenue

The impact of bills that are not fully collected is important in any decision analysis involving revenue. Hospitals typically collect less than 100 cents on the dollar. Unlike retail stores, which collect at the point of purchase, hospitals bill after a service has been rendered. This practice increases the risk of bad debts. Further, by practice and by statute (Hill-Burton), hospitals provide free care for some patients who are unable to pay and who have no insurance. Finally, the contractual adjustments for major third-party payors can amount to as much as 16 to 18 percent. Write-offs for discounts or contractual allowances, bad debts, and free or charity care reduce gross revenues substantially. The use of gross revenue in decision analysis will result in a wrong decision because it overstates the profitability of any opportunity. Consequently, only net revenue should be used.

DECISION MODELS

Mathematical models represent a tool that managers can use to support sound decision making. It is possible to model such things as nurse staffing, financial results, and third-party reimbursement. Manually prepared models, the pencil-and-paper kind, have given way to sophisticated computer-based models. These are fast and highly sophisticated, making short work of "what if?" exercises. In plotting a course of action, a manager can speed through several iterations and select the best of several possible courses of action.

Keep in mind some cautions when using modeling software. Make sure the workings of the model (how it makes the calculations, what the relationships among the various variables are, what the built-in assumptions are, and so forth) are fully understood before using it. Never accept the answer just because the computer said so. It is also advisable to understand the underlying decision algorithms in case the model is not available.

It is possible to custom-build a model using spreadsheet software. If this is the case, extreme care should be taken in defining the relationships that are critical to the success of the model. The "80-20 rule" applies to modeling: 80 percent of the result will be determined by 20 percent of the variables involved. Not all of the relationships must be defined, but those that are used must be very carefully defined.

ORGANIZATION OF FINANCIAL ANALYSIS

In order to be useful, financial analysis must be understandable. It must be neat and well organized. The true test is whether someone other than the preparer can look at the analysis and discern its message without the aid of the preparer. This means all information should be clearly labeled, and the presentation of data and calculations should be in the proper sequence.

To avoid confusion and clutter, summary figures (like total nursing cost) can be used if a properly referenced (e.g., "See worksheet A") support schedule containing the details (types and quantities of nurses, hourly rates, and so on) is attached. This is similar to the financial reporting technique of data reduction discussed in Chapter 2.

Widely available spreadsheet software packages can be helpful in organizing and presenting analysis. Prices vary with sophistication and compatibility with other software packages. The more sophisticated and compatible, the higher the price.

Regardless of the brand, spreadsheet packages basically offer one thing—the ability to manipulate data in a matrix organization far faster than can human hands. Financial analysis is therefore easier because adjustments can be made with a few key strokes. Analyses can be updated almost instantly to reflect the most current facts. "What if?" situations can be used to change the analyses, and the sensitivity of the analyses can be tested quickly (e.g., What happens if the collection rate drops by 5 percent?).

In selecting spreadsheet software, the following criteria should be considered:

1. How easy ("user-friendly") is the software to use? Make sure the package is not so complex and complicated that there will be a general reluctance to use it.

2. Does the spreadsheet have the capacity for its intended users? Most have sufficient capacity to support the organization of analysis, modeling, budgeting, and so on; a few do not.

3. What are other managers using? If there is a predominance of one brand of spreadsheet in an institution, it may be wise to purchase similar or compatible software so that data can be shared simply by exchanging floppy discs.

4. Price should also be a factor. Neither underbuy nor overbuy. Match software to needs. If the right package is not affordable, wait until it is rather than underbuy and be disappointed later.

5. After the software has been acquired, become familiar with the way it operates. Spreadsheet software can drastically improve a manager's effectiveness and make the management of the financial resource less difficult. The easiest way to become familiar is to "play" with the software on a Saturday or Sunday afternoon to avoid the usual interruptions of the business day.

Flying by the seat of the pants may have been perfectly acceptable in granddad's day, but today's manager needs to take advantage of analytical methods that support decision making and software packages that improve productivity.

REVIEW PROBLEMS

Problem #1

Use the following information about supply consumption to determine the usage and price variances. The department is considered to be 100 percent variable with volume. Actual units of service were 8,100 compared with a budget of 9,000.

	Usage		Dollar Amounts	
Drug	Actual	Budget	Actual	Budget
Item A	1,760	750	$7,920	$2,625
Item B	1,600	1,599	8,576	6,972
Item C	1,500	1,524	4,530	4,983
Item D	400	411	740	748
Item E	450	426	89,100	83,164
Item F	100	180	1,600	2,740
Item G	74	93	2,109	2,655
Item H	350	348	8,747	8,707
Item I	30	30	2,250	2,245
Item J	120	114	6,120	5,792
			$131,692	$120,631

Problem #2

Use variance analysis to determine the cause(s) of the salary variance. The department is considered 60 percent variable.

	Actual	Budget
Salaries	$457,600	$474,240
Paid Hours	41,600	39,520
Volume	66,500	70,000

Problem #3

Given the following information, explain the salary variance. Costs in the department are considered 50 percent variable.

	Actual	Budget
Salaries	$228,800	$237,120
Paid Hours	20,800	19,760
Volume	19,000	20,000

Problem #4

Department ABC is considered 100 percent variable with volume. The following information has been received. Calculate the efficiency and labor rate variances.

	Actual	Budget
Salaries	$451,000	$450,000
Paid Hours	36,080	37,500
Volume	99,000	90,000

Problem #5

A subordinate has come forward with a business venture concept that takes advantage of a piece of equipment currently performing 50 tests per month. This equipment has the ability to produce a total of 250 tests a month. This new business would have fixed costs of $200,000 per year for salaries and would consume $100 of supplies for each test performed.

The price charged would be $250 per test. The business office has indicated that the collection rate is 90 percent for insured patients and 50 percent for self-paying patients. The expected mix of patients is half insured and half self-pay.

What is the break-even point? Should this opportunity be pursued?

Problem #6

A new procedure can be offered at a price of $1,400. The patient population is anticipated to be 80 percent commercially insured patients and 20 percent self-pay. The expected collection rates are 90 percent for commercial insurance and 100 percent for self-paying patients. Each procedure consumes $288 of supplies. Fixed costs are anticipated to be $765,000. What is the break-even point?

Problem #7

Determine the break-even point for a procedure that can be offered at a price of $800. The anticipated patient population will be 40 percent commercially insured patients, 50 percent HMO, and the balance uninsured. The expected collection rates are 90 percent for commercial insurance, 80 percent for HMO, and, because the procedure is elective in nature, 100 percent for uninsured patients. Each procedure consumes $588 of supplies. Fixed costs are anticipated to be $400,000.

Problem #8

A hospital is considering the addition of digital angiography equipment at a cost of $1,100,000 for the equipment and $75,000 for renovations. Net patient revenue will average $700 per procedure. Incremental, fixed operating costs will be $90,000 per year. Procedure volumes are expected to grow during the first five years: 300 procedures in year one, 600 in year two, 700 in year three, 900 in year four, and 1,000 in year five. The hurdle rate is 10 percent. Calculate the net present value and the benefit/cost ratio. Should this investment be pursued?

Problem #9

ABC Medical Center is investigating the acquisition of state-of-the-art radiology equipment that will cost $925,000 for equipment and $250,000 for installation and renovations. The price for services is $50 per RVU, and the collection rate 80 percent. The addition to operating costs will be $80,000 for supplies and $10,000 for maintenance. Volumes will be as follows.

Year 1:	3,000 RVUs	Year 2:	6,000 RVUs
Year 3:	7,000 RVUs	Year 4:	9,000 RVUs
Year 5:	10,000 RVUs		

The hurdle rate is 10 percent. Calculate the net present value and the benefit/cost ratio. Should this investment be pursued?

Problem #10

A new lab machine will reduce operating costs while increasing revenue. The machine will allow a reduction of 2.5 FTEs (each earning $8.00/hour plus benefits at 20 percent) and a savings of $0.10 per CAP unit. The lab currently produces 1,008,000 CAP units each year. The machine will also allow the lab to produce additional volumes as follows.

Burn Unit	50,000 CAP Units
Adult Med/Surg	100,000 CAP Units
Clinics	20,000 CAP Units

The cost of reagents for the new machine is $0.40 per CAP unit. No added labor is needed to achieve the new volume.

Revenue is generated at a rate of $0.60 per CAP unit. The collection rate is 80 percent. The price of the machine, which has a useful life of three years, is $305,000. The hurdle rate is 20 percent. Calculate the net present value and the benefit/cost ratio. Should this investment be pursued?

Chapter 9

Managing Under Rate Control and Competition

Today, health care managers are faced with difficult challenges. Hospitals, nursing homes, and other health care providers are striving to survive in an environment that is constantly and rapidly changing. A new set of challenges develops each day.

A CLIMATE OF CHANGE

Over the course of the last two decades, the health care delivery system has undergone major changes involving every aspect of the system. There have been changes in the science and technology used to prevent and treat diseases; the locus of treatment and the facilities used to deliver health care; the numbers and skills of workers and the ways in which they must be treated; physician practice habits; the public's attitude toward health care and its expectations of the health care delivery system; and, of utmost concern to managers, reimbursement methodologies and emphasis.

From the reimbursement standpoint, a significant change has been the de-emphasis of retrospective cost-based reimbursement and the shift to prospective case-oriented approaches like Medicare's Prospective Payment System (PPS) and Maryland's Guaranteed Inpatient Revenue (GIR) System. The result has been a constraining of the amount of resources available to managers.

Over the past 10 years, the forces of rate control and competition have gained a strong foothold. Rate control seeks to hold down the cost of health care by controlling price and underlying cost, while competition focuses on changing demand patterns in order to influence price.

REGULATION AND RATE CONTROL

Federal and state regulations have been a part of health care for many years. From setting the requirements for registered nurse staffing in nursing homes to the width of corridors in hospitals, regulating bodies have sought to define how patient care would be rendered by establishing boundaries that limit the latitude of a health care provider. More recently, however, this regulatory apparatus has been directed at the cost associated with providing care. Figure 9-1 demonstrates the theoretical effect of rate control on the pace of cost escalation.

Rate control as a means of holding down the cost of care operates by establishing a review agency and charging it with the responsibility and authority to set rates (prices) that providers can charge. Generally, a review of hospital costs and volumes results in the establishment of a set of rates or prices for each service (radiology, routine care, and so on). Certain costs are disallowed as excessive or inappropriate. Emphasis is placed solely on price; no effort is made to alter demand patterns. Prices are set prospectively for a future period. In this way the rate of predicted cost escalation (the lightly shaded bars in Figure 9-1) is deflected. The difference between the lightly shaded bars and the "controlled

Figure 9-1
The Effect of Rate Control on the Cost of Health Care

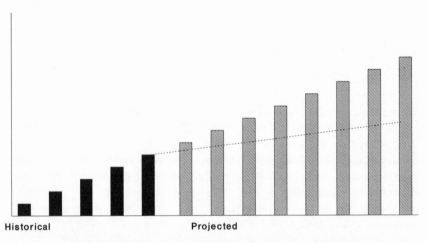

Historical   Projected

 Absent Rate Control   ······· Controlled Growth

Rate control acts to hold down the pace of cost escalation by reviewing costs to determine reasonableness and, based on that review, assigning prices that providers can charge. The rate of predicted cost escalation (the lightly shaded bars) based on historical, actual growth is restricted to that depicted by the dotted line. The difference between the lightly shaded bars and the line of "controlled growth" represents, theoretically at least, cost savings attributable to rate control.

growth" line represents, theoretically at least, the hypothetical cost savings attributable to rate control.

THE FORCES OF COMPETITION

Unlike rate control, competition functions as an external pressure to force prices down by changing the pattern of demand by diverting patients to less expensive providers. Health maintenance organizations (HMOs), for example, refer patients needing institutionalized care to providers with the lowest price per case. The incentive for providers is increased volumes in exchange for lowered price per case. Since price per case can be lowered by increasing volume, providers may lower prices in order to attract a greater volume of cases.

Given a free market economy (absent government intervention and control) that supports "perfect competition," a decrease in demand that results in an oversupply of goods or services will trigger a corresponding decrease in price, just as an increase in demand that creates a shortage of supply will produce a price increase.

To understand the workings of competition more fully, a two-hospital model may be helpful. West Side Memorial and East Side General are located in the center of the city. In 19X1, each has fixed costs of $60 million and variable costs of $40 million; each marks up cost by 15 percent to cover bad debts, discounts, and so on; and each has a volume of 20,000 cases (admissions) (Table 9-1). For purposes of this model, annual inflation is considered to be zero, the acuity or intensity of cases is equal at both hospitals, and there is no difference in the quality of care.

The following year there is a spontaneous shift of 1,000 admissions from East Side General to West Side Memorial. The result is an increase in cost and price per case at one hospital and a decrease at the other (Table 9-2). Now, instead of

Table 9-1
Comparative Cost Data

	West Side Memorial	East Side General
Fiscal Year 19X1		
Fixed Cost	$60,000,000	$60,000,000
Variable Cost		
($2,000 per case)	40,000,000	40,000,000
Total Cost	$100,000,000	$100,000,000
Cases	20,000	20,000
Cost per Case	$5,000	$5,000
Price per Case		
(after 15% mark−up)	$5,750	$5,750

Table 9-2
Comparative Cost Data

	West Side Memorial	East Side General
Fiscal Year 19X2		
Fixed Cost	$60,000,000	$60,000,000
Variable Cost		
($2,000 per case)	42,000,000	38,000,000
Total Cost	$102,000,000	$98,000,000
Cases	21,000	19,000
Cost per Case	$4,857	$5,158
Price per Case		
(after 15% mark−up)	$5,586	$5,932

the cost and price per case being equal at the two hospitals, West Side Memorial's are about 5 percent lower. West Side Memorial has become more competitive.

The next year a further shift of 2,000 cases is induced by a cost-conscious HMO (Table 9-3). Now, West Side Memorial has become even more competitive, with a difference in cost and price per case of about 17 percent.

At this point East Side General's position in the marketplace has become so uncompetitive that a further erosion of cases is inevitable. Such a reduction would only serve to worsen the situation. In effect, East Side General has entered a dangerous, downward death spiral that could be financially fatal if allowed to continue. The only option available is to reduce the cost and price per case in order to attract additional cases that in turn will help to reduce further the cost and price per case.

Assuming East Side General's strategy calls for a lowering of price per case by 18 percent to attract more business coupled with a reduction of fixed costs by 10 percent, the result, if successful, would be as shown in Table 9-4.

Table 9-3
Comparative Cost Data

	West Side Memorial	East Side General
Fiscal Year 19X3		
Fixed Cost	$60,000,000	$60,000,000
Variable Cost		
($2,000 per case)	46,000,000	34,000,000
Total Cost	$106,000,000	$94,000,000
Cases	23,000	17,000
Cost per Case	$4,609	$5,529
Price per Case		
(after 15% mark−up)	$5,300	$6,359

Table 9-4
Price per Case Comparison

Price per case (artificially reduced)	$5,213
Cases – prior to price reduction	17,000
– in response to price reduction	4,400
Total Cases	21,400
Fixed Cost (reduced by 10%)	$54,000,000
Variable Cost (at $2,000 per case)	42,800,000
Total Cost	$96,800,000
Total Cases	21,400
Cost per Case	$4,523
Comparison of Price per Case	
Artificially reduced price per case	$5,213
Price per case if based on lowered cost plus mark–up	5,202
Difference	$11

The price that would normally be calculated to be $5,202 (using cost, volume, and markup) is $11 lower than the artificially set price of $5,213. On a volume of 21,400 cases, this represents a positive contribution to the bottom line of over a quarter of million dollars ($12 × 21,400 = $256,800). The strategy has worked for East Side General, and those paying for health care have benefited as well. Caution must be exercised because the "real world" is far more complex than this simple model.

The beauty of competition from the institution's point of view is that pricing decisions and authority rest with the institution rather than an outside rate-setting authority. There is more freedom of movement in attracting business via pricing strategies.

One of the weaknesses of the competitive model for reimbursement is that, if not modified, it can be blind to certain societal goals and may achieve short-term savings at the expense of the general public's long-term interests. Competition based on price alone would place a dangerous and potentially fatal burden on those institutions with high costs resulting from teaching, the provision of care for the indigent, and their operation of regional specialty centers or trauma centers requiring high-priced technologies and expensive standby capabilities.

WHAT IT TAKES TO MANAGE

The recipe for successful management contains four essential ingredients: knowledge, planning, a businesslike approach, and, perhaps the most important, the desire to manage.

Knowledge

A manager must understand the following: the prevailing reimbursement rules and regulations, the quality and quantity of resources that the prevailing reimbursement methodology makes available (resource supply), the quantity and quality of resources needed (resource demand), and how to balance resource demand and supply (resource maximization).

The complex web of rules and regulations governing reimbursement is difficult to understand in complete detail. It is possible, however, to achieve a working familiarity that can be used to guide day-to-day activities. The regulations governing the operation of professional review organizations (PROs), for example, are complex and lengthy. However, day-to-day operations may require only that a manager understand and be guided by a few simple principles. A manager should never be afraid of asking for advice from the experts inside the organization who are more familiar with certain aspects of the regulatory environment.

Managers must also understand the bases used to include, or exclude, for that matter, various cost elements in the calculation of the reimbursement for service. How many minutes of radiology technician time were included in the price structure for a CT scan of the brain? What level of compensation was included? How much supply consumption was provided for? On a broader scale, managers must look at what resources were included in per case reimbursement rates. For a particular type of case, how many days of inpatient care were envisioned? What mix and intensity of ancillary usage were included? What level of acuity was included? In nonrevenue-producing departments, managers must examine and understand what elements were included in the department expense budget (in a sense this is their "revenue") and what level of work output was expected. This information represents resource availability. In many respects it is analogous to "supply" in the supply-and-demand equation.

As a next step, managers must understand what the customary way of operating includes. How many technician hours are involved in performing a CT scan of the brain? What level of compensation is paid? How many dollars of supplies are consumed? Similarly, in a per case situation, the use of routine and ancillary services customarily provided for a certain type of case must be understood. How many inpatient days? What mix and intensity of ancillaries? What acuity level? This information represents the customary "demand" for resources.

By comparing reimbursement (supply) with resource needs (demand), managers can determine if and where resource shortages exist as well as the order of magnitude of any shortages. An example of such a comparison is displayed in Table 9-5.

This comparison points to a possible resource shortage arising in inpatient care, medical/surgical supplies, the laboratory, and the operating room. An excess exists in pharmacy, radiology, anesthesia, respiratory therapy, and other items. The $550 net resource shortfall can be attacked in many ways. A reduction of spending could be instituted in the five shortfall areas, a proportionate reduc-

Table 9-5
Comparison of Resource Cost and Reimbursement
for a Hypothetical Diagnosis

Resources Consumed	Cost per Case	Reimbursement per Case	Difference (Unfavorable)
Inpatient Care	$7,290	$6,750	($540)
Med/Surg Supplies	706	568	(138)
Laboratory	726	524	(202)
Pharmacy	264	412	148
Radiology	720	741	21
Operating Room	2,910	2,889	(21)
Anesthesia	903	939	36
Respiratory	279	301	22
All Other Items	72	196	124
Total	$13,870	$13,320	($550)

tion could be instituted in all areas, and so on. Or, it could be decided that, based on a small volume of cases of this diagnosis, no action would be taken.

In order to take appropriate action, additional knowledge is essential. The characteristics of any item to be dealt with must be comprehended fully. What makes an expense item go up or down? What influence can management have on such behavior? All of the "who, what, when, where, why, and how" facts must be understood. Further, how the behavior will change under a variety of possible remedial circumstances must also be understood.

Finally, a manager's knowledge must be updated periodically by management information reports that indicate what is happening with all of the resource elements for which a manager is responsible.

Planning

Both operations planning (the annual operations budget) and strategic planning (three-to-five-year business planning) must be employed to develop and implement courses of action to support successful activities, remedy poor performance, or reposition for the future.

To be successful, managers must constantly strive to improve performance — essentially, to do more with less. This means that on a daily basis, managers will be taking action to achieve improvement by doing the following:

- Changing spending habits. Often, supplies are consumed out of force of habit, without a lot of thought. Such habitual behavior needs to be replaced by more appropriate cost-conscious behavior.

- Changing the demand for services through user education establishment or revision of ordering criteria and other techniques to reduce resource consumption.

- Substituting less expensive items. Managers must examine the potential to save by using less resource-intense technologies, lower-cost supplies, more cost-effective staffing patterns, and so on. The emphasis must be placed on achieving the desired result using the least costly resources.

- Examining staff composition to determine that only the absolutely necessary types and numbers of staff are present. In addition, managers must focus on creative personnel recruitment and retention practices and cost-effective work schedules.

- Reviewing procedures and practices to identify realistic alternatives that use resources more effectively. Such alternatives must be workable and acceptable; otherwise they will fail, and the resources used to identify and implement them will have been wasted.

- Searching for productivity gains throughout the organization. Since labor costs represent the largest single resource expenditure, methods that increase work output must be carefully studied.

- Critically reviewing current practices to determine what frills and extras might be eliminated. Here, the concentration is on "need to have" rather than "nice to have."

With the reimbursement environment changing as it does, even successful operations must be modified or changed from time to time to assure their continued success. Change, too, is involved in actions designed to remedy or reposition. Change often involves risk and often places a strain on the organization. Many times, it is resisted. Consequently, change must be carefully planned and implemented if it is to be successful.

A Businesslike Approach

While it is true that a health care facility cannot be compared to a manufacturing plant, there are many techniques that have been used successfully in other industries that have application in health care. It is possible for health care managers to adopt a businesslike approach while retaining the necessary human qualities. Some business techniques that have application in health care include capital infusion, subsidization, opportunism, and innovation.

Capital Infusion. Equipment can be used to perform tasks faster, more accurately, and less expensively. Equipment can be used to increase labor productivity, thus permitting a growth in volume without a corresponding growth in labor costs. A reduction of labor costs may also be possible. Care must be exercised, however, because in some cases capital infusion can lead to increased labor costs.

A computerized appointment scheduling system in the physical therapy department may increase productivity by eliminating unfilled appointment slots during which there may be no productivity. Further, such a system may speed patient flow from inpatient units so that length of stay is reduced, resulting in a less costly and, thus, more competitive or more profitable case.

The addition of equipment may support a "make versus buy" decision. A bone marrow aspiration kit purchased from the outside may be more costly than a kit manufactured in-house. Perhaps the addition of a gas sterilizer would allow this potential cost savings to be realized.

Some equipment reduces labor and supply costs. If the equipment is not too costly, the savings may be significant enough to justify acquiring the equipment. New or expanded equipment may allow the addition of new, more profitable, or less expensive business. It may allow an increase in capacity that results in economies of scale. Be wary, however, of expensive new equipment. Sometimes, the appeal of fancy bells and whistles can lead to the acquisition of some equipment that actually reduces productivity. High-technology equipment can be particularly attractive, but occasionally unnecessary.

Subsidization. Financial support can be given to a losing entity from a profitable entity. Thus, one department that loses money may be supported, or subsidized, by a department that runs a profit. Consider, for example, the case of a psychiatric outreach program that loses money but acts as a feeder of patients who are admitted to an inpatient acute psychiatric unit that makes a profit. If viewed in isolation, the outreach program might be abandoned. A subsidy from the profits of the acute psychiatric unit changes the picture (Table 9-6).

A common practice in business is to recognize that certain products, or entire product lines, are loss leaders that do not make a profit; however, they do contribute to the profitability of the rest of the business. In consumer electronics, for example, companies lose money on small parts, but they must offer these "loss leaders" if they are to be viewed as full-line companies and make large profits from high-priced hardware.

Opportunism. This involves quickly taking advantage of opportunities as they develop. Opportunism requires an orientation to rapid analysis and decision making. To be opportunistic, managers must be observant, energetic, and, most of all, not afraid to make a decision.

Innovation. This is required for the development of new and improved methods and practices. Especially in a rapidly changing reimbursement environment, innovation can be the difference between leading the pack and being lost in the dust. Be careful, however, to avoid trendy notions and fads that are not true innovations.

While it is appropriate to adopt a businesslike approach, this should not be confused with a ruthless win-at-all-costs approach. Health care involves people, both patients and workers, and the decisions made in managing the delivery of health care must be balanced by human needs.

Table 9-6
Subsidization

	Outreach Program	Inpatient Psychiatry Unit
Total Revenue	$200,000	$2,500,000
Total Expense	249,000	2,150,000
Profit or (Loss)	($49,000)	$350,000
Subsidy	50,000	(50,000)
Profit or (Loss) after Subsidy	$1,000	$300,000

The Desire to Manage

Finally, success hinges on the desire to manage. Lacking this single ingredient, the recipe will fail. The role of a manager is usually described with action words like planning, directing, leading, controlling, and so on. Acting involves a certain level of risk; mistakes can be made, even by the best of managers. So, to be successful as a manager requires an orientation to act and to be proactive and a willingness to take risks in order to achieve results. Lacking this, it is impossible for a person to be a successful manager.

In finance, the conventional wisdom is that risk and reward balance each other. The greater the reward, the greater the risk. The more secure or safe an investment is, the lower the rate of return. Conversely, investments offering a higher than usual return typically involve a higher than usual risk. This is true in management as well. To achieve a reward, a manager must take a risk. To achieve a substantial reward, a manager must take a substantial risk.

The worst managers, those who are the least successful, are those who are so afraid of making a mistake that they will risk nothing and, thus, will avoid acting. As a result they cannot be opportunistic or innovative because taking advantage of an opportunity or being an innovator means taking a risk and perhaps making a mistake.

The manager is an advocate, too, and this can cause problems for some managers who have difficulty striking a balance between supporting one position (the advocate's role) and supporting a different position once a decision has been made (the manager's role). It can be difficult for some managers to understand that the two roles are able to coexist. How is it possible for a manager to argue in favor of new lab equipment during the capital budget process only to turn around after the budget has been approved, without the lab equipment, and support and defend that decision? The answer rests in the fact that no manager is asked to play both roles at the same time. The advocacy role comes first as part of the decision-making process, while the manager role comes later on during the implementation process.

When being an advocate for anything, understand the constraints in the environment and be realistic with requests. Do not argue for what cannot be achieved. Advocate for the "cause" but understand when to back off. If challenged too strongly ("Obviously you don't understand"), fall back to filling the manager's responsibility to communicate. Remember the old sage: "Sometimes it's better to run away and live to fight another day." Do not be afraid to lose the battle so that later you can win the war.

OBSTACLES TO SUCCESS

Despite the presence of all the ingredients for success, obstacles can stand in the way, and success depends on a manager's ability to overcome the obstacles while continuing to work toward stated goals and objectives. Among these obstacles to success, most common are a lack of input to the original planning process, a lack of information, an overabundance of problems, and finally, the need to bring about change.

Not being involved in the planning process can place a manager in the position of being expected to deliver the impossible. The plant manager who is not consulted as the utilities budget is being prepared may not be able to reduce utility expenditures to the level inappropriately budgeted. This inability to "deliver" can lead to frustration, despair, and eventually the manager's resignation. If, however, the manager had been consulted, the outcome might have been far better. He or she might have convinced those constructing the budget that a reduction in utility costs was impossible but that other actions in other areas could yield the same cost savings.

Another major obstacle to any manager is the lack of quality management information. A good manager must always be reviewing how his or her department or section is operating, using a yardstick of some sort. This constant vigilance must be supported by a management information system that provides timely, accurate, and usable information. Managers who lack this kind of information support will be forced to manage by the seat of their pants, a style not highly recommended for today's health care managers.

From time to time, a manager will be thrust into a situation in which there are too many problems with which to deal. In many cases, the situation is inherited from a previous manager. Often, the situation involves a lack of prior management control and/or false expectations on the part of upper management. This could have been precipitated by sudden and dramatic increases in cost, unanticipated volume changes, and so on. In this situation a manager must take precautions not to despair. A deliberate approach to the problems, never losing sight of the light at the end of the tunnel, is the only approach that will lead to success. Setting an agenda for improvement and always moving forward, even with little steps, eventually build momentum for success. The key is to persevere.

Managers must be able to bring about change in response to changes in the health care delivery environment. Managing change is, perhaps, the most difficult task a manager will ever face because change, in and of itself, is a most difficult task. People, the instruments of change, are often reluctant to change ("We've always done it this way"; "Mrs. Norwich always liked it this way") and in some cases resist change quite strenuously. If management backs away from the necessary change, it is perceived as a victory for the status quo. The next time a change is to be introduced, even more difficulty will be encountered. Some managers, it seems, are particularly adept at bringing about change, while others flounder. For this latter group, assistance from the outside may be available.

Often circumstances are such that a solution to a problem cannot be found in a single department. Effort is required beyond a given manager's level in the organization or outside the manager's scope of responsibility. Such circumstances require accurate, timely communications both with peer-level managers as well as up through the organization structure. Refrain from telling the next layer of management what it wants to hear; rather, tell it what it needs to hear.

SUGGESTIONS FOR SUCCESS

While there is a recipe for successful management, there is no guarantee. All that is certain is that managers throughout the health care delivery system will be challenged as never before. The response to those challenges depends on the exact circumstances, the resources available, the ability of the manager, and so on. It is impossible to provide a troubleshooting list with problems and recommended solutions. It is possible, however, to offer a number of generic suggestions for consideration from time to time.

Since most of today's reimbursement methodologies employ a per case, rather than a per day, approach, management orientation must be changed to think in terms of the entire stay.

Managers must constantly remind themselves that their actions are not isolated to their own departments. Consider, for example, the laundry department head who saves money for his or her department by reducing the temperature of the wash water, the amount of chemicals used in processing the linen, and the temperature of the ironers. The result is a decrease in the laundry department's utility and supply costs. The resulting increase in the infection rate on the inpatient units because the linen is not as clean as before produces a spike in laboratory and drug usage that may never be connected with the laundry manager's actions.

Place emphasis on efficiency and effectiveness, not just productivity. Productivity is important and necessary, but it must be balanced against reimbursement. A laboratory capable of producing 23 different test results for patient Johnson may be more productive than a laboratory capable of producing only 16 tests; but if the reimbursing party will pay for only 15 tests, which lab is more efficient and effective?

Consideration should be given to alternative sites and methods for delivering care. Outpatient and same-day surgery reduces cost by cutting down on the number of inpatient days for a given surgical procedure. Such initiatives may provide an opportunity to increase revenue without a corresponding increase in cost. Innovation is the key in this regard.

Consideration should also be given to alternative scheduling. When are most hospital clinics open? During the day, Monday through Friday. When are most patients who have good insurance coverage, or the ability to pay out of pocket, most inconvenienced? During the day, Monday through Friday. When are most patients who have good insurance coverage, or the ability to pay out of pocket, least inconvenienced? Evenings and weekends. When should hospital clinics offer hours? Evenings and weekends.

Discharge planning has become a standard technique at many institutions. But how many institutions are practicing "admissions planning"? This seeks to manipulate elective admissions in order to cut down on the typical peaks and valleys of the inpatient census. It, in turn, allows staffing to be adjusted to a range of activity that has less deviation from the average. Compare Figure 9-2 with Figure 9-3. Notice that the average daily census remains unchanged. The staffing level, however, is reduced in response to the decrease in actual census fluctuation around the average.

Figure 9-2
Inpatient Census Activity

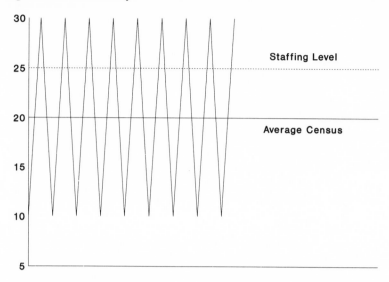

Wild fluctuations in the daily inpatient census pattern before admissions planning result in a certain staffing pattern.

Figure 9-3
Inpatient Census Activity

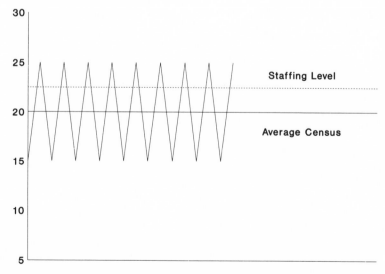

Admissions planning has the effect of achieving the same average daily census as in Figure 9-2, but because it results in a narrower range of census, the staffing level can be lowered slightly, resulting in savings.

In response to reimbursement pressures, has any consideration been given to predetermined, PRO-reviewed treatment protocols that would suggest the tests and procedures to be performed on day 1, day 2, and so on of a patient's inpatient stay? While the idea may seem like "cookbook" medicine, it might allow costs in routine cases to be reduced through standardization.

The medical record tells reimbursers what happened to the patient for whom they are expected to pay. If the medical record miscodes a surgical procedure or a diagnosis, reimbursement could be affected. A periodic audit of medical record coding quality may identify an opportunity for improvement.

Determining profitability on a product line basis could lead an institution to decisions to increase or decrease certain types of cases.

Marketing efforts tied to product line profitability can increase business in those areas that generate profits and can help turn marginal case types into more profitable ones. Given a proper level of volume, a financial loser could become a winner.

Market analysis could be used to determine more than simply which zip codes are most represented in a hospital's patient population. It is possible to determine which product lines (the MDCs) and products (the DRGs) are strongest in terms of market share. Further, market analysis can help determine which product lines and products have growth potential and which are in decline. This, in turn, can become a part of the decision-making process in allocating scarce resources.

Determining profitability on a physician-by-physician basis could lead an institution to decisions regarding the granting of privileges, the application of peer pressure, the allocation of additional resources, and so on. A linkage to the utilization review program is appropriate to assure proper patient care.

Examine departmental linkages to maximize synergistic relationships. Many institutions now link quality assurance with risk management under a single leader. Could even more be gained by linking admitting (responsible for the "input" of patients), quality assurance (responsible for the ongoing review of patient care delivery—"throughput"), and social work (responsible for discharge planning "output")? Would stronger linkages between inpatient units and ancillary departments for patient scheduling result in more efficient and effective therapy schedules? Could better working relationships prevent the dietary department from delivering breakfast for the patient who is fasting prior to a gastrointestinal (GI) study? Could computerized master scheduling tie together treatment protocols, available therapy time slots, diagnostic schedule, and the like to improve efficiency and effectiveness in the delivery of care.

Management information systems need to be enhanced to provide information that is supportive of a per case rather than a per day reimbursement orientation.

Operational audits or reviews can be used to examine departments on an ongoing basis to determine if improvements can be made. Comparing department operating results with those of similar departments at other institutions can also be helpful in this regard.

Industrial engineering techniques such as time-and-motion studies have resulted in improvement in the manufacturing environment. Industrial engineers are always on the lookout for better, faster, more effective ways of doing things. They bring sophisticated, quantitative methods to the task at hand. They are prepared by training and experience to improve process and "throughput." The techniques they use, modified to account for the human element, can lead to improvement in health care as well. Some providers are already employing the skills of management engineers (the title "industrial engineer" does not seem to be well received in health care) to achieve better operating results. In manufacturing, department heads relish the idea of an industrial engineer spending some time in the department looking for ways to do the job better. In hospitals, on the other hand, department heads are often defensive, and the relationship can become adversarial ("Why are *you* looking in *my* department?") rather than cooperative.

One technique is the development of comparative cost analyses to determine where improvement can be made and how much improvement is possible. A comparative analysis of the laundry operation at the ABC Nursing Home might look something like Table 9-7.

This kind of analysis indicates that the laundry department in question might be capable, all other things being equal, of producing laundry at $0.27 per pound if it were operated like Nursing Home ZZ. Where this analysis goes one step further, however, is in taking the best performer in each cost category and constructing the "best possible" profile, which, if achievable, could result in additional savings of $0.04 per pound.

How many hospitals have ever built a working model to test a technique, a delivery system, or a room configuration to see if it works? How many have ever built a model of anything?

Linked with industrial or management engineering, industrial cost accounting methods, which are different from the cost accounting methods employed by most health care providers, can establish standard cost profiles for many day-to-day activities. Application of this technique to medical/surgical supplies would result in departments' being charged for supplies on the basis of a standard price per item. Any deviation from this cost would be accounted for separately. In this

Table 9-7
Comparative Analysis of Laundry Cost per Pound

Cost Element	ABC Nursing Home	– – – Nursing Homes – – –			Best Possible
		XX	YY	ZZ	
Labor	$0.10	$0.13	$0.12	$0.09	$0.09
Linen Replacement	0.07	0.02	0.05	0.04	0.02
Chemicals	0.10	0.08	0.12	0.06	0.06
Other Supplies	0.08	0.05	0.03	0.05	0.03
Utilities	0.03	0.03	0.03	0.03	0.03
Total	$0.38	$0.31	$0.35	$0.27	$0.23

way unit and department managers could concentrate their efforts on supply usage rather than price. The purchasing department would be responsible for the price deviation. Responsibility would therefore be fixed at the control point—in the departments for usage and in purchasing for price. In manufacturing, for instance, this is the accepted practice for establishing accountability and management responsibility. It removes uncontrollable items from a manager's responsibility.

In hospitals, the focus of cost accounting has historically been on the past—what *did* something cost? In manufacturing, the concentration has been on the future—what *will* something cost? Standards exist for virtually everything in the manufacturing process. There are virtually no such standards in a hospital. In a manufacturing plant, variances from budgets or standards are scrupulously monitored, tracked down, and controlled. How many hospital department managers routinely calculate labor rate variance? How many know how to make the calculation? How many have ever calculated a labor efficiency variance? A materials usage variance? How many hospital directors of materials management have ever calculated a purchase price variance on the medical supplies they acquire for use throughout the hospital? If scarce and expensive resources require these calculations in manufacturing, should not resource scarcity and cost require the same in hospitals? Is not this a method of stretching resources to benefit more patients by wasting less? Does that not translate into better health care?

Sophisticated financial analysis tools are available to improve decision making and management control. Benefit/cost ratio analysis, break-even analysis, payback period calculations, and the like can be used to select the best alternative from among several options. Variance analysis can be used to determine if a hidden problem exists and can help in selecting the appropriate course of action. Regression analysis can be employed to develop trends and forecast future direction.

Information systems and automation can pay enormous dividends in health care. Information systems do not refer to routine billing and lab results reporting systems, and automation is not characterized by little R2D2s scurrying around sticking patients when it is time for their medications.

Information systems refers to separate, but fully integrated, systems to support financial, operational, and clinical management. It means tracking DRG performance versus reimbursement, tracking hospital performance against established quality norms, physician tracking in terms of admissions, length of stay, mortality indexes, patient progress on predetermined treatment protocols, and so on. It means "throughput" planning and scheduling on a massive scale, not just the same tired old discharge planning that has been around for years.

An analogy may help focus on the kind of all-encompassing information systems envisioned. With all of its diverse staff and services, all of its diverse resources—its physicians, nurses, and other skilled and unskilled workers—its physical plant, its supplies and equipment, a hospital is similar in many ways to a concert orchestra. Left unattended, as an orchestra is before the conductor raps his baton, there is chaos. Anyone who has attended a concert has heard the din before the orchestra leader taps the baton. The difference between before and after is that the conductor *orchestrates* the various resources so that the outcome of the musicians' effort is music and not noise!

The complex and complicated workings of a hospital also must be orchestrated, and the use of powerful, integrated systems can do the orchestrating far better than human hands. Obviously, the computer must be subordinate to humans, but once the human mind determines what tune to play, the computers can make sure it is played flawlessly.

Automation is essential to the solution of worsening labor shortages—and not just skilled professionals, but unskilled workers as well. Automation in health care means infusing machinery and technology to produce work with far less human effort. Multiplex pumps can control several IV solutions, varying dosages, keeping records, and alerting staff when a problem arises. Automatic, computer-driven unit dose preparation and dispensing systems allow pharmacy staff to concentrate their efforts on drug usage and effectiveness rather than the manufacturing and assembly process. Dictation systems that generate a typed note directly from the physician's spoken word without the need for transcriptionists can reduce or stretch manpower and make information available faster. Voice-driven scheduling systems can take a simple physician order, "Upper GI series for Mr. Johnson," and with no further human intervention convert it to an appointment in radiology the following morning, schedule the escort messenger to take Mr. Johnson to radiology and return him when the procedure is completed, issue an NPO (nothing by mouth) order a specified number of hours before the procedure, cancel breakfast and schedule a makeup meal for later in the day, and so on. Robots linked with computers can be used to fill and deliver supply orders, remove infectious waste, and deliver meals. There are other examples, and the limit on such advances rests solely with the ability to imagine what could be.

Finally, incentives for managers can have a place in improving operations. A management bonus may have the most effect but may not be politically possible because of the nature of business. There remain, however, other forms of incentives that can be just as effective. Make it easier for managers who "deliver" to compete for scarce resources—a larger share of the capital equipment budget, additional expense budget funds, a lower cost reduction target, and so on.

PRODUCT LINE MANAGEMENT

Restructuring to support the concept of product line management can lead to improved results. Product line management divides a hospital's business into distinct product lines just as an automobile manufacturer might separate its business into five product lines—subcompact cars, compact cars, intermediate cars, light-duty trucks, and recreational vehicles. There are several available models for dividing hospital business.

Currently in vogue is a division based on 492 diagnosis-related groups (DRGs). It is difficult to imagine any hospital effectively managing that many product lines. The DRGs, nonetheless, represent a hospital's products, and they do fall within a product line framework. That framework is found in the significantly more limited major diagnostic categories (MDCs). Just 23 of these groups account for essentially all of the diagnosis-related groups. By using the MDCs, the number of products has not been reduced at all, but the number of distinct product lines to be managed has been trimmed to a far more manageable number. Table 9-8 lists the major diagnostic categories and the number of DRGs grouped within each.

Using this approach, it is possible to manage 25 product lines, each of which has from 3 to 50 products. Again, this is analogous to the auto manufacturer with only five manageable product lines. Within each, however, there may be dozens of products (convertible models, station wagons, two-doors, four-doors, front-wheel drives, 4×4s, and so on) just as there may be dozens of diagnosis-related groups in each hospital product line. The argument that all admissions, even those in the same DRG, are different and, therefore, that there are thousands, even millions of products, thus making product line management impossible, is invalid. The solution rests with computerized information systems that currently exist outside the health care industry but that could be introduced and put to good use eliminating waste and reducing cost. In the auto industry, for example, the number and combination of options available on any individual automobile require management to track millions of possible combinations. Their computer systems do the tracking routinely and could be imported to track and manage patients.

Another approach to the division of hospital services into product lines is the division along the more classical department lines. In this model the business might be divided into medicine, surgery, pediatrics, psychiatry, neuroscience, ophthalmology, oncology, and so on.

Once product lines have been defined, the concentration shifts to the assignment of management to each of the product lines. All of the tools and strategies of management must now be focused at the product line level as well as at the traditional organization and department levels. Planning, marketing, financial analysis, and the like must be geared to support each product line.

Business decisions relative to the success or failure of individual product lines can be based on volume and profit position. This requires a sophisticated system to account for all revenues and costs on a product line basis and to produce individualized product line profit-and-loss statements. Lacking the ability to provide product line-specific financial information compromises the whole notion of product line management.

If the proper financial information is available, it is possible to construct a volume/profit matrix and track performance of each product line. Decisions involving such areas as resource allocation, marketing emphasis, and pricing can be based, in part at least, on the relative performance position of each line. Figure

Table 9-8
Major Diagnostic Categories (MDCs)

MDC	Description	Number of DRGs
1	Diseases and Disorders of the Nervous System	35
2	Diseases and Disorders of the Eye	13
3	Diseases and Disorders of the Ear, Nose & Throat	31
4	Diseases and Disorders of the Respiratory System	30
5	Diseases and Disorders of the Circulatory System	45
6	Diseases and Disorders of the Digestive System	40
7	Diseases and Disorders of the Hepatobiliary System and the Pancreas	18
8	Diseases and Disorders of the Musculoskeletal System and Connective Tissue	50
9	Diseases and Disorders of the Skin, Subcutaneous Tissue and Breast	28
10	Endocrine, Nutritional and Metabolic Diseases and Disorders	17
11	Diseases and Disorders of the Kidney and Urinary Tract	32
12	Diseases and Disorders of the Male Reproductive System	19
13	Diseases and Disorders of the Female Reproductive System	17
14	Pregnancy, Childbirth, and the Puerperium	19
15	Newborns and Other Neonates with Conditions Originating in the Perinatal Period	9
16	Diseases and Disorders of the Blood and Blood Forming Organs	8
17	Myeloproliferative Disorders	17
18	Infectious and Parasitic Diseases	9
19	Mental Diseases and Disorders	9
20	Substance Use and Substance Induced Organic Mental Disorders	6
21	Injuries, Poisoning, and Toxic Effects of Drugs	17
22	Burns	7
23	Factors Influencing Health Status and Other Contacts with Health Services	7
24	Multiple Significant Trauma	4
25	Human Immunodeficiency Virus (HIV) Infections	3
26	Other DRGs Associated with All MDCs	10

9-4 displays such a matrix. Only a handful of product lines is used for purposes of illustration. The volume/profit matrix is divided into four quadrants: high volume/high profit (HVHP), low volume/high profit (LVHP), low volume/low profit (LVLP), and high volume/low profit (HVLP). From a business standpoint, the preference would be for those MDCs located in the most appealing quadrant—high volume/high profit. From a strategic planning point of view, attempts might be made to increase the profitability of MDC 1 and MDC 12 in order to reposition them to the HVHP quadrant. MDC 14 might be tolerated and subsidized because of a desire to serve the community or because the product line is required if the hospital wishes to market itself as full service. It is possible that a business decision could be made to abandon MDC 14 because it is in the LVLP quadrant and to divert resources to MDC 11 in order to increase the volume of business in that product line.

If one assumes that a case orientation will be a fundamental part of reimbursement for health care services for the foreseeable future, it is safe to say that product line management will be a part of prudent management for some time to come.

Figure 9-4
Volume/Profit Matrix

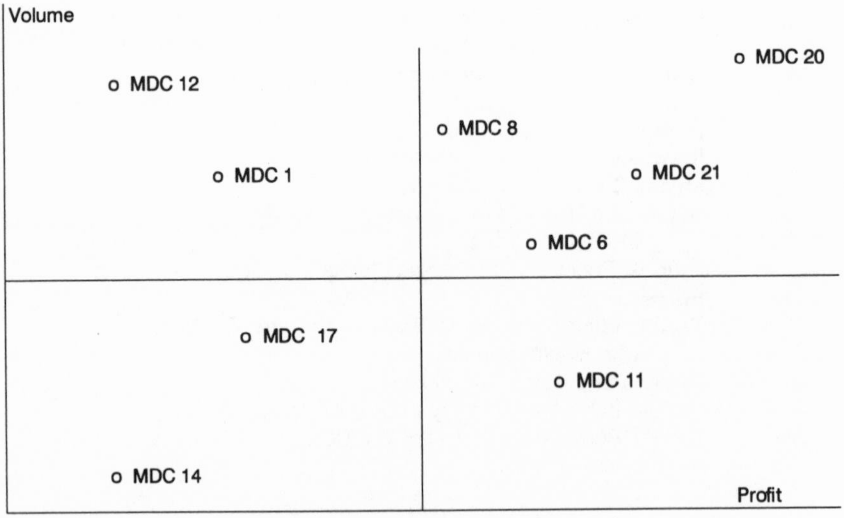

The volume/profit matrix is divided into four quadrants (clockwise from upper right): high volume/high profit (HVHP), low volume/high profit (LVHP), low volume/low profit (LVLP), and high volume/low profit (HVLP).

A FINAL WORD ABOUT MANAGING

Managing in the current environment is not easy. The challenges are frequent, and sometimes a manager may feel overwhelmed. But it is possible to be a successful manager if one wants to manage, is prepared to make mistakes, and is willing to take risks to achieve rewards.

Chapter 10

Productivity

Productivity can be viewed from two different perspectives. It is usually described as the amount of output derived from a unit or quantity or resource. For example, the number of laboratory CAP workload units per technician hour is a statement of productivity. Productivity can also be described as the amount of resources needed to derive a single unit of output (e.g., eight nursing hours per patient day). Of the two definitions, the former is preferred because it deals with output as a final product.

Productivity should never be confused with working harder. It is quite possible, given a lack of equipment, to work very hard but not be very productive. In a hospital laboratory using a manual reporting system based on the manual transcription of thousands of test results, individuals may be working harder but be less productive than their peers in a comparable, fully automated lab. Often, the expression "wheel spinning" is used to describe hard work but nonproductive efforts.

These days, "working smarter" equates with productivity. The point to remember is that managers must focus on output in determining if productivity is high or low, not simply on whether the staff is working hard or not. If the staff is working hard and output is low, emphasis needs to be placed on means of improving the way in which they go about their jobs. Approaches such as streamlining procedures, eliminating or reducing redundant tasks, and using machines to support human effort should be considered as ways to improve productivity.

IMPORTANCE OF PRODUCTIVITY

The more constraints there are on resource availability, the more important productivity becomes. For managers seeking to do more with less, an emphasis on improving productivity can mean the difference between success and failure. The importance of productivity is not a recent phenomenon. Historically, economic rewards have accrued only to those individuals who have increased their productivity. In some cases economic rewards have increased at a greater rate than productivity, and this has occasioned a decrease in the buying power of the individual's income. This is referred to as inflation.

Competitive health care reimbursement methodologies employed by HMOs and some incentive systems, like Medicare's prospective payment system (PPS) and Maryland's guaranteed inpatient revenue (GIR) approach, reward productivity increases while penalizing decreases and maintenance of the status quo. From the standpoint of competition, institutions able to increase productivity levels will be able to increase the amount of care they can deliver from the same amount of resources. Consequently, these institutions will be able to hold costs and prices constant or perhaps even lower them. In turn, this leads to an improved competitive position.

INCREASING PRODUCTIVITY

When any organization looks for improvements in productivity, the search must begin at the departmental or cost center level. The leadership of the organization can inspire productivity improvement by requiring it of all managers, by providing incentives to encourage increases, by rewarding increases, and, most importantly, by providing an environment that is conducive to improving productivity.

The first step toward improvement is to achieve an understanding of the existing level of productivity. This knowledge allows managers to determine where improvements are likely to be made.

Productivity statements should be incorporated into the annual budget for each department or cost center. Doing so increases awareness and makes a strong statement of the overall institutional philosophy. This, in turn, has the effect of establishing a level of expectation throughout the organization. As a preliminary to the budgeting process, the development of organizational and departmental goals and objectives should establish targets for productivity improvement.

What is the right amount of productivity? How can a manager know if his or her department's level of output is lower or higher than it ought to be? A number of techniques are available.

Observation, simply keeping one's eyes open, can be beneficial, even if not entirely scientific. More than simply looking to see if the staff is "working hard or hardly working," the technique of observation can help a manager get a feel for whether the staff is being helped or hindered by procedures, work methods, and equipment. Frequent, random observations can lead to a gross sense of what is happening in a department. If workers are observed 10 times and on five occasions are having difficulty with a particular procedure, one can then conclude, in a very rough way, that half of their potential productivity is being wasted by the procedure. If it could be modified to be more "worker-friendly," an increase in productivity could be achieved. Thus, observation can help a manager choose those areas to be targeted for improvement. If a similar 10 random observations turned up the fact that on six occasions the workers were playing cards, it might indicate that a change in staff could lead to an increase in productivity.

Management engineering can be used to determine objective productivity standards and to examine work methods to discover if improvement is possible and, if so, to what degree. If management engineering talent is not available within the institution, outside consulting help may be a possibility. This can be expensive, but the benefits often outweigh the cost. If this is the only way to identify productivity improvements, it should be given serious consideration.

The same analytical technique used to compare cost profiles can be used to compare productivity profiles. Standards for multifunction operations can be developed using this technique and a building-block approach. As an example, consider the manager of the imaging department at Our Only Memorial Hospital, who wants to determine how the man-hours used to perform a certain radiologic procedure stack up against the competition. One way is to compare the total man-hours with those of several other similar operations. The initial analysis may consist of a comparison of overall radiology relative value units (RVUs) and technician staffing to develop a sense of the general productivity level (Table 10-1).

At this point the manager knows that the department's productivity is better than that of three hospitals, worse than that of four, and better than the group average by about 9 percent. But this level of analysis provides no clues about specific procedures. The next level of analysis may be more helpful.

By comparing Our Only with the three hospitals closest in productivity, the manager is able to determine that from 10 to 50 percent more man-hours are used to perform the procedure at Our Only Memorial (Table 10-2). This level of analysis, however, yields information only at the level of total man-hours. A better

Table 10-1
Comparative Productivity Data

Hospital	Units of Service (RVUs)	Staffing Level (FTEs)	Productivity (RVU per FTE)
AA	262,479	33.0	7,953.9
BB	251,860	29.1	8,655.0
CC	155,714	21.9	7,110.2
DD	275,732	32.2	8,563.1
EE	812,140	132.3	6,138.6
FF	201,733	21.7	9,296.5
GG	202,395	22.4	9,035.5
Our Only	291,061	35.8	8,130.2
Total	2,453,114	328.4	
Average			7,469.9

Table 10-2
Man-hours Comparison—Imaging Procedure #2894 (Time in Hours)

		Amount of Deviation	
Hospital	Man−hours	Man−hours	Percent
AA	2.6	−0.7	−26.9
BB	3.0	−0.3	−10.0
DD	2.2	−1.1	−50.0
Average	2.6	−0.7	−26.9
Our Only	3.3		

Table 10-3
Productivity Comparison—Procedure #2894 (Time in Man-hours)

Work Elements	Our Only Memorial	Comparison Hospitals			Best Possible
		AA	BB	DD	
Task #1	0.5	0.8	0.7	0.4	0.4
Task #2	0.7	0.2	0.5	0.4	0.2
Task #3	1.0	0.8	1.2	0.6	0.6
Task #4	0.8	0.5	0.3	0.5	0.3
Task #5	0.3	0.3	0.3	0.3	0.3
Total	3.3	2.6	3.0	2.2	1.8

Table 10-4
Productivity Standard—Procedure #2894 (Time in Man-hours)

Work Elements	Productivity Standard	Comments
Task #1	0.5	Continue current practice
Task #2	0.4	Use video program to supplement tech for informed consent process (Hospital DD)
Task #3	0.8	Modify set−up routine (Hospital AA)
Task #4	0.5	Computerize records keeping (Hospital DD)
Task #5	0.3	Continue current practice
Total	2.5	

approach is to use an analysis that breaks down the procedure into its various tasks and compares these (Table 10-3).

With this analysis in hand, the manager knows on which tasks to concentrate his or her efforts if improvement is to be achieved and can also use the data to establish a new standard for man-hours by constructing a hybrid from the best practices of his or her and other departments (Table 10-4).

At this juncture the newly developed standard is ready for implementation, which must be handled very carefully because change is involved.

Managers must be farsighted. Productivity improvements do not happen over-night. They take time to develop, plan, implement, monitor, and adjust. The pre-ceding imaging department productivity improvement could not come about quickly. Time would be needed to develop information about Our Only's imaging department, to gather comparative data, to analyze the productivity differences as well as understand the implications, and to construct the right productivity standard. Planning would have to be involved because several changes in proce-dure would have to be mapped out with specific responsibility assignments and target dates in order to set the stage for implementation of this new work method.

The implementation phase would need to be carried out carefully. Change can be traumatic for staff and is often resisted. Careful implementation can avoid both the trauma and the resistance. Changes must be nearly transparent to patients, who must always be the first concern. Following implementation, the new work method or procedure must be monitored closely to make certain all is functioning as planned. Problems that arise must be dealt with quickly. Adjustments will be dictated mainly by the problems that arise, but some fine-tuning may be of value even if no problems are encountered.

Productivity should not be viewed as management's responsibility alone. Everyone should be involved because everyone has a stake in the success of the institution, which is dependent on maintaining and improving productivity. Staff nurses, pharmacists, lab and radiology technicians, housekeepers, aides, physi-cians, accountants, clerks, cooks, physical and occupational therapists, and all the other professionals and nonprofessionals can make valuable contributions. None should be excluded. Incentives can be offered that reward those whose con-structive suggestions are implemented. Traditional cost improvement programs can be just as effective when adapted to become productivity improvement pro-grams.

Make productivity a part of the performance review and appraisal system. Re-wards can be built into compensation systems to allow greater salary increases to those managers and workers responsible for increasing productivity and lesser in-creases (perhaps even decreases) for those not achieving increased productivity.

Specialization may be helpful in boosting productivity. Grouping like tasks may allow for economies of scale. Be careful, however, because too much spe-cialization can result in boredom and burnout among the work force. This could lead to a decrease in productivity. Pay attention to workers. It has been demon-strated that workers will respond when they can see that management cares about them. Money is not the only motivator of any work force. This is not a new concept driven by today's environment. The famous wire room experiment at Western Electric's Hawthorne Works in the 1930s pointed out the need for man-agement to be attentive to the needs and concerns of workers.[1]

Capital infusion, the addition of machines to help workers, is another tech-nique that can be transplanted from the industrial environment. While automated laboratory analyzers and computerized scheduling systems quickly come to mind as examples of equipment that increases productivity, less sophisticated examples may be just as effective. Two-way radios can dramatically increase the effectiveness and productivity of a patient escort service. Any task performed by workers has the potential to benefit from capital infusion. Imagination and open-mindedness are the only real limiting factors in identifying improvements.

If productivity is to be increased—or merely maintained, for that matter—a system must be developed to report results periodically (just as the financial results are reported periodically). This closes the loop in the process of developing, planning, implementing, and so on by measuring progress in achieving goals and sustaining performance.

Finally, make sure that subordinate managers are given enough time and ample support to bring about improvements. Not all changes happen overnight, and it is necessary for a manager to know that his or her superiors are both patient and supportive, up to a point. Two leadership styles that lend themselves particularly well to improving productivity are participatory management, which involves others in the decision-making process, and situational leadership, which attempts to match leadership style to the situation at hand.

PRODUCTIVITY IMPROVEMENT VERSUS QUALITY

Are high levels of productivity and high levels of quality mutually exclusive? Will managers have to sacrifice quality to achieve productivity improvements? The answer to both of these questions is a resounding no! So long as the output product or service is not altered, increased productivity will yield improved quality. Consider a clinical laboratory that schedules blood drawing on a lab-by-lab basis. The chemistry lab's phlebotomist awakens patient Johnson to draw a specimen. A bit later, patient Johnson is interrupted by a second phlebotomist who draws blood for the hematology lab. An improvement in productivity would result in scheduling a single phlebotomist who draws blood for both labs. The change to the blood-drawing procedure results in increased productivity while at the same time improving the quality of service—patient Johnson is bothered only once and, because a single needle stick is substituted for two sticks, the chance of infection is reduced, thereby increasing clinical quality as well. The result: increased productivity in the lab and two increases in quality at the bedside.

As managers work in the total quality management environment with its emphasis on continuous quality improvement and worker empowerment, the techniques discussed in this chapter can be used just as easily in matters of quality as they can in matters of productivity. The drive to improve both quality and productivity can be complementary, if managers only allow it.

STATISTICS – UNITS OF MEASURE

A wise man once observed that there are three kinds of falsehoods: lies, damned lies, and statistics. The point he was trying to make was that statistics can often be manipulated to prove any point. If, for example, the average length of stay is increasing, one could argue that efficiency is decreasing; after all, it is taking more time to treat each case. On the other hand, it could be argued that the length of stay is up because the patients are sicker and require more care.

It is important to remember that statistics can be helpful only when used wisely. Statistics are merely mathematical expressions of facts. They can serve three purposes: first, as a statement of activity; second, as a measure of productivity; and third, as a tool for managing resources.

A Statement of Activity

Statistics make very simple, convenient statements of business activity. Consider this simple, almost eloquent, statement: "over 50 billion sold." This single statistic conveys a great deal of information about the McDonald's fast-food restaurant chain; it is a high-volume operation, it has been around for a long time, it is popular, and so on. Similarly, a statistic like patient days tells about the output of a nursing unit.

But does either statistic present a complete picture? Were all "50 billion" served identically? Did some purchase a burger and a soft drink while others purchased more or less? Were all patient days the same? Were some more or less acutely ill than others?

What benefit do these statistics serve if they do not present the complete picture? They can be used quite effectively to demonstrate trends, to make comparisons, and to help develop relationships. There must, however, be a reasonable level of understanding of the particular statistic being used to avoid arriving at an unreasonable conclusion. Consider the scenario of a nursing unit that has experienced a major growth, expressed in terms of patient days, over the last three years (Table 10-5).

One could examine the growth and determine that patient day volumes have increased by 10 percent each year. Further, that trend could be projected into 19X4, with the resulting estimate of volume set at 17,004 patient days (15,458 + 10% or 15,458 + 1,546 = 17,004).

However, a reasonable understanding might provide the following background against which to examine the three years of volume statistics. This unit was not open for all of 19X1; it was a newly opened unit. Its volumes grew during 19X1 and 19X2 as staff was added, referral patterns established, and so on. Finally, in

Table 10-5
Patient Day Volume Data (Three-Year Trend)

Year	Patient Days
19X1	12,775
19X2	14,052
19X3	15,458

19X3, its occupancy achieved the preopening target level and stabilized. Further, this unit has only 45 beds, which yield a maximum of 16,425 bed days (365 calendar days × 45 beds). Clearly, now, the estimate of 17,004 patient days is erroneous. It exceeds unit capacity and is therefore unreasonable. The point that must be remembered is that there is a clear need to understand the statistic and what it means and to understand the context in which it is used.

A list of statistics that are generally accepted as standard units of measure is contained in Appendix 5. Units of measure such as these are used externally when reporting actual or budget data to regulatory agencies, third-party payers, and so on. Internally, they may be included in a monthly financial report, department performance reports, the institution's annual report, and so on.

A Measure of Productivity

Statistics can be used "as is" to provide information about productivity. When the same statistic is viewed over time, several facts may be discerned. A careful review of the data in Table 10-6 yields the following facts. Last year's volume was just less than 11,400 patient days. Over the years, volume has grown consistently about 2 percent per annum with no fluctuation.

More knowledge can be gained by combining this statistic with another (admissions) and deriving a third (length of stay) (Table 10-7).

It is now possible to determine that patient days are increasing as a function of an increasing length of stay. Fewer patients are being treated, 1,420 admissions in

Table 10-6
Patient Day Volume Data (Five-Year Trend)

Year	Patient Days
19X1	10,500
19X2	10,710
19X3	10,920
19X4	11,140
19X5	11,360

Table 10-7
Patient Days, Admissions, and Length of Stay Data

Year	Patient Days	Admissions	Length of Stay
19X1	10,500	1,480	7.1 Days
19X2	10,710	1,467	7.3
19X3	10,920	1,456	7.5
19X4	11,140	1,428	7.8
19X5	11,360	1,420	8.0

19X5 versus 1,480 in 19X1; but it is taking almost one full day longer to treat them. This information speaks to productivity rather than just activity. Assuming, for purposes of demonstration, that there had been no changes in severity of illness, that all cases were identical; one could conclude from this newly developed information that while volume has increased, productivity has apparently decreased.

Often, it is possible to compare a department's statistical profile with that of other similar departments, with national or regional averages, or with standards developed using management (industrial) engineering techniques. In the setting of a nursing unit, it would be possible to collect and compare such statistics as nursing hours per patient day, productive hours as a percent of total paid hours, turnover rates, and so on. It is also possible to modify the standard, traditional "patient day" using any of the available patient acuity measurement systems to produce a hybrid "weighted patient day." This could be used to compare and understand differences from one nursing unit to another. Although comparable data from other institutions may be impossible to obtain, weighted patient day volumes could be collected and compared internally over time to develop acuity and productivity trend data for use in staffing models and decision making.

An important point to keep in mind when using statistical profile data to measure productivity is to use statistics that measure productivity, not just activity. Often, this involves adding time, man-hours, or some other resource modifier to standard units of measure. Table 10-8 displays two kinds of statistics, one describing activity and one describing productivity.

A Tool for Managing Resources

To manage resources properly and to exercise the manager's responsibility to plan, organize and staff, direct or lead, and control, it is necessary to understand

Table 10-8
Statements of Activity and Productivity Measures

Department	Statement of Activity	Productivity Measure
Admitting	Number of Admissions	Average processing time per admission or admissions per FTE
Nursing Unit	Patient days, admissions, or weighted patient days	Productive nursing hours per patient day, productive vs. total paid hours, or productive hours per weighted patient day
Laboratory	CAP Workload Units	CAP units per lab tech hour worked
Respiratory Therapy	Relative Value Units (RVUs)	RVUs per hour worked

what has happened, what is happening, and what may happen. Statistics can be helpful in this regard.

It is possible to develop relationships between various resources and a given statistic. Simply stated, ratios are developed between a statistic or unit of measure and the various resources (medical/surgical supplies, drugs, reagents, office supplies, staff time and salaries, and so on) consumed in providing a service. The assignment of resources to each product or procedure is based on a fairly detailed review of actual operations and results in several useful outcomes.

Managers obtain a better, fuller understanding of departmental operations. In order to assign resources properly, it is necessary to understand the "who, what, when, where, why and how" of resource use. This increased understanding should translate into better management.

A detailed relationship between the statistic and resource consumption can be segregated into several natural categories (supplies, services, man-hours and salaries, and so on) and into specific types within natural expense categories (4×4s, normal saline, D5W, phlebotomy butterflies, and so on within the category of supplies). This level of detail can be helpful in examining performance and in preparing budgets and other projections.

Finally, it is possible to develop a file of standard purchase prices that can be used to determine if the reason for any difference between actual and budgeted spending for supplies and services results from price, usage, or a combination of the two. Management efforts can then be directed appropriately.

DEVELOPING A RELATIVE VALUE UNIT

In those departments that offer a multiplicity of products or procedures, it is possible to develop a system of relative value units (RVUs). The starting point is a detailed resource consumption matrix. It is possible to understand this more easily by using the model of a department that performs several different procedures. For this department a resource consumption matrix would look something like Table 10-9.

With this level of information available, it is possible to budget for control purposes in detail (for Na citrate, for transfer sets, and so on) or in the aggregate (a single amount of supplies) in a far more accurate manner. It is also possible to compare actual monthly spending with a dollar amount exactly calculated to meet the level of activity actually experienced. The following example may serve to illustrate this point.

The budget for the therapeutics department at XYZ Memorial Hospital was based on 40 procedures (10 of each of the procedures the department performs). The supply budget was projected, based on this level and mix of activity, to be $5,000. Actual results are displayed in Table 10-10. Was supply consumption properly managed?

At first glance, supply consumption appears to be unfavorably high by $1,875

Table 10-9
Resource Consumption Matrix

| | Procedures | | | |
Resources	#1	#2	#3	#4
Supplies –				
Tubing	XX	XX	XX	XX
Centrifuge bowls	XX	XX	XX	XX
Patient prep set	XX	XX	XX	XX
Volex	XX			
Na citrate	XX	XX	XX	XX
Transfer pack	XX	XX	XX	XX
Butterflies	XX	XX	XX	XX
Normal saline	XX			
Transfer set	XX	XX	XX	XX
T–2000	XX			
Transfer bags	XX			
Minor consumables	XX		XX	
Total	$275	$50	$100	$75
Lab Testing –				
White Count	XX		XX	XX
Differential	XX	XX		XX
Electrolytes	XX	XX		XX
Hematocrit			XX	XX
Total	$75	$50	$25	$150
Staffing –				
Supervision	XX	XX	XX	XX
Professional	XX	XX	XX	XX
Technical	XX	XX	XX	XX
Total	$100	$50	$25	$75
Grand Total	$450	$150	$150	$300

Summary Resource Consumption Matrix

	#1	#2	#3	#4
Supplies	$275	$50	$100	$75
Lab Testing	75	50	25	150
Staffing	100	50	25	75
Total	$450	$150	$150	$300

Table 10-10
Volume Data

Procedure	Actual	Budget
# 1	20	10
# 2	10	10
# 3	5	10
# 4	5	10
Total	40	40

Med/Surg Supplies Consumed	$6,875	$5,000
Variance from Budget – Dollars		($1,875)
Variance from Budget – Percent		−37.5 %

($6,875 – $5,000) when compared with the budget. The volume of procedures (40) is as budgeted. But is it the same level of activity? Is the mix of procedures important? The use of the resource consumption matrix could provide a different, more accurate insight (Table 10-11).

Using the predetermined standard for supply consumption, it is possible to calculate a revised budget amount ($6,875) that reflects the fact that the actual mix of procedures differed from the budget. By comparing the revised budget with actual results, it can be seen that there is no unfavorable supply consumption.

Building the RVU

Taking this a step further, it is possible to develop an RVU for almost any department. Ratios are developed among the various products and procedures in a department based on their individual utilization or resources. The detailed analysis used to develop the resource consumption matrix provides the necessary base information.

Again using the example of the XYZ Memorial Hospital therapeutics depart-

Table 10-11
Budget Adjustment Worksheet

Procedure	Actual Quantity	Supply Standard	Revised Budget
# 1	20	$275	$5,500
# 2	10	50	500
# 3	5	100	500
# 4	5	75	375
Total	40		$6,875

Actual Supply Consumption	6,875
Variance Adjusted for Mix	$0

ment, the starting point would be the summary resource consumption matrix (Table 10-12).

The procedure consuming the least amount of resources (Procedure #2) is assigned a value of 1 RVU, and the amount of resources associated with it is then divided into the resources associated with all of the other procedures to determine their RVU values. Thus, Procedure #1 is assigned an RVU value of 3 ($450 ÷ $150 = 3), Procedure #3 is assigned an RVU value of 1 ($150 ÷ $150 = 1), and Procedure #4 is assigned an RVU value of 2 ($300 ÷ $150 = 2).

Use of such a relative value unit system to track volumes can be seen in the comparison presented in Table 10-13. It appears that volume is constant over time at 110 procedures every month, but overlaying these volume data with relative value unit weights paints an entirely different picture (Table 10-14).

Table 10-12
Relative Value Unit Calculation

Summary Resource Consumption Matrix

Resources	#1	#2	#3	#4
	— — — — Procedures — — — —			
Supplies	$275	$50	$100	$75
Lab Testing	75	50	25	150
Staffing	100	50	25	75
Total	$450	$150	$150	$300
Relative Value Units	3	1	1	2

Table 10-13
Therapeutics Department: Monthly Volume Comparison–Procedures

Procedure	January	February	March
# 1		100	60
# 2	90		40
# 3	10		5
# 4	10	10	5
Total	110	110	110

Table 10-14
Therapeutics Department: Monthly Volume Comparison–RVUs

Procedure	January	February	March
# 1	0	300	180
# 2	90	0	40
# 3	10	0	5
# 4	20	20	10
Total	120	320	235

It can be seen that the three months have very different levels of activity when expressed in RVUs. February volume is more than two and a half times that of January, while March represents a decrease of over 23 percent from February.

Before any system of RVUs can be used as a management tool, it must be thoroughly tested and verified. Only after it has been proven to be accurate can it be used confidently to measure and predict volumes and control costs.

Achieving success in today's "do more with less" environment requires managers to monitor productivity closely and to seek improvement wherever and whenever possible. Remember that tools are available to measure productivity, and methods exist to increase it.

NOTE

1. For more information, see Elton Mayo, *The Human Problems of an Industrialized Civilization* (New York: Macmillan, 1933); F. J. Roethlisberger and W. J. Dickson, *Management and the Worker* (Cambridge, MA: Harvard University Press, 1939).

Chapter 11

Negotiating the Budget

Perhaps no words strike as much fear in the heart of a manager as the simple notation in his or her calendar: Budget Meeting—2:00 P.M. to 4:00 P.M. Whether to negotiate a budget for an upcoming year, review performance-to-date versus the current budget, or simply to be briefed on the forms to be used in requesting the budget for next year, anxiety, apprehension, fear, and downright panic are some of the emotions that managers experience in preparing for a budget meeting. It does not have to be that bad. The meeting can be a very positive experience.

SETTING THE AGENDA

The key to any successful meeting is a predetermined agenda. Whether formally prepared and distributed or merely kept in the minds of the person who chairs the meeting and the participants, the agenda acts as a guideline for discussion and as an aid in keeping the meeting on track. Even a brief agenda of perhaps three or four items contributes to a smoother, more productive meeting.

A budget meeting called to discuss a single issue, for example, quite often will deal with several topics that are intertwined within the issue. A meeting called to discuss the single issue of actual expense spending versus budget will likely deal with such topics as patient acuity, volume, staffing, and supply utilization.

If possible, offer to prepare the agenda for the meeting. Volunteering that "I could prepare a brief agenda if you think it would be helpful" sets a tone of cooperation that can help smooth away any confrontational feelings that may be present. It tells the reviewer that the manager being reviewed is interested in a productive meeting. It also allows the manager being reviewed to prepare the agenda with issues or topics listed in the sequence that best serves his or her purposes.

When formulating the agenda, positive items should be listed first, and negatives should follow. This allows a buildup of favorable momentum before the discussion turns to the negatives. Positive aspects of performance should be accentuated. Managers should tactfully blow their own horns. They should demonstrate the kind of return the organization has achieved by investing resources in their departments. This can be accomplished anecdotally or, more persuasively, by displaying a departmental P&L.

The transition from positive to negative items on the agenda should be accomplished with a transitional summary of the positive accomplishments. Negatives or problems should be addressed as challenges with which to deal. This removes, to a degree, the negativism and frames the issues with a positive action orientation. The manager with more staff than budget should deal with the challenge of reducing FTEs rather than the problem of overstaffing.

This is not to imply that negative aspects or performance can be glossed over by the use of semantics. Problems must be dealt with honestly, and managers must be prepared to discuss the genesis of a problem and the steps to resolution that they are taking or plan to take. The manager who talks of the challenge of reducing FTEs rather than the problem of overstaffing must be prepared to discuss how the extra employees came to be hired in the first place and what steps are being taken to reduce the FTE count (hiring freeze, attrition, and so on).

Occasionally, during the course of a meeting, a manager may encounter a hidden agenda. This refers to the issue that one of the meeting participants wishes to discuss and share information about but that was hidden when the formal agenda was prepared. Often the issue is a volatile or controversial one in which this participant has a keen interest. Consider the following scenario.

The executive director, chief of operations, finance director, and director of nursing are meeting to discuss year-to-date performance compared with budget. Overall, the director of nursing has overspent the budget by about 1 percent. The chief of operations has information indicating that supply consumption is considerably over budget and that usage of supplies, not price, is the culprit. There is no formal agenda, but the director's intent is to review the performance of his three subordinates and determine if remedial action is necessary. After the meeting has progressed beyond the preliminary stages, the chief of operations deftly inserts the fact that his supply room personnel are having a difficult time keeping pace with nursing's supply consumption by stating, "We can hardly keep the units stocked, they're consuming supplies so fast."

Now the once-hidden agenda is no longer hidden. It is out on the table, and it is likely that the director of nursing will be challenged to explain supply consumption; defend it, if possible; and tell what steps are being taken to correct the situation.

In this scenario, the chief of operations wanted to apply pressure and wanted that pressure to be a surprise. If resolving the problem of supply consumption was important, it would have been far more profitable for him to talk with the executive director in advance to make sure this issue was put on the agenda and with the director of nursing so that some preparation could have been made to discuss the issue from nursing's vantage point.

The importance of dealing appropriately with a hidden agenda cannot be over-emphasized. One method is to review performance critically and determine if there are any "skeletons in the closet" that might pose a problem. If there are, be prepared to explain and defend them and indicate the actions taken, or soon to be taken, to remedy the situation. Sometimes a premeeting phone call or visit can unearth a clue that an issue will surface unannounced at the meeting. If so, preparation can be made. In any event, do not be defensive and do not appear surprised. Treat the subject as though it was a planned agenda item.

The best method of dealing with hidden agendas is to avoid them entirely by fostering open communications and respect throughout the organization. Everyone shares in this responsibility.

PRESENTATION QUALITIES

Any presentation, whether at a budget meeting or at a meeting of the local civic association, benefits from a confident, relaxed, and knowledgeable presenter. The effect is that the audience is more open to the presentation and less likely to challenge the presenter. The cohesiveness of a unified presentation can be achieved only when the presenters have planned, rehearsed, and strategized about what is to be said, who will cover various points, when certain facts will be used, what supporting documents will be used, and so on.

Understanding the audience and their biases, expectations, and ability to comprehend what is being presented is essential for the success of the presentation. Information should be presented in a way that the audience will understand. This allows the presenter to concentrate his or her energy on the facts of the presentation without having to educate the audience. If the presentation is to result in a decision being made, a few well-placed premeeting sales calls may be helpful in winning over some key members of the audience to the presenter's point of view even before the presentation. Sometimes, the reaction of these members of the audience can sway others.

Essential to the success of any presentation is a smooth delivery. This can be accomplished only by practice. Rehearse the presentation. If several persons are to present pieces of it, rehearse as a group. In that way each person becomes more familiar with what the others will be presenting, and the individuals will be better able to support each other during the presentation. Someone in the group can be designated to play devil's advocate during rehearsal and challenge parts of the presentation to simulate possible live presentation reaction. If an individual is the sole presenter, an associate can fill this same role. In this way, the presentation will have been tested in private. A rehearsal prior to the real meeting can help discover problems in the handouts, missing facts, mistakes, and so on that can be fixed in order to avoid embarrassment during the meeting.

Last, a little bit of psychology can go a long way. To borrow from the vernacular, get "psyched up" about the presentation. A well-constructed presentation that has been rehearsed and tested should result in a positive meeting. A presenter who truly feels confident, relaxed, and knowledgeable will infect the room with those same feelings.

PRESENTATION TECHNIQUES

A presentation can be enhanced by employing informational handouts to emphasize the message and make it easier for the listener to understand and remember the presentation. Obviously, these should support the presenter's position. A list of actions taken or planned, a brief program description, even the meeting agenda itself are examples of handouts that can help support a presentation. The handouts should serve a purpose. Do not use a handout to state the obvious or some fact that need not be supported by a handout. A handout that merely tells the number of nursing hours per patient day serves no purpose. However, a handout that provides a comparison (with other institutions, national standards, and so on) or that shows the trend over time can be very helpful in explaining the current state of affairs in the nursing department and can be used effectively to support and justify a staffing budget request.

The best informational handouts are simple and tightly focused. They should be brief, using key words. A telegraphic approach (employing "bullets" like advertising fliers) is better than a rambling narrative, which should be avoided. If a narrative must be used, pick out the key words, phrases, and concepts and mark them with a fluorescent yellow highlighter so they stand out from the text. Make sure they do not contradict each other. This can happen when several presenters split up the work of preparing the handouts (another good reason to practice the presentation).

Should the handouts be bound into a booklet or distributed one at a time? There are pros and cons to either approach. The answer depends on the number of persons attending the meeting as well as the number of handouts used.

In a budget meeting, which can have dozens of handouts, it is probably advisable to bind them together, number the pages, and distribute them at the beginning of the meeting. This avoids the disruptive process of distributing so many handouts during the course of the meeting. This is not to say that even with the booklet approach there will not be some individual handouts that the presenter holds in reserve in case a particular unscheduled issue comes up. The risk of this approach is that people may not be looking at the right page at the right time, and it can be more difficult to focus the listener's attention.

The other approach, one-at-a-time distribution, can be used when only a few handouts are used. The advantage is that attention can be focused on a single issue without competition from other handouts. To avoid any confusion, clearly identify handouts that look similar by using simple, straightforward titles.

Construct informational handouts so the audience can understand them. The presenter must know the audience's baseline of understanding of the subject and construct the handouts accordingly. A handout that only the presenter under-stands is worthless at best and may be harmful in the final analysis.

Rather than an anecdotal response, a facts-and-figures handout can help defend against a hidden agenda. It need not be distributed unless necessary. This cer-tainly would give the impression that the problem is not a surprise and that a pru-dent manager is on top of the situation.

Far better than tables of numbers, a good graph or chart can make a strong vis-ual impression. The old adage "a picture is worth a thousand words" applies in this instance. Rather than merely comment that a recent change in price has af-fected patient volume, a graph such as the one in Figure 11-1, showing increases and decreases in volume linked to price changes, will dramatically emphasize the point.

Graphs can be used in combination with tables of numbers to provide a hand-out that has the complete numerical story in addition to a pictorial display of one

Figure 11-1
Price Changes and Patient Volumes

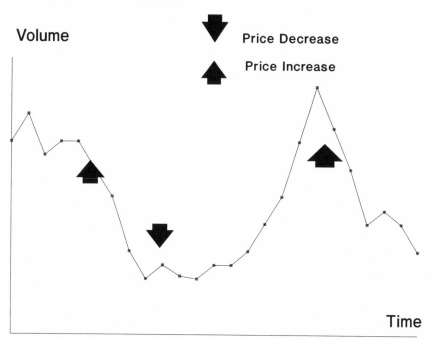

A graph such as this that depicts patient volume on a time line with three known price actions indicated by markers can be effective in supporting an argument that patient volume is price-sensitive and that increases in price may result in a revenue decrease. Further, it might be argued that a loss could result from the combination of decreased revenues and the failure to eliminate fixed costs.

or two pertinent facts. A table of historical patient volumes can be combined on a single page with a graph that depicts the pattern or trend that is masked in the table of numbers.

When preparing a graph, the choice of vertical or horizontal format should be a conscious decision. A vertical display emphasizes a trend, while a horizontal orientation de-emphasizes a trend. Figure 11-2 displays an upward trend using 10 data points in a horizontal orientation—the width exceeds the height of the graph. Figure 11-3 displays the identical data in a vertical orientation—the height exceeds the width. Which looks more positive, the horizontal or the vertical? The human eye perceives the trend graphed vertically as having a greater slope and thus as more positive despite the fact that the data are identical. The selection of a vertical or horizontal orientation cannot make good news out of bad news, but it can provide emphasis or de-emphasis.

Make sure the graph is easily understood. If a presenter is forced to spend a lot of time explaining what it means, its effectiveness is lost.

STRATEGIES FOR SUCCESS

The primary strategy involves understanding the expectations of upper management, the constraints on the system, and the latitude allowed in managing resources.

In any venture, understanding what is expected is critical to success. The bud-

Figure 11-2
Horizontal Display

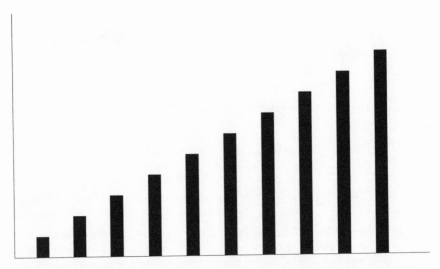

Using a horizontal display of data elements causes a trend line to flatten out as it crosses the X axis, the width of which exceeds the height of the Y axis.

Figure 11-3
Vertical Display

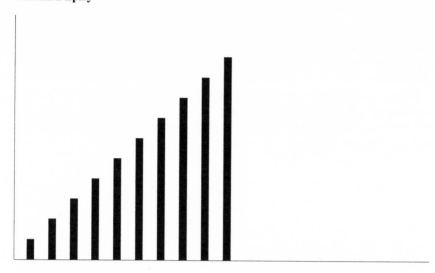

The vertical orientation of this graphic display of the same data used in Figure 11-2 causes the eye to perceive the trend as more positive.

get to be negotiated must be consistent with upper management's expectations. Do not seek budget resources for a new program that is at odds with organizational goals and objectives. A request for funds to open and operate an outpatient skin cancer clinic will likely meet with disapproval if the overall objective of the organization is gradually to divest itself of clinic programs. Further, such a request may lead to the questioning of a manager's fundamental understanding of the organization and of his or her ability to be entrusted with resources.

Refrain from asking for resources that are not available. Constraints on the ability to generate revenue, whether because of competition, regulation, or general business conditions, must be understood. If funds are available to support only 60 housekeepers, it serves no purpose to ask for 62 or 63. In essence, be realistic.

It is also important to understand budget latitude. Can the budget for contract services be converted to salary dollars by a department manager, or is a higher level of authority needed for such a maneuver? Is emphasis placed on compliance with the budget on a line item-by-line item basis, or is overall performance against the total budget amount all that is considered? This must be understood because it defines a manager's latitude. The style of management will differ if line item compliance is necessary.

A secondary strategy involves maneuvering the reviewer in such a way that he or she makes the point or mandates the action that the presenter had as an objective. This is not the same as the overt act of winning someone over to a position.

It is, rather, the subtle art of manipulation. This is very difficult, and there are few managers with the skill to accomplish it.

Finally, two strategies can be used in a defensive way. The uniqueness of a department or unit can be stressed so that comparison with other departments, with national averages, and so on is made difficult. The technique of presenting only supportive data rather than all the facts and figures available can also be employed defensively.

The use of fallacious data should be avoided at all cost. Making up "facts" to support a request is bad business. If information is not available, say so. If a mistake was made in the management of resources, admit it. In the long run, honesty and trust will be rewarded.

Appendix 1
Solutions to Review Problems

Chapter 2

Problem 1

Current Ratio
  = Total Current Assets ÷ Total Current Liabilities
  = $24,114,321 ÷ $11,791,848
  = 2.04

Working Capital
  = Total Current Assets - Total Current Liabilities
  = $24,114,321 - $11,791,848
  = $12,322,473

Quick Ratio
  = (Total Current Assets - Inventory) ÷ Total Current Liabilities
  = ($24,114,321 - $2,023,155) ÷ $11,791,848
  = 1.87

Average Age of Accounts Receivable (Gross, Net and Net-Net) Multi Step Approach

Gross Revenue per Day
  = Gross Revenue ÷ Calendar Days
  = $77,185,080 ÷ 365
  = $211,466

Net Revenue per Day
  = Net Revenue ÷ Calendar Days
  = $70,234,733 ÷ 365
  = $192,424

Average Age of Accounts Receivable - Gross
  = Gross Receivable ÷ Gross Revenue per Day
  = $10,950,068 ÷ $211,466
  = 51.8 days

Average Age of Accounts Receivable - Net
  = Net Receivable ÷ Net Revenue per Day
  = $9,596,368 ÷ 192,424
  = 49.9 days

Average Age of Accounts Receivable - Net-Net
    = (Net Receivable - 3rd Party Advances) ÷ Net Revenue per Day
    = ($9,596,368 - 1,319,451) ÷ 192,424
    = 43.0 days

Accounts Receivable Turnover
    = 365 days ÷ Average Age of Accounts Receivable

Accounts Receivable Turnover (Gross)
    = 365 days ÷ 51.8 days
    = 7 times

Accounts Receivable Turnover (Net)
    = 365 days ÷ 49.9 days
    = 7.3 times

Accounts Receivable Turnover (Net-Net)
    = 365 days ÷ 43.0 days
    = 8.5 times

Return on Investment
    = Net Operating Gain ÷ Total Assets or
    = (In this Case) "Excess of Revenues over Expenses" ÷ Total Assets
    = $3,467,099 ÷ $66,497,106
    = 0.052 or 5.2%

Collection Rate
    = Net Patient Revenue ÷ Gross Patient Revenue
    = $70,234,733 ÷ $77,185,080
    = 0.9099 or 91%

Operating Margin Ratio
    = Operating Gain ÷ Total Operating Revenue or
    = (In this Case) "Excess of Revenues over Expenses" ÷ Gross Patient
Revenue
    = $3,467,099 ÷ $77,185,080
    = 0.0449 or 4.5%

Problem 2

Average Inventory Value
    = (Inventory at 6/30/X2 + Inventory at 6/30/X1) ÷ 2
    = ($2,145,673 + $2,023,155) ÷ 2
    = $2,084,414

Inventory Turnover
   = Annual Inventory Purchases ÷ Average Inventory Value
   = $15,528,884 ÷ $2,084,414
   = 7.45 times

Problem 3

Inventory Age
   = 365 ÷ Inventory Turnover
   = 365 ÷ 7.45
   = 49 days

Value of 1 Day of Inventory
   = Current Inventory Balance ÷ Inventory Age
   = $2,145,673 ÷ 49
   = $43,789

Cash Provided by Reducing Inventory Age to 30 Days
   = $43,789 x (49 days - 30 days)
   = $43,789 x 19
   = $831,991

Chapter 5

Problem 1

FTE Requirements:
Patient Days Planned   5,400
Hours per Patient Day   x   6
Total Hours Needed   32,400 (A)

Hours per Year per FTE   2,080
Productive Time   x   85.00%
Productive Hours per FTE   1,768 (B)

FTEs Needed = (A / B) = 18.32579 Rounded to: 18.5

Rank	Name	FTE Value	Rates @ 11/4/X0	Rates @ 7/1/X1	Base Salary	Salary Increase	Salary Budget
RNs	Abelein	1.0	$14.30	$15.16	$31,529	$315	$31,844
	Brenchley	1.0	13.80	14.63	30,426	304	30,731
	Brownstein	0.5	13.50	14.31	14,882	149	15,031
	Colson	1.0	14.00	14.84	30,867	309	31,176
	Cottingham	0.5	12.75	13.52	14,056	141	14,196
	Cyr	1.0	14.20	15.05	31,308	313	31,621
	Vacant Positions	13.5		13.00	365,040	3,650	368,690
	Total	18.5			$518,108	$5,181	$523,289

Problem 2

FTE Requirements:

"Hands on" hours per patient day	6
Times Patient days in the budget	3,600
Productive hours required	21,600
Divide by Hours per FTE	2,080
FTEs required before gross up	10.38
Divide by Productivity Rate	80.00%
Total FTEs Required	12.98

Rounded to the nearest whole FTE   13.0

Name	FTE Value	Rates @ 4/1/X1	Rates @ 7/1/X1	Base Salary	Salary Increase	Salary Budget
King	1.0	$14.00	$14.84	$30,867	$309	$31,176
Law	1.0	13.80	14.63	30,426	304	30,731
Rogers	1.0	13.50	14.31	29,765	298	30,062
Ruby	1.0	14.00	14.84	30,867	309	31,176
Russell	0.5	12.75	13.52	14,056	141	14,196
Vacant Positions	8.5		13.00	229,840	2,298	232,138
	13.0			$365,821	$3,658	$369,479

Problem 3

FTE Requirements:

Units of Service Planned	3,000	
Hours per Unit of Service	5	
Total Hours Needed	15,000	(A)

Hours per Year per FTE	2,080	
Productive Time	85.00%	
Productive Hours per FTE	1,768	(B)

FTEs Needed = (A / B) = 8.484163   Rounded off to 8.5

Name	FTE Value	Rates @ 3/8/X2	Rates @ 7/1/X2	Base Salary	First Raise	Second Raise	Salary Budget
Critz	1.0	$14.50	$15.37	$31,970	$1,119	$169	$33,258
Zeri	0.4	13.50	14.31	11,906	417	$63	12,386
Goel	1.0	15.00	15.90	33,072	1,158	$175	34,405
Taft	0.5	13.75	14.58	15,158	531	$80	15,769
Freeman	0.6	14.60	15.48	19,314	676	$102	20,092
Vacant Positions	5.0	13.00	13.78	143,312	5,016	$760	149,087
Total	0.0			$254,732	$8,916	$1,350	$264,997

Problem 4

Two Approaches to Calculating the Volume Budget

Number of Beds	75	Number of Beds		75
Calendar Days	x 365	Occupancy Rate	x	0.8
Bed Days Available	27,375	Average Census		60
Occupancy Rate	x 0.8	Calendar Days	x	365
Patient Days Budget	21,900	Patient Days Budget		21,900

Supplies and Services Budget Worksheet

FIXED EXPENSES

EXPENSE ACCOUNT	BASE PERIOD AMOUNT	BASE PERIOD MONTHS	AMOUNT PER MONTH	BUDGET PERIOD MONTHS	BASE BUDGET AMOUNT	INFLATION RATE	INFLATION AMOUNT	FINAL BUDGET AMOUNT
Office Supplies	$500	5	$100.00	12	$1,200	0.10	$120	$1,320
Books & Periodicals	50	5	10.00	12	120	0.10	12	132
Miscellaneous	1,000	5	200.00	12	2,400	0.10	240	2,640
TOTAL FIXED	$1,550	5	$310.00	12	$3,720	0.10	$372	$4,092

VARIABLE EXPENSES

EXPENSE ACCOUNT	BASE PERIOD AMOUNT	BASE PERIOD UNITS	AMOUNT PER UNIT	BUDGET PERIOD UNITS	BASE BUDGET AMOUNT	INFLATION RATE	INFLATION AMOUNT	FINAL BUDGET AMOUNT
Med/Surg Supplies	$18,000	9,000	$2.00	21,900	$43,800	0.10	4380	48,180
Stock Drugs	13,500	9,000	1.50	21,900	32,850	0.10	3285	36,135
TOTAL VARIABLE	$31,500	9,000	$3.50	21,900	$76,650	0.10	$7,665	$84,315
GRAND TOTAL	$33,050				$80,370	0.10	$8,037	$88,407

Problem 4 continued

SALARY BUDGET WORKSHEET

POSN or RANK	INCUMBENT	FTE VALUE	CURRENT HOURLY RATE	INCREASE BEFORE START OF FYX2		RATE AT START OF FY 19X2	BASE SALARY BUDGET FY 19X2	INCREASE AFTER START OF FYX2		BUDGETED SALARY INCREASE	TOTAL SALARY BUDGET FY 1991
				AMOUNT	DATE			AMOUNT	DATE		
H.N.		1.0	$20.00	10.00%	1/1/91	$22.00	$45,760	8.00%	1/1/92	$1,830	$47,590
RNs	One	1.0	$15.00	10.00%	1/1/91	$16.50	$34,320	8.00%	1/1/92	$1,373	$35,693
	Two	1.0	$15.00	10.00%	1/1/91	$16.50	34,320	8.00%	1/1/92	1,373	35,693
	All others	48.0	$15.00	10.00%	1/1/91	$16.50	1,647,360	8.00%	1/1/92	65,894	1,713,254
	TOTAL RNs	50.0					$1,716,000			$68,640	$1,784,640
	TOTAL	51.0					$1,761,760			$70,470	$1,832,230
	BENEFITS (20%)										$366,446

220

Problem 5

SALARY BUDGET WORKSHEET

POSN or RANK	INCUMBENT	FTE VALUE	CURRENT HOURLY RATE	INCREASE BEFORE START OF FYX7		RATE TO START FY19X7	BASE SALARY BUDGET FY19X7	INCREASE AFTER START OF FYX7		SALARY INCREASE	TOTAL SALARY BUDGET FY19X7
				AMOUNT	DATE			AMOUNT	DATE		
Tech I	Bull	1.0	$9.80	4.00%	5/1/X6	$10.19	$21,199	4.00%	5/1/X7	$141	$21,341
	Jones	1.0	9.80	4.00%	5/1/X6	10.19	21,199	4.00%	5/1/X7	141	21,341
	Carroll	1.0	10.00	4.00%	5/1/X6	10.40	21,632	4.00%	5/1/X7	144	21,776
	Kulis	0.8	9.70	4.00%	5/1/X6	10.09	16,786	4.00%	5/1/X7	112	16,898
	Condon	1.0	9.40	4.00%	5/1/X6	9.78	20,334	4.00%	5/1/X7	136	20,470
	Kennedy	0.2	9.90	4.00%	5/1/X6	10.30	4,283	4.00%	5/1/X7	29	4,312
	Lewiston	0.5	9.50	4.00%	5/1/X6	9.88	10,275	4.00%	5/1/X7	69	10,344
	Smith	0.5	9.60	4.00%	5/1/X6	9.98	10,383	4.00%	5/1/X7	69	10,453
	Vacant Positions	4.0			5/1/X6	9.40	78,208	4.00%	5/1/X7	521	78,729
	TOTAL TECH I	10.0					$204,301			$1,362	$205,663
Tech II	Swartz	0.8	$8.60	2.00%	7/1/X6	8.77	$14,597				$14,597
	Johansson	1.0	8.70	2.00%	7/1/X6	8.87	18,458				18,458
	Vacant Positions	2.2			7/1/X6	$8.50	38,896				38,896
	TOTAL TECH II	4.0					$71,951				$71,951
	DEPARTMENT TOTAL	21.0					$276,251			$1,362	$277,613

221

Problem 6

Number of Shifts per Week:

Day	14
Evening	7
Night	5
Total	26
Hours per Shift	x 8
Hours per Week	208
Weeks per Year	x 52
Hours per Year	10,816

FTE Conversion = 10,816 / 2,080

= 5.20

Productive FTEs = 5.20 / 80%

= 6.50

Base Salary Calculation

	6.5 FTEs
x	2,080 Hours per FTE
	13,520
x	$8.00 Hourly Rate
	$108,160

Premium Pay Calculation

Premium Shifts per Week:

Day	4
Evening	7
Night	5
Total	16
Hours per Shift	x 8
Hours per Week	128
Weeks per Year	x 52
Hours per Year	6,656
Hourly Premium	x $1.00
	$6,656

Base Salary	$108,160
Premium Pay	6,656
	$114,816

222

Problem 7

Staffing Requirements = 21,000 procedures / 2,000 procedures per FTE = 10.5 FTEs

INCUMBENT	FTE VALUE	CURRENT RATE 4/20/X1	INCREASE BEFORE START OF FY 19X2		RATE TO START YEAR	BASE SALARY BUDGET	INCREASES SCHEDULED AFTER START OF YEAR				SALARY INCREASE #1	SALARY INCREASE #2	TOTAL SALARY BUDGET
			AMOUNT	DATE			#1 AMT	DATE	#2 AMT	DATE			
Milligan	1.0	$10.00	6.00%	5/1	$10.60	$22,048	$0.50	1/1	6.00%	5/1	$520	$231	$22,799
Gomez	0.5	9.60	6.00%	6/1	10.18	10,583	$0.50	1/1	6.00%	6/1	260	56	10,899
Ripken,B.	1.0	9.80	6.00%	7/1	10.39	21,607	$0.50	1/1		7/1	520		22,127
Worthington	1.0	9.20		12/1	9.20	19,136	6.00%	12/1	$0.50	1/1	670	520	20,326
Anderson	0.8	9.60		12/1	9.60	15,974	6.00%	12/1	$0.50	1/1	559	416	16,950
Davis,G.	0.2	9.00		12/1	9.00	3,744	6.00%	12/1	$0.50	1/1	131	104	3,979
Dempsey	0.5	9.50		4/1	9.50	9,880	$0.50	1/1	6.00%	4/1	260	156	10,296
Ripken,C.	1.0	9.75		4/1	9.75	20,280	6.00%	1/1	$0.50	4/1	520	320	21,120
Horn	0.7	9.00		10/1	9.00	13,104	6.00%	10/1	$0.50	1/1	590	364	14,058
Evans	0.3	9.10		10/1	9.10	5,678	6.00%	10/1	$0.50	1/1	256	156	6,090
Vacant	3.5				9.00	65,520	$0.50	1/1			1,820		67,340
TOTALS	10.5					$207,555					$6,105	$2,322	$215,982

Problem 8

Rank & Name	FTE	Rates of Pay		Salary Budget Amounts		
		12/20/X7	7/1/X8	Routine	Increase	Total
R.N.s –						
Arnold	1.0	$11.80	$12.27	$25,526	$255	$25,781
Balog	1.0	11.80	12.27	25,526	255	25,781
Chalmers	1.0	12.00	12.48	25,958	260	26,218
Coffey	0.8	11.70	12.17	20,248	202	20,450
Davila	1.0	11.40	11.86	24,660	247	24,907
DeMeester	0.2	11.90	12.38	5,148	51	5,200
Escobar	0.5	11.50	11.96	12,438	124	12,563
Heaton	0.5	11.60	12.06	12,547	125	12,672
Vacant	6.0	11.40	11.86	147,963	1,480	149,443
Total	12.0			$300,014	$3,000	$303,014
Aides –						
Baker	0.8	$8.60	$8.77	$14,597		$14,597
Caldwell	1.0	8.70	8.87	18,458		18,458
Vacant	3.2	8.50	8.67	57,708		57,708
Total	5.0			$90,762		$90,762
Premium Payments –		Hours	Rate			
Charge – Routine (832 shifts x 8 hours)		6,656	$2.50	$16,640		$16,640
Charge – Holiday (10 holiday shifts)		80	2.50	200		200
Agency (16 hours/week x 13 weeks)		208	35.00	7,280		7,280
Overtime (24 hours/week x 13 weeks)		312	12.14	3,788		3,788
Total				$27,908		$27,908
Grand Total	17.0			$418,684	$3,000	$421,684

Chapter 8

Problem 1

Actual Volume = 8,100 units
Budgeted Volume = 9,000 units
Volume Change = -10%
Variable Expense Factor = 100%
Volume Adjustment Factor = -10%

| | Usage | | | Volume Adjusted | Volume Adjusted Usage Variance | Unit Price | | | Variance | | |
Drug	Actual	Budget	Volume Adjustment	Budget	(Unfav)	Actual	Budget	Variance (Unfav)	Usage (Unfav)	Price (Unfav)	Total (Unfav)
Item A	1,760	750	-75	675.0	-1085	$4.50	$3.50	($1.00)	($4,883)	($675)	($5,558)
Item B	1,600	1,599	-159.9	1,439.1	-160.9	5.36	4.36	(1.00)	(862)	(1,439)	(2,302)
Item C	1,500	1,524	-152.4	1,371.6	-128.4	3.02	3.27	0.25	(388)	343	(45)
Item D	400	411	-41.1	369.9	-30.1	1.85	1.82	(0.03)	(56)	(11)	(67)
Item E	450	426	-42.6	383.4	-66.6	198.00	195.22	(2.78)	(13,187)	(1,066)	(14,253)
Item F	100	180	-18	162.0	62	16.00	15.22	(0.78)	992	(126)	866
Item G	74	93	-9.3	83.7	9.7	28.50	28.55	0.05	276	4	281
Item H	350	348	-34.8	313.2	-36.8	24.99	25.02	0.03	(920)	9	(910)
Item I	30	30	-3	27.0	-3	75.00	74.84	(0.16)	(225)	(4)	(229)
Item J	120	114	-11.4	102.6	-17.4	51.00	50.81	(0.19)	(887)	(19)	(907)
								Total	($20,140)	($2,984)	($23,124)

Problem 2

Actual Volume:	66,500		
Budget Volume:	70,000		
Variable Expense Factor:	0.60 or (60%)		
Volume Change:	−0.05 or (−5%)		
Volume Adjustment Factor:	−0.03 or (−3%)		

Description	Actual	Budget	Variance (Unfavorable)
Salaries	$457,600	$474,240	$16,640
Volume Adjustment		(14,227)	(14,227)
	$457,600	$460,013	$2,413
Hours	41,600	39,520	(2,080)
Volume Adjustment		(1,186)	(1,186)
	41,600	38,334	(3,266)
Labor Rate	$11.00	$12.00	$1.00

Labor Rate Variance	$38,334
Efficiency Variance	(35,922)
Total	$2,413

Problem 3

Actual Volume:	19,000
Budget Volume:	20,000
Variable Expense Factor:	0.5 or (50%)
Volume Change:	−0.05 or (−5%)
Volume Adjustment Factor:	−0.025 or (−2.5%)

Description	Actual	Budget	Variance (Unfavorable)
Salaries	$228,800	$237,120	$8,320
Volume Adjustment		(5,928)	(5,928)
	$228,800	$231,192	$2,392
Hours	20,800	19,760	(1,040)
Volume Adjustment		(494)	(494)
	20,800	$19,266	(1,534)
Labor Rate	$11.00	$12.00	$1.00

Labor Rate Variance	$19,266
Efficiency Variance	(16,874)
Total	$2,392

Problem 4

Actual Volume:	99,000
Budget Volume:	90,000
Variable Expense Factor:	1.00 or (100%)
Volume Change:	0.10 or (10%)
Volume Adjustment Factor:	0.10 or (10%)

Description	Actual	Budget	Variance (Unfavorable)
Salaries	$451,000	$450,000	($1,000)
Volume Adjustment		45,000	45,000
	$451,000	$495,000	$44,000
Hours	36,080	37,500	1,420
Volume Adjustment		3,750	3,750
	36,080	41,250	5,170
Labor Rate	$12.50	$12.00	($0.50)

Labor Rate Variance	($20,625)
Efficiency Variance	64,625
Total	$44,000

Problem 5

Payor	Share (Percent)	Collection Rate (Percent)	Aggregate Rate
Insured	50.00	90.00	45.00%
Self Pay	50.00	50.00	25.00%
Total	100.00		70.00%
Gross Revenue per Unit			$250.00
Net Revenue per Unit			$175.00

Variable Cost Per Unit	$100.00
Fixed Costs	$200,000.00
Capacity	2,400

Break−even Point = $200,000 / $75 = 2,667

Do not Pursue: Capacity is Less than Break−even Point

Problem 6

Payor	Share (Percent)	Collection Rate (Percent)	Aggregate Rate
Commercial	80.00%	90.00%	72.00%
Self Pay	20.00%	100.00%	20.00%
Total	100.00%		92.00%
Gross Revenue per Unit			$1,400.00
Net Revenue per Unit			$1,288.00

Variable Cost Per Unit	$288.00
Fixed Costs	$765,000.00

Break−even Point = $765,000.00 / $1,000.00 = 765

Problem 7

Payor	Share (Percent)	Collection Rate (Percent)	Aggregate Rate
H M O	50.00%	80.00%	40.00%
Commercial	40.00%	90.00%	36.00%
Self Pay	10.00%	100.00%	10.00%
Total	100.00%		86.00%
Gross Revenue per Unit			$800.00
Net Revenue per Unit			$688.00

Variable Cost Per Unit	$588.00
Fixed Costs	$400,000.00

Breakeven Point = $400,000.00 / 100.00 = 4,000

Problem 8

PRESENT VALUE OF THE INVESTMENT

YEAR	CONSTRUCTION	EQUIPMENT	INSTALLATION	OTHER	TOTAL INVESTMENT	PRESENT VALUE FACTORS	INVESTMENT PRESENT VALUE
0		$1,100,000	$75,000		$1,175,000	1.000	$1,175,000
1						0.909	
2						0.826	
3						0.751	
4						0.683	
TOTAL		$1,100,000	$75,000		$1,175,000		$1,175,000

PRESENT VALUE OF THE BENEFIT

YEAR	REVENUE INCREASES	REVENUE DECREASES	EXPENSE INCREASES	EXPENSE DECREASES	TOTAL BENEFIT	PRESENT VALUE FACTORS	BENEFIT PRESENT VALUE
1	$210,000		$90,000		$120,000	0.909	$109,080
2	420,000		90,000		330,000	0.826	272,580
3	490,000		90,000		400,000	0.751	300,400
4	630,000		90,000		540,000	0.683	368,820
5	700,000		90,000		610,000	0.621	378,810
TOTAL	$2,450,000		$450,000		$2,000,000		$1,429,690

NET PRESENT VALUE $254,690
BENEFIT/COST RATIO 1.217
INVESTMENT SHOULD BE PURSUED

Problem 9

PRESENT VALUE OF THE INVESTMENT

YEAR	CONSTRUCTION	EQUIPMENT	INSTALLATION	OTHER	TOTAL INVESTMENT	PRESENT VALUE FACTORS	INVESTMENT PRESENT VALUE
0	$250,000	$925,000			$1,175,000	1.000	$1,175,000
1						0.909	
2						0.826	
3						0.751	
4						0.683	
TOTAL	$250,000	$925,000			$1,175,000		$1,175,000

PRESENT VALUE OF THE BENEFIT

YEAR	REVENUE INCREASES	REVENUE DECREASES	EXPENSE INCREASES	EXPENSE DECREASES	TOTAL BENEFIT	PRESENT VALUE FACTORS	BENEFIT PRESENT VALUE
1	$120,000		$90,000		$30,000	0.909	$27,270
2	240,000		90,000		150,000	0.826	123,900
3	280,000		90,000		190,000	0.751	142,690
4	360,000		90,000		270,000	0.683	184,410
5	400,000		90,000		310,000	0.621	192,510
TOTAL	$1,400,000		$450,000		$950,000		$670,780

NET PRESENT VALUE ($504,220)
BENEFIT/COST RATIO 0.571
INVESTMENT SHOULD NOT BE PURSUED

230

Problem 10

PRESENT VALUE OF THE INVESTMENT

YEAR	CONSTRUCTION	EQUIPMENT	INSTALLATION	OTHER	TOTAL INVESTMENT	PRESENT VALUE FACTORS	INVESTMENT PRESENT VALUE
0		$305,000			$305,000	1.000	$305,000
1						0.833	
2						0.694	
3						0.578	
4						0.482	
TOTAL		$305,000			$305,000		$305,000

PRESENT VALUE OF THE BENEFIT

YEAR	REVENUE INCREASES	REVENUE DECREASES	EXPENSE INCREASES	EXPENSE DECREASES	TOTAL BENEFIT	PRESENT VALUE FACTORS	BENEFIT PRESENT VALUE
1	$81,600		$68,000	$150,720	$164,320	0.833	$136,879
2	81,600		68,000	150,720	164,320	0.694	114,038
3	81,600		68,000	150,720	164,320	0.578	94,977
4							
5							
TOTAL	$244,800		$204,000	$452,160	$492,960		$345,894

NET PRESENT VALUE $40,894
BENEFIT/COST RATIO 1.134
INVESTMENT SHOULD BE PURSUED

231

Appendix 2
Formulary

Current Ratio =
    Total Current Assets ÷ Total Current Liabilities

Quick Ratio =
    (Total Current Assets - Inventory) ÷ Total Current Liabilities

Net Revenue Per Day =
    Net Revenue ÷ Calendar Days

Gross Revenue Per Day =
    Gross Revenue ÷ Calendar Days

Average Age of Accounts Receivable - Gross =
    Gross Receivable ÷ Gross Revenue per Day

Average Age of Accounts Receivable - Net =
    Net Receivable ÷ Net Revenue per Day

Average Age of Accounts Receivable - Net/Net =
    (Net Receivable - 3rd Party advances) ÷ Net Revenue per Day

Accounts Receivable Turnover =
    365 Days ÷ Average Age of Accounts Receivable

Inventory Turnover =
    Annual Inventory Purchases ÷ Average Inventory Value

Inventory Age =
    365 Days ÷ Inventory Turnover

Average Age of Accounts Payable =
    Accounts Payable ÷ (Annual Credit Purchases ÷ 365)

Return on Investment =
    Net Operating Gain ÷ Total Assets

Return on Investment =
    Net Operating Gain ÷ Total Investment

Average Rate of Return =
    Average Profit ÷ Average Investment

Operating Margin Ratio =
    Operating Gain ÷ Total Operating Revenue

Collection Rate =
    Net Patient Revenue ÷ Gross Patient Revenue

Average Payback Period =
    Net Investment ÷ Average Annual Cash Inflow

Net Present Value =
    Present Value of Cash Inflows - Present Value of Investment

Benefit/Cost Ratio =
    Present Value of Cash Inflows ÷ Present Value of Investment

Break-Even Point =
    Fixed Cost ÷ (Net Revenue Per Unit - Variable Cost per Unit)

Average Daily Census =
    Patient Days ÷ Calendar Days

Average Length of Stay =
    Patient Days ÷ Admissions or Discharge

Occupancy Rate =
    Average Daily Census ÷ Beds

Bed Days =
    Available Beds x Calendar Days

Full-Time Equivalent (FTE) =
    Payroll Hours Paid ÷ Standard FTE Hours

Standard FTE Hours =
    40 Hours per week, 520 per quarter, 1,040 per half year, or 2,080 per year

Nursing Hours per Patient Day =
    Total Productive Hours ÷ Patient Days in Same Period

Productive Hours =
    Total Paid Hours - Nonproductive Hours

Nonproductive Hours =
    Vacation, Sick, Holiday, and all other hours paid, but not worked

Volume Change Factor =
    (Actual Volume - Budget Volume) ÷ Budget Volume

Volume Variance =
     (Actual Volume - Budget Volume) x Actual Rate

Rate Variance =
     (Actual Rate - Budget Rate) x Budget Volume

Labor Rate Variance =
     (Actual Rate - Budget Rate) x Adjusted Budget Hours

Efficiency Variance =
     (Actual Hours - Adjusted Budget Hours) x Actual Rate

Usage Variance =
     (Volume Adjusted Budgeted Usage - Actual Usage) x Actual Price

Price Variance =
     (Budgeted Price - Actual Price) x Volume Adjusted Budgeted Usage

Appendix 3
Budget Timetable

Event(s)

Chief executive establishes overall goals and objectives to include volume targets, rates of inflation, labor contract settlements (if unionized), salary increase parameters, profit target, dollar limits for equipment and facility improvements, and so on.	-17 weeks
Guidelines for operating and capital budgets issued to departments. Includes schedule of due dates for various budgets.	-16 weeks
Departments prepare operating and capital budgets including new program and budget adjustment requests.	-16 weeks to -12 weeks
Operating and capital budgets submitted to Budget Office and Capital Review Committee via appropriate administrative hierarchy.	-12 weeks
Budget Office performs nonjudgmental technical review of submitted budgets and prepares for budget review meetings. Capital Review Committee performs similar review of equipment and improvements requests.	-12 weeks
Budget meetings with departments to review their requests for operating and capital funds.	-10 weeks to -6 weeks
Capital Review Committee makes determination of which requests to recommend for funding.	-6 weeks
Executive level of organization makes final determination of funding for operating and capital budgets, to include new programs and budget adjustments.	-4 weeks
Budget Office prepares supportive analysis for presentation to governing body for final approval.	-2 weeks
Presentation of budget to governing body for approval.	Last board meeting before start of budget year.

*The ultimate responsibility for the institution's operations rests with the governing body. It delegates authority to management. Consequently, the approval authority for the operating and capital budgets rests with the governing body. Management must obtain its approval prior to implementing the new budget. Because the meeting schedule varies from institution to institution, this sample budget timetable's time frames are expressed in terms of weeks prior to the board meeting at which the budget will be presented for approval. "-12 weeks" represents, for example, an event that should take place 12 weeks prior to that governing board meeting.

Appendix 4
Present Value Table

(The Present Value of $1 Received in a Future Year)

Year	1%	2%	3%	4%	5%	6%	7%	8%	9%	10%
1	0.990	0.980	0.971	0.962	0.952	0.943	0.935	0.926	0.917	0.909
2	0.980	0.961	0.943	0.925	0.907	0.890	0.873	0.857	0.842	0.826
3	0.971	0.942	0.915	0.889	0.864	0.840	0.816	0.794	0.772	0.751
4	0.961	0.924	0.888	0.855	0.823	0.792	0.763	0.735	0.708	0.683
5	0.951	0.906	0.863	0.822	0.784	0.747	0.713	0.681	0.650	0.621
6	0.942	0.888	0.837	0.790	0.746	0.705	0.666	0.630	0.596	0.564
7	0.933	0.871	0.813	0.760	0.711	0.665	0.623	0.583	0.547	0.513
8	0.923	0.853	0.789	0.731	0.677	0.627	0.582	0.540	0.502	0.467
9	0.914	0.837	0.766	0.703	0.645	0.592	0.544	0.500	0.460	0.424
10	0.905	0.820	0.744	0.676	0.614	0.558	0.508	0.463	0.422	0.386
11	0.896	0.804	0.722	0.650	0.585	0.527	0.475	0.429	0.388	0.350
12	0.887	0.788	0.701	0.625	0.557	0.497	0.444	0.397	0.356	0.319
13	0.879	0.773	0.681	0.601	0.530	0.469	0.415	0.368	0.326	0.290
14	0.870	0.758	0.661	0.577	0.505	0.442	0.388	0.340	0.299	0.263
15	0.861	0.743	0.642	0.555	0.481	0.417	0.362	0.315	0.275	0.239
16	0.853	0.728	0.623	0.534	0.458	0.394	0.339	0.292	0.252	0.218
17	0.844	0.714	0.605	0.513	0.436	0.371	0.317	0.270	0.231	0.198
18	0.836	0.700	0.587	0.494	0.416	0.350	0.296	0.250	0.212	0.180
19	0.828	0.686	0.570	0.475	0.396	0.331	0.277	0.232	0.194	0.164
20	0.820	0.673	0.554	0.456	0.377	0.312	0.258	0.215	0.178	0.149
21	0.811	0.660	0.538	0.439	0.359	0.294	0.242	0.199	0.164	0.135
22	0.803	0.647	0.522	0.422	0.342	0.278	0.226	0.184	0.150	0.123
23	0.795	0.634	0.507	0.406	0.326	0.262	0.211	0.170	0.138	0.112
24	0.788	0.622	0.492	0.390	0.310	0.247	0.197	0.158	0.126	0.102
25	0.780	0.610	0.478	0.375	0.295	0.233	0.184	0.146	0.116	0.092
30	0.742	0.552	0.412	0.308	0.231	0.174	0.131	0.099	0.075	0.057
35	0.706	0.500	0.355	0.253	0.181	0.130	0.093	0.067	0.049	0.035
40	0.672	0.453	0.307	0.208	0.142	0.097	0.067	0.046	0.032	0.022
45	0.639	0.410	0.264	0.171	0.111	0.073	0.047	0.031	0.021	0.014
50	0.608	0.372	0.228	0.141	0.087	0.054	0.034	0.021	0.013	0.008

Year	11%	12%	13%	14%	15%	16%	17%	18%	19%	20%
1	0.901	0.893	0.885	0.877	0.870	0.862	0.855	0.847	0.840	0.833
2	0.812	0.797	0.783	0.769	0.756	0.743	0.731	0.718	0.706	0.694
3	0.731	0.712	0.693	0.675	0.658	0.641	0.624	0.609	0.593	0.579
4	0.659	0.636	0.613	0.592	0.572	0.552	0.534	0.516	0.499	0.482
5	0.593	0.567	0.543	0.519	0.497	0.476	0.456	0.437	0.419	0.402
6	0.535	0.507	0.480	0.456	0.432	0.410	0.390	0.370	0.352	0.335
7	0.482	0.452	0.425	0.400	0.376	0.354	0.333	0.314	0.296	0.279
8	0.434	0.404	0.376	0.351	0.327	0.305	0.285	0.266	0.249	0.233
9	0.391	0.361	0.333	0.308	0.284	0.263	0.243	0.225	0.209	0.194
10	0.352	0.322	0.295	0.270	0.247	0.227	0.208	0.191	0.176	0.162
11	0.317	0.287	0.261	0.237	0.215	0.195	0.178	0.162	0.148	0.135
12	0.286	0.257	0.231	0.208	0.187	0.168	0.152	0.137	0.124	0.112
13	0.258	0.229	0.204	0.182	0.163	0.145	0.130	0.116	0.104	0.093
14	0.232	0.205	0.181	0.160	0.141	0.125	0.111	0.099	0.088	0.078
15	0.209	0.183	0.160	0.140	0.123	0.108	0.095	0.084	0.074	0.065
16	0.188	0.163	0.141	0.123	0.107	0.093	0.081	0.071	0.062	0.054
17	0.170	0.146	0.125	0.108	0.093	0.080	0.069	0.060	0.052	0.045
18	0.153	0.130	0.111	0.095	0.081	0.069	0.059	0.051	0.044	0.038
19	0.138	0.116	0.098	0.083	0.070	0.060	0.051	0.043	0.037	0.031
20	0.124	0.104	0.087	0.073	0.061	0.051	0.043	0.037	0.031	0.026
21	0.112	0.093	0.077	0.064	0.053	0.044	0.037	0.031	0.026	0.022
22	0.101	0.083	0.068	0.056	0.046	0.038	0.032	0.026	0.022	0.018
23	0.091	0.074	0.060	0.049	0.040	0.033	0.027	0.022	0.018	0.015
24	0.082	0.066	0.053	0.043	0.035	0.028	0.023	0.019	0.015	0.013
25	0.074	0.059	0.047	0.038	0.030	0.024	0.020	0.016	0.013	0.010
30	0.044	0.033	0.026	0.020	0.015	0.012	0.009	0.007	0.005	0.004
35	0.026	0.019	0.014	0.010	0.008	0.006	0.004	0.003	0.002	0.001
40	0.015	0.011	0.008	0.005	0.004	0.003	0.002	0.001	0.001	0.001
45	0.009	0.006	0.004	0.003	0.002	0.001	0.001	0.001	0.000	0.000
50	0.005	0.003	0.002	0.001	0.001	0.001	0.000	0.000	0.000	0.000

Year	21%	22%	23%	24%	25%	26%	27%	28%	29%	30%
1	0.826	0.820	0.813	0.806	0.800	0.794	0.787	0.781	0.775	0.769
2	0.683	0.672	0.661	0.650	0.640	0.630	0.620	0.610	0.601	0.592
3	0.564	0.551	0.537	0.524	0.512	0.500	0.488	0.477	0.466	0.455
4	0.467	0.451	0.437	0.423	0.410	0.397	0.384	0.373	0.361	0.350
5	0.386	0.370	0.355	0.341	0.328	0.315	0.303	0.291	0.280	0.269
6	0.319	0.303	0.289	0.275	0.262	0.250	0.238	0.227	0.217	0.207
7	0.263	0.249	0.235	0.222	0.210	0.198	0.188	0.178	0.168	0.159
8	0.218	0.204	0.191	0.179	0.168	0.157	0.148	0.139	0.130	0.123
9	0.180	0.167	0.155	0.144	0.134	0.125	0.116	0.108	0.101	0.094
10	0.149	0.137	0.126	0.116	0.107	0.099	0.092	0.085	0.078	0.073
11	0.123	0.112	0.103	0.094	0.086	0.079	0.072	0.066	0.061	0.056
12	0.102	0.092	0.083	0.076	0.069	0.062	0.057	0.052	0.047	0.043
13	0.084	0.075	0.068	0.061	0.055	0.050	0.045	0.040	0.037	0.033
14	0.069	0.062	0.055	0.049	0.044	0.039	0.035	0.032	0.028	0.025
15	0.057	0.051	0.045	0.040	0.035	0.031	0.028	0.025	0.022	0.020
16	0.047	0.042	0.036	0.032	0.028	0.025	0.022	0.019	0.017	0.015
17	0.039	0.034	0.030	0.026	0.023	0.020	0.017	0.015	0.013	0.012
18	0.032	0.028	0.024	0.021	0.018	0.016	0.014	0.012	0.010	0.009
19	0.027	0.023	0.020	0.017	0.014	0.012	0.011	0.009	0.008	0.007
20	0.022	0.019	0.016	0.014	0.012	0.010	0.008	0.007	0.006	0.005
21	0.018	0.015	0.013	0.011	0.009	0.008	0.007	0.006	0.005	0.004
22	0.015	0.013	0.011	0.009	0.007	0.006	0.005	0.004	0.004	0.003
23	0.012	0.010	0.009	0.007	0.006	0.005	0.004	0.003	0.003	0.002
24	0.010	0.008	0.007	0.006	0.005	0.004	0.003	0.003	0.002	0.002
25	0.009	0.007	0.006	0.005	0.004	0.003	0.003	0.002	0.002	0.001
30	0.003	0.003	0.002	0.002	0.001	0.001	0.001	0.001	0.000	0.000
35	0.001	0.001	0.001	0.001	0.000	0.000	0.000	0.000	0.000	0.000
40	0.000	0.000	0.000	0.000	0.000	0.000	0.000	0.000	0.000	0.000
45	0.000	0.000	0.000	0.000	0.000	0.000	0.000	0.000	0.000	0.000
50	0.000	0.000	0.000	0.000	0.000	0.000	0.000	0.000	0.000	0.000

Year	31%	32%	33%	34%	35%	36%	37%	38%	39%	40%
1	0.763	0.758	0.752	0.746	0.741	0.735	0.730	0.725	0.719	0.714
2	0.583	0.574	0.565	0.557	0.549	0.541	0.533	0.525	0.518	0.510
3	0.445	0.435	0.425	0.416	0.406	0.398	0.389	0.381	0.372	0.364
4	0.340	0.329	0.320	0.310	0.301	0.292	0.284	0.276	0.268	0.260
5	0.259	0.250	0.240	0.231	0.223	0.215	0.207	0.200	0.193	0.186
6	0.198	0.189	0.181	0.173	0.165	0.158	0.151	0.145	0.139	0.133
7	0.151	0.143	0.136	0.129	0.122	0.116	0.110	0.105	0.100	0.095
8	0.115	0.108	0.102	0.096	0.091	0.085	0.081	0.076	0.072	0.068
9	0.088	0.082	0.077	0.072	0.067	0.063	0.059	0.055	0.052	0.048
10	0.067	0.062	0.058	0.054	0.050	0.046	0.043	0.040	0.037	0.035
11	0.051	0.047	0.043	0.040	0.037	0.034	0.031	0.029	0.027	0.025
12	0.039	0.036	0.033	0.030	0.027	0.025	0.023	0.021	0.019	0.018
13	0.030	0.027	0.025	0.022	0.020	0.018	0.017	0.015	0.014	0.013
14	0.023	0.021	0.018	0.017	0.015	0.014	0.012	0.011	0.010	0.009
15	0.017	0.016	0.014	0.012	0.011	0.010	0.009	0.008	0.007	0.006
16	0.013	0.012	0.010	0.009	0.008	0.007	0.006	0.006	0.005	0.005
17	0.010	0.009	0.008	0.007	0.006	0.005	0.005	0.004	0.004	0.003
18	0.008	0.007	0.006	0.005	0.005	0.004	0.003	0.003	0.003	0.002
19	0.006	0.005	0.004	0.004	0.003	0.003	0.003	0.002	0.002	0.002
20	0.005	0.004	0.003	0.003	0.002	0.002	0.002	0.002	0.001	0.001
21	0.003	0.003	0.003	0.002	0.002	0.002	0.001	0.001	0.001	0.001
22	0.003	0.002	0.002	0.002	0.001	0.001	0.001	0.001	0.001	0.001
23	0.002	0.002	0.001	0.001	0.001	0.001	0.001	0.001	0.001	0.000
24	0.002	0.001	0.001	0.001	0.001	0.001	0.001	0.000	0.000	0.000
25	0.001	0.001	0.001	0.001	0.001	0.000	0.000	0.000	0.000	0.000
30	0.000	0.000	0.000	0.000	0.000	0.000	0.000	0.000	0.000	0.000
35	0.000	0.000	0.000	0.000	0.000	0.000	0.000	0.000	0.000	0.000
40	0.000	0.000	0.000	0.000	0.000	0.000	0.000	0.000	0.000	0.000
45	0.000	0.000	0.000	0.000	0.000	0.000	0.000	0.000	0.000	0.000
50	0.000	0.000	0.000	0.000	0.000	0.000	0.000	0.000	0.000	0.000

Appendix 5
Standard Units of Measure

Activity	Unit of Measure
Inpatient:	
Medical/Surgical Acute	Patient Days
Pediatric Acute	Patient Days
Acute Psychiatric	Patient Days
Obstetrics Acute	Patient Days
Intensive Care Unit	Patient Days
Coronary Care Unit	Patient Days
All Others	Patient Days
Outpatient:	
Emergency Services	Number of Visits
Clinic Services	Number of Visits
Ancillary:	
Labor and Delivery	Number of Procedures
Operating Room	Surgery Minutes
Anesthesiology	Anesthesia Minutes
Pharmacy	Prescriptions
Laboratory Services	Workload Measurement Units
Blood Bank	500 cc Units
Electrocardiography	Relative Value Units
Cardiac Cath	Number of Procedures
Diagnostic Radiology	Relative Value Units
CT Scanner	Number of Procedures
Radiology-Therapeutic	Relative Value Units
Nuclear Medicine	Relative Value Units
Respiratory Therapy	Relative Value Units
Pulmonary Function Testing	Relative Value Units
Electroencephalography	Relative Value Units
Physical Therapy	Relative Value Units
Occupational Therapy	Hours of Service
Speech-Language Pathology	Number of Treatments
Recreational Therapy	Number of Treatments
Audiology	Number of Procedures
Psychiatric Services	Number of Treatments
Renal Dialysis	Number of Treatments
Support Services:	
Dietary Services	Number of Patient Meals
Cafeteria	Equivalent Number of Meals Served
Laundry and Linen	Number of Dry and Clean Pounds Processed
Social Services	Admissions or Cases Opened
Plant Operations & Maintenance	Number of Gross Square Feet
Ambulance Services	Number of Occasions of Service
Housekeeping	Number of Square Feet Serviced
Escort Service	Number of Trips

*This does not represent an all-inclusive list of activities or units of measure. It is also possible that some institutions may use more or different units of measure. Managers may refer to Chapter 10 for a guide to developing a more appropriate unit of measure if such is the case.

Glossary

Accrual Basis. The basis on which an accountant typically views the revenues and expenses of a business firm. This usually means that revenues are recognized at the time they are earned and expenses are recognized at the time they are incurred. The actual cash flows (in for revenue and out for expenses) may not occur until a later time.

Acid Test Ratio. A measure of liquidity calculated by dividing a firm's current assets minus its inventory by its current liabilities. The higher the ratio, the better.

Allocation of Overhead. In preparing financial statements, rate requests, and so on, it is necessary to assign overhead expenses to patient care areas on the basis of some statistical factors (labor hours, square feet, and so on). This assignment is called the allocation.

Benefit/Cost Ratio. Sometimes called a profitability index. This ratio is used to evaluate capital expenditure proposals. It is obtained by dividing the present value of cash inflows by the present value of the investment in the project. If the ratio is equal to or greater than one, the project is acceptable. If the ratio is less than one, the project should be rejected.

Capital Budgeting. The total process of generating, evaluating, selecting, and following up on capital expenditure alternatives.

Capital Expenditure. An outlay made for the purchase of a fixed asset (plant, equipment, and so on) from which benefits will be received for a length of time greater than one year.

Case-Mix. The makeup, by diagnosis, of a health program's caseload. The case-mix directly influences the length of stay as well as the intensity, cost, and scope of services provided by a hospital or other health program.

Cash Budget. A statement of various cash receipts and disbursements expected by a firm during the coming year; this is generally prepared on a month-by-month basis. It is a short-term financial planning tool. By determining the net cash flows for each period (month) and adjusting for any beginning cash, the firm can determine when financing will be required and when surpluses will be available for investment.

Cash Flows. The actual payment or receipt of dollars by the organization. Cash flows do not necessarily occur at the point at which an obligation (expense) is incurred or a charge is made to a patient. Financial managers generally operate using a cash flow point of view because cash is the lifeblood of the firm.

Certificate of Need (CON). Certification issued by a governmental body to an individual or organization proposing to construct, expand, or modify a health facility or offer a new or different health service usually involving more than a minimum capital expenditure or change in bed capacity. The issuance of such certification recognizes that the facility or service, when available, will be needed by those for whom it is intended. It is a condition of licensure of the facility or service and is intended to avoid unnecessary duplication of facilities and services that frequently leads to increased cost of health care and lower quality of care.

Coinsurance. A cost-sharing requirement that provides that the subscriber will assume a portion or percentage of the costs of covered services.

Commercial Paper. Short-term, unsecured promissory notes issued by corporations with a high credit standing. The maturity ranges up to 270 days, and the yield is often higher than that of other marketable securities.

Copayment. Type of cost sharing in which the insured pays a specified flat amount per unit of service, and the insurer (carrier) pays the rest of the cost.

Cost Center. An accounting method whereby all costs attributable to a particular activity, department, or program within an institution (e.g., a hospital burn center) are segregated for accounting or reimbursement purposes.

Cost Sharing. Provisions of a health insurance policy that require the insured, or covered, individual to pay some portion of his or her covered medical expenses. Deductibles, coinsurance, and copayments are all forms of cost sharing.

Cross-Subsidization. The practice of allocating at least a portion of the higher costs associated with the provision of a particular health service or with a particular cost center in the overall financial operation of a health care facility to other services or cost centers that are usually less costly. Cross-subsidization is normally accomplished through an adjustment of the rates for each service.

Current Ratio. A measure of liquidity calculated by dividing current assets by current liabilities. The higher the ratio, the more liquidity.

Debt Service. Amount for required principal and interest payments.

Deductible. The amount of loss or expense that must be incurred by the insured before benefits are paid by the insurer.

Discount Rate. The rate at which a series of future cash flows are adjusted in order to determine their present value. It is sometimes referred to as the opportunity rate or opportunity cost of capital in capital budgeting.

Endowment Funds. Funds restricted by their donors to income-producing investments, only the income from which may be spent.

First-Dollar Coverage. Coverage that begins with the first dollar of expense incurred by the subscriber for covered services. Such coverage, therefore, has no deductibles, although it may have copayments or coinsurance.

Fiscal Year (FY). Any 12-month period for which annual accounts are kept.

Fixed Costs. Costs that are a function of time rather than the level of activity.

Health Care Financing Administration (HCFA). Federal agency within the Department of Health and Human Services responsible for administering Medicare, Medicaid, and quality assurance programs.

Health Maintenance Organization (HMO). An entity with four essential attributes: (1) an organized system for providing health care in a geographic area, which accepts the responsibility to provide or otherwise assure the delivery of (2) an agreed-upon set of basic and supplemental health maintenance and treatment services to (3) a voluntarily enrolled group of persons, and (4) to be reimbursed for services through a predetermined, fixed, periodic prepayment made by, or on behalf of, each person or family unit enrolled in the HMO without regard to the amounts of actual services provided.

Hill-Burton. Legislation and its programs for federal support of construction and modernization of hospitals and other health facilities, beginning with Public Law 70-725, the Hospital Survey and Construction Act of 1946. This law, as amended, provided for surveying state needs, developing plans for construction of hospitals and public health centers, and assisting in constructing and equipping them. Until the late 1960s, the program expanded in dollars and scope.

Hospital Insurance Program (Part A). The compulsory portion of Medicare, which automatically enrolls all persons aged 65 and over entitled to benefits under the Old-Age, Survivors, Disability and Health Insurance Program (OASDHI) administered by the Social Security Administration; persons under 65 eligible for disability for over two years; and insured workers and their dependents requiring renal dialysis or transplantation. The program pays, after various cost-sharing requirements are met, for inpatient hospital care and care in skilled nursing facilities and home health agencies after a period of hospitalization. The program is financed through a payroll tax levied on employers, employees, and the self-employed.

Incentive Reimbursement. A scheme that provides payment for the health services rendered, generally by an institution, and that provides added financial rewards if certain conditions are met. Such a scheme is intended to promote and reward increased efficiency and cost containment with better care or at least without adverse effect on the quality of care rendered.

Indirect Cost. A cost that cannot be identified directly with a particular activity, service, or product of the program experiencing the cost. Indirect costs usually are allocated to patient care areas on the basis of some statistical factor.

Internal Rate of Return (IRR). A sophisticated way of evaluating capital expenditure proposals. The discount rate that causes the net present value of a project to equal zero. Thus, if a project's internal rate of return is greater than the cost of capital, the project is acceptable; otherwise, it is rejected.

Liquidity. The ability to pay bills as they come due. This is directly related to the level of cash and securities owned by the hospital.

Major Medical. Insurance designed to offset the heavy medical expenses resulting from catastrophic or prolonged illness or injuries. Generally, such policies do not provide total coverage but do provide benefit payment of 75 to 80 percent of all types of medical expenses above a certain base amount paid by the insured. Most major medical policies sold as private insurance contain maximums on the total amount that will be paid (such as $50,000); thus, they do not provide complete protection against catastrophic costs, as catastrophic health insurance does.

Medicaid. Federal-state programs established under Title XIX of the Social Security Act and/or Kerr-Mills programs that finance payments to providers of health care services for low-income persons eligible under the law. Subject to broad federal guidelines, states determine the benefits, program eligibility, rates of payment for providers, and methods of administering the programs. Often referred to as the Medical Assistance program.

Medicare. A nationwide federal health insurance program, established under Title XVIII of the Social Security Act, for people aged 65 and over, for persons who have been eligible for Social Security disability payments for at least two years, and for certain persons who need kidney transplantation or dialysis. Medicare is available to these groups without regard to income. It consists of two separate but coordinated programs—a compulsory Hospital Insurance Program (Part A) and an optional Supplementary Medical Insurance Program (Part B).

Net Present Value. The most common of the sophisticated tools for evaluating capital expenditure proposals. It is calculated by subtracting the present value of the investment required by a project from the present value of the projected cash inflows. If the project's net present value is greater than zero, the project should be accepted; otherwise, it should be rejected.

Nonrevenue-Producing Cost Centers. Support or overhead units, such as dietary services, that provide necessary services to other hospital departments but generate no patient revenues themselves.

Per Diem Cost. Literally, cost per day. Refers, in general, to hospital or other inpatient institutional costs per day or for a day of care. Hospitals occasionally charge for their services on the basis of a per diem rate derived by dividing their total costs by the number of inpatient days of care given. Per diem costs are, therefore, averages and do not reflect true cost for each patient. With this approach patients who use few hospital services (typically those at the end of a long stay) subsidize those who need much care (those just admitted). Thus, the per diem approach is said to give hospitals an incentive to prolong hospital stays.

Present Value. The value of a future sum or a stream of dollars discounted at a specific rate. The process of finding the present value is, in reality, the reverse of the compound earnings process.

Prospective Reimbursement. A contractual agreement between third-party payers and hospitals or other health programs in which amounts or rates of payments are established in advance for the coming year and the programs are paid these amounts regardless of the costs they actually incur.

Reimbursement. The process by which health care providers receive payment for their services. Because of the nature of the health care environment, providers are often reimbursed by third parties who, for the most part, represent their patients. See also incentive reimbursement and prospective reimbursement.

Restricted Funds. Monies such as plant and endowment funds limited to specific uses by donors or outside agencies.

Revenue Bond. A bond payable solely from the revenue generated from the operation of the project being financed. In the case of hospital revenue bond financing, the bonds typically are payable from the gross receipts of the hospital.

Revenue-Producing Cost Center. Hospital departments providing direct services to patients (such as laboratory and X-ray services) and thus generating revenue. See also nonrevenue-producing cost centers.

Semivariable Costs. Costs that are fixed over a certain range of volume and change to a different level beyond that volume.

Stop-Loss Limit. A specified dollar amount of covered services in excess of the deductible, at which point the level of reimbursement by the plan increases to 100 percent.

Third-Party Payer. Any public or private organization that pays or insures specific health or medical expenses on behalf of beneficiaries or recipients (e.g., Blue Cross and Medicaid). The individual (first party) generally pays a premium for such coverage in all private and some public programs. The organization (third party) then pays bills from the care provider (second party) on behalf of the insured. Such payments are referred to as third-party payments.

Unrestricted Funds. Monies that have no external restrictions and can be used for any legitimate purpose.

Variable Costs. Costs that vary directly with the level of activity. They are a function of volume, not time.

For Further Reading

Donald F. Beck, *Basic Hospital Financial Management*, 2nd ed., Aspen Publishers, 1989.

Howard J. Berman, *The Financial Management of Hospitals*, 7th ed., Health Administration Press, 1990.

Steven B. Eastaugh, *Health Care Finance: Economic Incentives and Productivity Enhancement*, Auburn House, 1992.

Truman H. Esmond, *Budgeting for Effective Hospital Resource Management*, American Hospital Publishing, 1990.

John G. Nackel, George M. J. Kis, and Paul J. Fenaroli, *Cost Management for Hospitals*, Aspen Publishers, 1987.

Sandra H. Pelfrey, *Basic Accounting for Hospital Based Nonfinancial Managers*, Delmar Publishers, 1992.

Charles E. Phelps, *Health Economics*, HarperCollins Publishers, 1992.

L. Venn Seawell, *Hospital Financial Accounting: Theory and Practice*, 2nd ed., Kendell/Hunt Publishing, 1987.

Index

About the Author

WILLIAM J. WARD, JR., is Vice President—Operations and Secretary at the Francis Scott Key Medical Center, a Johns Hopkins Health System member institution, in Baltimore. He holds faculty appointments at the University of Maryland School of Nursing and the Johns Hopkins University School of Hygiene and Public Health. Ward has over 20 years of experience in management, health care, and finance. His first textbook, *An Introduction to Health Care Financial Management*, was published in 1989. Articles that he has authored have appeared in such journals as *Health Care Management Review*, *Healthcare Financial Management*, and *Management Review*. He has written and conducted numerous seminars covering various aspects of financial management in health care. His professional affiliations include the American College of Healthcare Executives, the Maryland Association of Health Care Executives, and the Healthcare Financial Management Association.